HITLER'S HENCHMEN

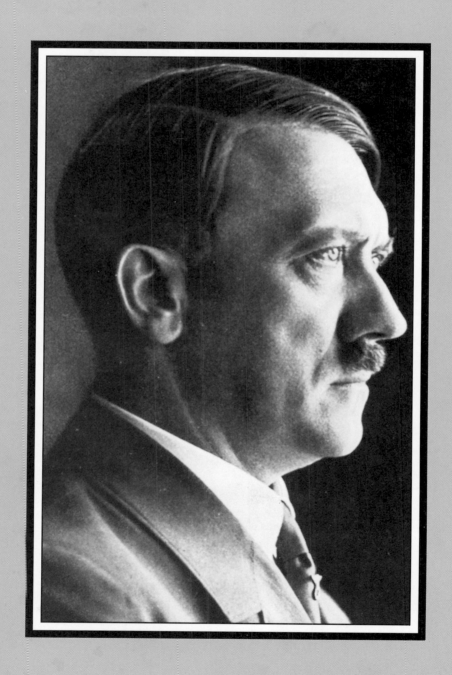

HITLER'S HENCHMEN

Dr. Henk van Capelle
Dr. Peter van de Bovenkamp

WARFARE

Page 1: *Adolf Hitler, a formal studio portrait.*

Pages 2-3: *Hitler salutes a column of the SA in 1931.*

These pages: *The Führer watches a marchpast of his bodyguard, the Leibstandarte Adolf Hitler.*

Published by Warfare
An imprint of Grange Books
Universal Books Limited
The Grange
Grange Yard
London SE1 3AG

Copyright © 1990 Bison Books Ltd

Produced by
Bison Books Ltd
Kimbolton House
117A Fulham Road
London SW3 6RL

ISBN 1-85627-0009

Printed in Hong Kong

10 9 8 7 6 5 4 3 2 1

CONTENTS

JOSEPH
GOEBBELS
1897-1945

Left: *Joseph Goebbels, the Third Reich's Minister of Propaganda.*

Above: *Goebbels and Hitler attend a gymnastics display in Stuttgart, 1933.*

Joseph Goebbels contributed as no other to the National Socialist creed, thereby managing to turn the 'messiah' of this movement, Adolf Hitler, into an idol in the eyes of millions of followers. Goebbels was the brain behind the Nazi propaganda machine in Germany and the conquered territories. It was Goebbels who invented the 'war of nerves' and, in a subtle manner, gave barefaced lies the appearance of truth. He was the man who promised the Germans a '1000 Year Reich' in which, as *Herrenvolk*, they would be able to rule over the 'inferior peoples.' Even up to the end of the war, with German defeat becoming more and more inevitable and German cities being transformed into burning ruins, Goebbels still managed to inspire a fanatical belief in the Führer and final victory. After the suicide of the man he worshipped, Joseph Goebbels also chose a self-inflicted death.

On 1 May 1945, when Russian shells had already hit the Reich Chancellery, flames flared up and consumed two bodies lying in the chancellery's garden. They were the bodies of Goebbels, Minister of Propaganda during Hitler's reign, and his wife,

Magda. Shortly before, Magda Goebbels had, with the help of a doctor, poisoned her six children, of whom the eldest was 12 years old and the youngest four. Hitler had put an end to his life and that of his young bride the day before. With the man to whom he had devoted himself dead, the life of one who had become burdened with guilt in the service of Adolf Hitler was also over.

In Nazi Germany propaganda grew into an extremely effective weapon in the maintenance and defense of the regime. Propaganda was, in a sense, the only original idea that made the rise and establishment of the Nazi regime possible. It was more than just an instrument of power; it was a part of the essence of Nazism.

The German propaganda machine managed to influence the people in an extremely cunning way. Use was made on a massive scale of the radio, newspapers, magazines, films and movie news. The Nazis organized numerous mass meetings, flag processions, parades and election rallies, whereby the uniforms and the thundering 'Sieg Heils' incited a feeling of ecstasy among millions of Germans for their country and, especially, for Adolf Hitler. The brain behind Nazi propaganda was Joseph Goebbels, one of the most intelligent leaders of the Third Reich. It was Goebbels who created the image of Adolf Hitler as the undisputed Führer, an idol in the eyes of the majority of Germans. It was Goebbels who, on a grand scale, applied the techniques of this completely new kind of mass propaganda, with its glorification of the German people and their old myths and legends.

In the first years of National Socialism no one thought that Goebbels would be able to cope with the immense task which had come to rest on his shoulders. In spite of his physical handicap – his left leg was 10cm shorter than the right – he knew how to fascinate

millions of Germans, not least women. Goebbels' genius lay in devising and disseminating propaganda which had no moral boundaries; the ultimate goal justified all means. He idolized German nationalism, although he frequently shocked friends and acquaintances with the contempt he felt for the masses. His idol was not Germany or the German people, but Adolf Hitler, for whom he sacrificed truth, honor and, ultimately, his life (even though he despised Hitler in those last days).

In his painfully accurate diaries Goebbels wrote that his feelings for his Führer were 'holy and unassailable.' After one of Hitler's speeches he wrote: 'He spoke in a brave and mystical manner; it seemed like a sermon.' Further on, in a surge of affection, he wrote: 'The day will come when the masses will cry: "crucify him!" Then we shall remain loyal and as rigid as iron and we shall shout

Left: *Goebbels looks on as Hitler takes the salute during the NSDAP's Party Day, Nuremberg, 1927.*

Below left: *Goebbels and Göring are driven to the opening of the Reichstag following their electoral success, 13 October 1930.*

Right: *Hitler and Goebbels pose for the camera with members of the Hattinger art group, November 1926.*

Below right: *Goebbels, the arch orator, in full flow.*

and sing Hosanna.' Feelings such as these gave Goebbels the inspiration to drag the masses along in their belief in the Führer and the Third Reich.

Goebbels, like Hitler, had a good eye for detail. For ceremonies in which Hitler participated each element, each proceeding, was prepared by Goebbels and approved by Hitler. Sophisticated methods were used time and time again: close-order marching, a child with a bunch of flowers, artillery salutes, views of white-bearded veterans from the wars of 1864, 1866 and 1871, martial music, and the dramatic arrival of the Führer. In the large stadiums all lights would be extinguished shortly before the Führer's arrival – except for the one lighting his entrance.

This mixture of sentimental performance and military bombast was presented to the masses with clockwork precision. These compelling and dazzling events were the result of sober and calculated planning. Goebbels observed, regarding this: 'Such large official ceremonies always depend on the smallest detail.' Once, while in a frank mood, Goebbels divulged the difference between himself and Hitler, thereby explaining why Hitler was so dangerous: Hitler also actually believed in what he said. Goebbels never believed in what he said and hid this fact behind a veil of cynicism.

Goebbels was born on 29 October 1897 in Rheydt, a small industrial town in the Rhineland. His father was the director of a small textile factory, his mother a devout Catholic. Goebbels, whose full name was Paul Joseph, had two brothers and one sister. During the relatively peaceful years around the turn of the century, it seemed that the young Goebbels would enjoy a tranquil and secure youth. One day, however, when Joseph was four years old, he was sitting on the sofa in the '*gute Stube*,' the sitting room on the first floor of his parents' house. Suddenly, and for no apparent reason, he started to cry, so heartbreakingly that a doctor was sent for. Joseph had polio and the doctor advised immediate surgery. The operation could not prevent a crippled left foot and a left leg that would remain thin and weak for the rest of his life. From then on he had to wear special shoes, braces and bandages.

Because of this handicap and its visible effects, Goebbels became a quiet boy who withdrew into himself because he was unable to join in games with the neighborhood children or his brothers and sister. Being physically their inferior, the young Goebbels developed his intellectual powers so that he could show himself to be superior in this aspect. He would criticize at every opportunity. His continual hateful remarks earned him the reputation of being arro-

gant and difficult to get along with. Joseph started to devour books, especially the works of Cicero and Virgil. To his mother, this passion indicated that he might become a priest and, even later, a bishop. But the priest Joseph came in contact with knew after a few hours that he did not believe in God. Young Goebbels was unsuited to an ecclesiastical education. However, a compromise was found. On finishing high school he received a grant from the Catholic Albert Magnus Society to study for two years at a German university.

Joseph was almost 17 when World War I broke out on 1 August 1914. He was one of the schoolboys who volunteered for the German Army, but the inevitable pronouncement was: *kriegsuntauglich* – unsuitable for military service. He locked himself up in his attic room and refused to speak to anyone for two days. Later, when he was at university and his limp was noticed, he would hint that it was from a war injury. Goebbels, as did many German students then, went to quite a number of universities, eight in all.

Following defeat in the war, Germany was struck by a second disaster – rampant inflation which brought bankruptcy to large

Above right: *Goebbels pictured behind his desk at the Ministry of Propaganda, 2 February 1933.*

Right: *Hitler, Göring and other Nazi dignitaries attend one of Goebbels' carefully orchestrated military parades.*

Above, far right: *Goebbels pictured at the Obersalzberg, a still taken from a cine-film.*

Far right: *Goebbels addresses a rally of the SA, Berlin, 1931.*

sections of the population. Goebbels also suffered from poverty, and his face became heavily lined because of it. Contrary to most other students, he declared that he was no longer interested in politics. Literature attracted him much more. He carried out extensive research on the German romantics.

He wrote his dissertation in 1922 on the romantic period: 'Wilhelm von Schütz – A Contribution to the History of Romantic Drama.' When he later became Minister of Propaganda he had his official biographers change the title to 'The Political School of Thought in the Early Romantics,' giving his literary studies a political tinge.

Slowly but surely feelings of nationalism began to grow in the young Goebbels, a result of his flight from almost everything that surrounded him in those days: his family, his hometown, the leftist intellectuals, the leftist press and his communist friend of several years, Flisges (a badly wounded and much decorated war veteran). When Goebbels became a nationalist he betrayed everything he had previously adhered to. His chauvinism was peppered with mysticism. He began to believe that Germany had a special mission to fulfill and, after some time, came to the conclusion that non-Germans were by nature inferior, and therefore of no importance. In consequence, he broke off all contact with Jews as, according to him, they were not Germans.

Nationalism made him zealous for war; if one people (or race) was superior to others then the inferior would have to either submit to or be destroyed by the superior people. In those days Munich was the unquestioned center for all nationalist movements and conspiracies. When Goebbels returned there in 1922 (he had earlier studied there), he soon became a member of the NSDAP. Adolf Hitler spoke at a mass meeting organized by the NSDAP. Goebbels was among the audience: 'At first he spoke hesitantly

and timidly as though he was searching for the right words to formulate his ambitious thoughts. Then, suddenly, his speech picked up momentum. I was seized. I listened. The crowd started to stir. I became alternately hot and cold. A flame went through me. This was a command. At that moment I was reborn. Now I knew which path to take!' What was it that drew Goebbels to Hitler? It was that Hitler displayed no doubts that he believed in what he preached. Goebbels had never encountered anyone with such unquestioning and rock-solid belief other than his mother. After the meeting Goebbels went to a table near the exit and applied to join the National Socialist German Workers' Party.

Goebbels soon became Gregor Strasser's secretary, the man responsible for NSDAP activities in northern Germany. In 1925 important differences of opinion arose between the National Socialists in the south (with Munich as their center) and those in the north. A meeting was held for all northern party officials. The discussion became so heated that Goebbels at one point cried out: 'I propose that the insignificant, bourgeois Adolf Hitler be thrown out of the party.' The corruption and the confusing reports about the party in the south had undermined Goebbels' faith in Hitler and he had reached a point of no longer accepting Hitler's leadership.

Goebbels was also unable to digest the fact that Hitler no longer considered socialism to be the most important principle of the NSDAP. The Führer no longer emphasized the party program's basic principles, such as the expropriation of large-landownership, the splitting up of the large department stores, the nationalization of banks and industry, the abolition of interest, and so on. A group of party leaders led by Gregor Strasser and Goebbels wanted to hold on to these principles at any cost. A division threatened the party.

For Hitler, collaboration with the communists was in direct conflict with everything he stood for. Besides, the NSDAP was supported on a large scale by industry in the south and could not afford to maintain the party without their support. In February 1926 Hitler decided to bring the northern leaders back to the 'Munich' line. He convened a meeting in Bamberg in south Germany which was to take place on a weekday. The northern leaders were unable to get away, and only Strasser and Goebbels attended the meeting. The 'rich' southern leaders were there in force and Strasser and Goebbels had to yield to their superior numbers. They finally agreed to the Hitler line. The Führer realized that he did not have their wholehearted support and decided to do everything within his means to win Goebbels over. In April 1926 Goebbels was invited to visit Bavaria and was given the opportunity of delivering a speech in the Burgerbräu-keller, where the putsch of 1923 had been hatched.

In Munich Goebbels was collected by limousine, slept in the most expensive hotels and was received with the greatest respect by Hitler and the southern leaders. Hitler tried everything to convert Goebbels from the 'socialist' party line and turn him into a loyal

follower. It did not take long for Hitler to succeed. By Hitler's birthday on 20 April 1926, Goebbels wrote (to Hitler): 'You have finally made me see the light.' In August Goebbels, who had spent most of the summer on the Obersalzberg, officially broke with Strasser. In an article in the *Völkischer Beobachter* he calls Strasser and his followers 'the revolutionaries of the word and not the deed.' He also described Hitler as an instrument of the 'Divine Powers' who would create history with a new passion. Hitler's reward for this show of devotion was not long in coming. At the end of October he appointed Goebbels Gauleiter for Berlin. Hitler knew only too well that the young intellectual and demagogue would come into his own in the busy and turbulent streets of the capital.

On arrival in Berlin, Goebbels found a corrupt and divided local NSDAP department. There were hardly any members and the communists and socialists were by far the larger movements in the capital. In early 1927, speaking to only 600 party members he said: 'We must break through the wall of anonymity. The Berliners can insult us, slander us, beat us, as long as they talk about us. Today we are 600 strong, but in six years time there will be 600,000 of us.' He kept his word. The battle began. Goebbels gave his first speech

on 11 February 1927. Fighting broke out with the communists almost immediately. By the time the police arrived there were 12 wounded SA men and 75 wounded anti-Nazis, mostly communists. Goebbels calmly stood on the podium during the uproar, which won him the respect of the rough SA men.

Goebbels' speeches were very different from Hitler's. What took Hitler 100 words to express, took Goebbels only 10. He did not stir up the masses as did Hitler, but he knew how to convince them. Press comments on the fighting, though not very flattering, could be read on all the front pages, which was exactly what Goebbels had hoped for. Three days later their headquarters received 2600 membership applications and 500 requests for admission to the SA. Goebbels now knew that his tactics had been right.

When fighting between the SA and the anti-Nazis became more serious Goebbels was banned from public speaking. He then decided to start up his own paper, thus providing himself with a platform which he was denied as a speaker. *Der Angriff* was founded. Goebbels used the same methods which had attracted audiences to his rallies. First, blood-red posters with only two words, *Der Angriff*, and a large question mark were put up on the billboards. A few days later new posters announced: '*Der Angriff* takes place on 4 July.' Only on the third poster could one read that it was about a new weekly that would appear every Monday. Initially the paper had a limited circulation of 2000 copies, but when his ban on public speaking was lifted in October, the number of subscriptions increased rapidly.

According to Goebbels it was propaganda that brought the desired results, other methods were wrong. It was pointless to argue that propaganda was crude, vile and unsporting for this was not at issue; propaganda was the forerunner of an organization and an organization the forerunner of the state and, finally, propaganda always aims at a goal. On 9 January Hitler appointed Goebbels head of propaganda for the entire nation.

Above: *The Brandenburg Gate at night, swathed in, and surrounded by, Nazi iconography.*

Left: *A poster calling for a 'free' Germany, one unfettered by the restrictions imposed by the Treaty of Versailles.*

This page: *Examples of the all-pervasive nature of Nazi propaganda, including an ashtray with swastika (top left), toy soldiers (top center and above), a candle (top right), a bottle of wine (above, far left), and a tie (above left).*

Left: *Two clasps and a chain in Nazi Party colors.*

Goebbels' first assignment was to convince the masses that Hitler was their savior. He was mainly occupied with the psychological preparations for the mass rallies. Before a Nazi speaker started his speech, the audience would have to be put in the right frame of mind. Goebbels turned political rallies into shows of pomp. Marching, uniformed SA, martial music, party songs, light effects, flags and flying colors heightened the mood. Goebbels' star was Hitler. On 16 November 1928, Hitler gave his first Berlin speech. The address took two hours and 55 minutes and the Führer raged on and on about the 'betrayal of Versailles,' the republic and the existing order. There was a lot of singing and parading with flags and banners. The crowds were wild with enthusiasm.

At the Reichstag election, which was held on 14 September 1930, there was talk of landslides within the political parties. The Nazis got 6.4 million votes (18 percent of the vote) and saw their number of seats in the Reichstag increase from 12 to 104, out of the

Left: *Hitler and Goebbels attend a memorial service for Horst Wessel in Berlin, 22 January 1933. Wessel was a young Nazi activist killed in February 1930.*

Below left: *Hitler and Goebbels at an event celebrating May Day 1933. Field Marshal von Blomberg, Vice-Chancellor von Papen and State Secretary Meissner are also in attendance.*

Right: *Hitler's new government photographed for posterity shortly after winning the 1933 election. Goebbels and Göring, the Minister of the Interior, flank their Führer.*

seats available.

The success of the NSDAP was felt everywhere. Goebbels was interviewed several times by the German, as well as the foreign, press, and sales of Hitler's book *Mein Kampf* increased. Financial worries now belonged to the past. Goebbels remained aggressive and came up with new stunts: for example, he challenged Reich Chancellor Brüning to a public debate. The Reich Chancellor refused to appear on a platform with a National Socialist. Whereupon Goebbels played a recording of a speech given by Brüning and stopped it when he wanted to reply to his invisible opponent. The papers were full of it.

From a technical point of view the propaganda campaigns became increasingly more refined. Elections were held again on 7 July 1932 and the NSDAP won 230 seats. The social democrats came second and the communists third. Even Goebbels thought that they had reached their peak. On 1 August he wrote in his diary: 'A brief breathing space to consolidate our position and then we shall have to take hold of the reins and show what we are capable of.' A few days later he wrote prophetically: 'Once we are in power we shall never give it up, except if we are carried out of our ministries as bodies.'

On 30 January 1933, von Hindenburg had no other choice than to appoint Hitler Reich Chancellor. Hitler's 'cold' coup d'etat had succeeded: a takeover of power from within, without a revolution or a civil war. The conservatives von Papen and Hugenberg, both members of Hitler's new cabinet, thought that they had control of this 'half-baked' Reich Chancellor. Hitler the revolutionary, who for years had been preaching that if the German people would only give him an opportunity he would put an end to all their economic and social sufferings, had now been given his chance.

Many leaders in industrial and governmental circles thought that the responsibilities of governing would change Hitler into a moderate, acceptable and bourgeois Reich Chancellor. The majority of Germans thought that his political opinions, encompassing such ideas as *Lebensraum*, anti-Marxism and anti-Semitism had been propaganda devices and simply did not believe that he was serious. However, there were writers already pointing out the horrible dangers which lay behind Hitler and his NSDAP, dangers which had to be taken seriously. These writers, Hesse, Werfel, Brecht, Mann, Zweig, Lillach and many others, were either prosecuted or forced to flee the country. Their work, described as degenerate literature, was burned shortly after Hitler's assumption of power on 30 January 1933.

Goebbels became Minister of Propaganda in Hitler's first cabinet. His ministry was situated in the heart of Berlin, at Wilhelm-splatz, across from the Reich Chancellery where Hitler resided. After an extensive renovation, Goebbels boasted that he was in charge of the smallest but most efficient ministry. He had a modern, streamlined, fast and efficient system in mind. In 1933 the ministry consisted of 300 civil servants and 500 employees. Goebbels chose his co-workers with care. His heads of departments were given a free hand and he expected a considerable amount of initiative from them.

His top assistants were Otto Dietrich as press officer and Max Aman, Hitler's sergeant during World War I and head of *Eher Verlag*, the Nazi Party's publishing company. Being the person in charge of the press and chairman of the press room, Aman had the power to suppress or forbid any publication that did not comply with the conditions the Nazis had dictated. All Jewish-run publishing houses were either dismantled or handed over to Aryan hands. Many newspapers and magazines were bought up by *Eher Verlag* or acquired by expropriation. After a time the Nazis controlled two-thirds of all newspapers and magazines published in Germany, and the others had to observe strict regulations. Three main German newspapers, the *Berliner Tageblatt*, the *Frankfurter Zeitung* and the *Deutsche Allgemeine Zeitung*, remained independent in name, but became mouthpieces for Nazi propaganda. Their independence was insisted upon by the Ministry of Foreign Affairs in order to maintain their reputation and serve as a means of presenting the 'new Germany' to the world.

After several years the entire German news service was bent to the Nazis' will. Newspapers only published official stories and were given strict instructions concerning the tone and content of their articles and items. Although it took some time before the newspapers were fully in Goebbels' hands, control of the radio was automatic since in Germany, as in most other European countries, the radio had always been state controlled. Radio became an extremely important element in the propaganda machine.

All aspects of German artistic life came under the Reich Culture Chamber after 22 September 1933. The purpose of this institution was the furtherance of 'German culture' and to bring together artists from all fields in a single organization under the control of the Reich. Every artist had to become a member of the culture chamber for his particular field. The rules and regulations of these chambers had the same weight as ordinary legislation. Each chamber, such as those for the visual arts, music, literature, theater and film, had the right to refuse membership or to expel individuals for political reasons. Any artist who had a reputation for being against the Nazi regime, or of having a critical attitude toward it, was prohibited from carrying out his or her work. These same reg-

ulations also applied to the press and the radio.

These measures had a profound effect on cultural life in the Third Reich. Art was totally subordinated to Nazi doctrine. Goebbels and his ministry determined what was to be performed at the theater, which books were published, which films could be shown and which art exhibitions were permitted. The only art form that did not have to submit entirely was music, which benefited from a rich and age-long tradition in Germany. The works of Jewish composers, such as Mendelssohn, were, however, forbidden. Contrary to many other artists, most musicians remained in Germany, a fact which Goebbels exploited by creating a flourishing music life which compensated for the decline of other art forms.

Goebbels exercised a unique form of power in Nazi Germany. Not the power that could form the policies of the Reich as Hitler had, or the power to arrest people and have them deported to concentration camps as Himmler had. Goebbels had the power to decide what people could read, see, hear and think. The exercise of this power was a task that suited Goebbels' talents, for he knew as no other how to persuade and convince people.

Hero worship and the adoration of the new order continued to play an important role in Nazi propaganda. On the one hand, this new order was maintained by the ruthless exercise of force but on the other by legislation that the people found agreeable. It was Goebbels who introduced national holidays, such as May Day and the 'Erntedant,' the harvest celebration. These holidays, which became more and more inflated and extensive, offered excellent opportunities for speeches and for showing the people how fortunate they were to be living under National Socialism. With these holidays, Goebbels also created a Nazi tradition, and after a few years it seemed to most Germans that they had been celebrating them all their lives – as though the Nazis had always been in power.

Holidays and so on were meant to create the impression abroad of stability, unity and the pride the German people felt for the achievements of National Socialism. Propaganda abroad, which had cost a lot of money, was a failure. Goebbels did not have a realistic picture of the views prevalent in other countries, where mass hysteria was not deemed impressive and the reports of those who had escaped the Nazi regime were more credible.

Goebbels was more successful with his overseas efforts during the Olympic Games held in Berlin in 1936. Everything possible was done to give foreign participants and visitors the impression that the German people stood as one behind Hitler and National Socialism. During the time of the Games the tone of the newspapers was milder and even the notices stating which bars, hotels and beaches were out of bounds to Jews were removed. Goebbels, Göring and von Ribbentrop gave banquets for thousands of guests and the Americans and British, especially, were impressed by their impeccable organization. Many started to doubt the stories of the persecution of the Jews, the concentration camps and the torture chambers.

On 30 October 1939, Goebbels stood on the Sportpalast podium which had been built for the Games. Hitler was giving a speech in which he praised Goebbels: 'I never would have been able to win over Berlin without you, my valued Dr Goebbels. I would not have been able to create our propaganda machine without you. Your name will live on in German history!'

Shortly afterward the German economy changed over to the mass production of military goods. The realization of Hitler's *Lebensraum* plans had begun, starting a new chapter in Goebbels' propaganda program. The people had to be prepared for war and that war had to be justified.

The campaigns against domestic enemies and the Jews were overshadowed by those which had to add force to German territorial demands. There was fierce agitation in the newspapers

against the injustice of the Treaty of Versailles, and more and more attention was directed toward the 'cruel fate' of the pan-Germans in Czechoslovakia and Poland, and the 'historical unity' of Germany and Austria. The bragging newspaper headings had to convince the Germans that their country was treated badly by the international community and that Germany was in great danger.

The propaganda had started with 'Germany Awake' and 'The Jews are our Misfortune,' but soon the emphasis was laid on 'Blood and Soil' and 'People without Living Space' and 'Guns for Butter.'

The cinema was to have a very special influence on Goebbels, for he was extremely fond of beautiful movie stars. This was no secret and there were soon stories going round Germany of his re-

Above, left to right: *A sequence of photographs taken in Berlin's Lustgarten on 25 August 1934 demonstrating the Minister of Propaganda's dramatic speaking style.*

Right: *Goebbels makes the Nazi salute during the singing of the* Horst Wessel *at a function commemorating Hitler's first year in office at the Berlin Sportpalast, 30 January 1934.*

lationships with these stars. One, with the young Czech actress Lida Baarova, developed into a serious love affair. His wife, Magda, also heard about it and she eventually considered divorce. They were already living apart since Magda had forbidden her husband to set foot in their country house in Schwanenwerder. After Magda Goebbels went to see Hitler to ask for his permission for a divorce, Hitler intervened. He sent for Goebbels and asked him how things stood. Goebbels answered that he was in love with Baarova and that he wanted to marry her.

Hitler became extremely agitated. How could he, the German Minister of Propaganda, get divorced? Quite out of the question, Hitler said. Goebbels replied that he had carefully thought it over and completely understood that under the circumstances he could no longer remain Minister of Propaganda. He asked permission to resign and to get a divorce in order to marry Lida Baarova. He would like to be sent to Japan as German ambassador. Hitler went into one of his notorious rages; he raved like a madman. His roaring culminated in the words: 'Those who make history may not have a private life!' Goebbels persisted. Hitler finally agreed to allow Goebbels to divorce Magda and remarry should he feel the same way a year later. But he was not allowed to see his beloved Baarova during that year.

Goebbels had to give his word of honor that he would obey. Baarova's house was under continuous Gestapo surveillance; Himmler was sure that Goebbels would break his word. Goebbels' throne was shaky and many party leaders, among them Himmler, Göring and von Ribbentrop, had their eyes on his job. Goebbels never saw Baarova again, for she was the victim of a cold and calculated boy-

cott. She finally gave up all hope of ever marrying Goebbels and left Berlin at the end of 1938.

Even though Goebbels had always spoken and written aggressively, he did not want a war. He realized that Germany would be taking unnecessary risks, that his own position of power would be weakened and that of the military strengthened. Despite the victories of 1940 Goebbels said: 'We must not fool ourselves. It will be a long and difficult war. Its outcome will not depend on boisterous victory parties but on a determination to do one's daily duty.' His skeptical attitude did not, however, prevent him from switching the Third Reich's propaganda machinery over to Hitler's military needs. Goebbels was probably the only Nazi leader who correctly judged the length and the gravity of the war.

Goebbels considered movies to be the most important medium for the manipulation of the public. Each program, both the official and the rare, acceptable foreign movie, was preceded by the *Wochenschau* (newsreel), a news bulletin which greatly emphasized the military successes of the German forces. When the military situation worsened, the tone of the *Wochenschau* was dominated by the heroic battle of Germany against 'the western supporters of Jewish capitalism' and against 'the red hordes of Bolshevism.'

A similar development took place on the radio, which usually broadcast classical music. Radio programs would suddenly be interrupted by so-called *Sondermeldungen* (special reports), which were sent out simultaneously on all stations, including those in the occupied territories. These *Sondermeldungen aus Führerhauptquartier* (special reports from the Führer's headquarters) all started with the same words: '*Das Oberkommando der Wehrmacht gibt*

Far left: *Goebbels announces that France has handed back the Saarland without demanding any concessions to an audience at Berlin's Kroll Opera House, 6 January 1935.*

Above: *Hitler and Goebbels in Leipzig, 6 March 1934.*

Left: *Goebbels, Hitler and Röhm accept the cheers of a Leipzig crowd, 16 July 1933.*

Far left: *Goebbels prepares to give Christmas gifts to 500 Berlin children, 1936.*

Left: *Goebbels admires a photograph of himself, part of an exhibition entitled 'The 10-Year Struggle for Berlin,' 30 October 1936.*

bekannt' (The High Command announces). Initially, military successes were glorified in the *Sondermeldungen*, but later in the war they consisted of no more than announcements in a dry and sluggish tone of 'tactical retreats' or 'reorganizations at the front.'

The *Sondermeldung* was not Goebbels' invention, but Hitler's, who personally formulated the texts of the first 'announcements' and indicated how they were to be presented. Each began with a fanfare overture. The announcements were carefully prepared. How many seconds did a mother need to rush out of the kitchen to the radio? How long did it take for a father to warn his children? After a measured lapse, the special announcements were read out to the German people. These fanfares and the reported victories undoubtedly had a hypnotic effect on the Germans and, together with the unremitting propaganda, created a practically uncritical and cowed population.

In 1941 something happened which even the resourceful Goebbels could not explain: the sudden flight of Rudolf Hess, Deputy Führer of the NSDAP and, officially, second in power in the Third Reich. Instead of giving guidelines, Goebbels told his associates that he was ill and then retreated to his country estate. His press officer, Otto Dietrich, had to handle the situation. Eventually he announced that Hess, in a state of insanity and driven by pacifist motives, had flown to England. When Goebbels heard the statement he nearly had a breakdown. How could anyone say that Hess,

Right: *Goebbels greets Hitler as he arrives at the Deutschlandhalle on 29 November 1935.*

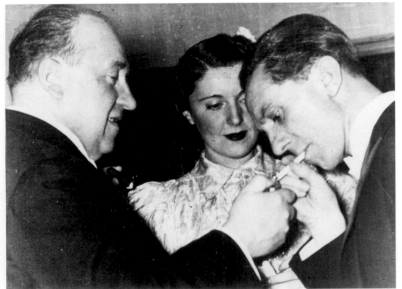

Hitler's deputy, had fled abroad and had gone mad? He did not, however, have a better explanation.

Meanwhile, the war was turning against Germany. The string of victories ended when the Sixth Army surrendered at Stalingrad on 2 February 1943. Germany had maneuvered herself into a 'total war.' It was a turning point, and the years of defeat and the horrors of total war began.

Goebbels now described his articles, speeches, circulars, directives, diaries and the leadership of the Ministry of Propaganda as 'intellectual warfare.' He saw himself as a general, his ministry as a general staff and his propaganda war as important as the war at the front. He worked day and night, often sleeping on a bed in his office. The more grave the war became for Germany the more convinced Goebbels was, that a catastrophe was imminent.

The aerial bombardment of Germany increased. Unlike Hitler and Göring, Goebbels appeared where things were at their worst. His official residence was hit during the air raids on Berlin, his

Above left: Goebbels accepts a light at a social engagement, 1937.

Left: A photograph taken to celebrate Goebbels' fortieth birthday on 29 October 1937 showing his wife Magda and two of his children, Helga and Helmuth.

Above right: Frau Goebbels captured on film with her children.

Below right: A small child gives the Minister of Propaganda a gift on his fortieth birthday.

ministry was badly damaged and his Gauleiter office suffered fire damage.

The newspapers, initially not allowed to take too much notice of the bombardments, were finally ordered to focus their attention on them. Goebbels invented the term 'terror attack.' The German people were led to believe that the Allies had, without any provocation, decided to kill German women and children from the air. He counted on the German people's forgetfulness, for it was only a few years earlier that they had been so enthusiastic about the news of 'burning London.' During the final years of the war Goebbels changed his approach. This man, whose magnificent command of the German language was unequaled, restricted himself to a minimum of sharply outlined sentences. His favored expressions were: 'It is clear that,' 'There is no doubt that,' and 'Firsthand information.'

The German people had to be informed of Field Marshal von Paulus' defeat and surrender at Stalingrad. Goebbels insisted that the news be given frankly and without frills. The people had to know that the fate of their motherland was at stake and that they could choose between Bolshevism or final victory. The defeat at Stalingrad was made public on 3 February 1943. A wave of dismay and fear swept over the Reich. Goebbels did not change his tactics and the disaster was announced in a special radio broadcast, with an orchestra playing the melancholy German soldier's song 'Ich hatte einen Kameraden' ('I had some comrades').

Goebbels' radio commentator and right-hand man, Fritsche, then spoke. He embellished nothing and was even critical. The German people were shocked and appalled. Would Goebbels succeed? London and Washington doubted his sanity, and Dr Dietrich took to his bed with a nervous breakdown. Himmler made preparations to take over all censorship and Goebbels' ministry. But Goebbels' experiment was a great success. The people came to terms with the defeat and began working together in the belief that defeat and sacrifices had a purpose. Goebbels announced: 'The army of the dead has not surrendered its weapons; it marches along with the ranks of the German soldiers.' And the German people swallowed it all! From that moment Goebbels could do what he liked with the facts.

Shortly after his announcement Goebbels wanted Hitler to speak to the people. But Hitler refused – he did not want to stand on any podium before the situation had improved. Goebbels had to deliver a long speech himself to encourage the people to make a superhuman effort. He prepared his entire speech. He asked the people whether they were prepared to make the greatest sacrifices as part of 'total war' that would eventually lead to a German victory.

The arrangements for Goebbels' speech, which would be broadcast throughout Germany and the occupied territories, were carefully planned. The audience consisted of loyal party members dressed in civilian clothes to give the impression that a cross-section of the entire German population was present. On entering the packed Sportpalast, Goebbels knew that this one speech could either reverse or worsen the situation. It was the best speech he had ever delivered. He spoke in a calm and confident manner, and made it seem as though he was having an intimate conversation with his family and friends. He did not prevaricate but outlined the situation at the front in plain terms. Goebbels declared that the fighting on the Eastern Front was a struggle between western civilization and Bolshevism. Two thousand years of western culture were at stake. The situation was extremely critical and total war was the only solution. The most radical measures were, according to him, hardly sufficient to achieve final victory.

He stirred up the crowd, provoked cheers and at the height of his speech addressed the audience directly, asking them 10 carefully formulated questions. When he asked them if they were willing to make the most extreme sacrifices, they thundered their assent. Germany, the occupied territories, and the whole world could hear

Far left: *Goebbels and Hitler in conversation, 1938.*

Left: *Goebbels and Hitler attend an architectural exhibition, 10 December 1938.*

Below: *Hitler greets Sudeten Germans at the Berghof in 1938; Goebbels keeps in the background.*

how Goebbels' questions were answered with deafening applause. The questions all concerned the same subject: was the people's belief in final victory and Hitler still undaunted, and were they willing to make the necessary sacrifices? Because of the numerous interruptions it took almost an hour to ask all the questions.

At the end of his speech Goebbels stated: '*Der Nation ist bereit. Der Führer hat befolen und wir werden ihn folgen.*' ('The nation is prepared, the Führer has ordered and we shall follow him.') The frenzied crowd carried him off the podium on their shoulders. Goebbels remained perfectly calm. Magda and six of his staff members were waiting for him. He was hoarse and could only whisper. Goebbels showed his contempt for the masses to this small group: 'What utter madness! If I had ordered them to jump out of the fourth-floor window they would have done so!'

The revival of German morale was, however, short-lived. Constant Allied bombing was transforming many German cities into smoldering ruins. In his meticulously kept diaries, Goebbels became less certain about the outcome of the war. On 1 May 1943, after a period of heavy bombing, he wrote: 'If this continues in such a way we shall have to face the serious consequences which, in the long run, will be unbearable.' Goebbels was becoming convinced that a war on two fronts would prove fatal to Germany and he urged Hitler to enter into negotiations with one of the Allied camps to limit the war to one front.

In speeches and articles Goebbels accused certain groups of taking a cowardly stand by calling for the opening of peace negotiations. In actuality, Goebbels was also looking for a way to get out of an increasingly hopeless situation. On 10 September 1943, shortly after Italy's capitulation, he wrote in his diary: 'We are being confronted with the problem of which side to turn to first – to the Moscow or the Anglo-American side. One way or another we shall have to come to terms with the fact that it will be very difficult to continue the war against both parties.' Goebbels presented this suggestion to Hitler. Hitler reckoned that they would stand a better chance coming to terms with the English. Goebbels disagreed as he regarded Stalin as a practical politician and Churchill as a 'romantic adventurer one could not speak sensibly to.'

There had been cautious discussions between the Germans and the Russians in March 1943. Stalin had sent an envoy to Stockholm, in neutral Sweden, who was empowered to conclude an armistice on condition that Hitler withdraw his troops from the Soviet Union and Poland. Although an unofficial move, its details

appeared in Swiss newspapers. It is very likely that Goebbels knew of this episode and had tried to get Hitler to sign an armistice. There are quite a few reasons for this assumption. For example, Goebbels said: 'Stalin is the only man who is leading a total war, the only man who survived 15 years of exile in Siberia and still had enough energy to maneuver himself into the position of an authoritarian ruler.' One can imagine Goebbels' shock when Hitler rejected the peace proposals and forfeited the possibility of putting

Left: *Goebbels entertains foreign statesmen accompanied by von Ribbentrop (far left), Admiral Raeder (fifth from left) and Dr Frick (second from right), 26 November 1941.*

Right: *The Italian Minister for Culture, Pavolini, salutes Nazi Party heroes buried in Munich during a visit to meet Goebbels, 17 March 1942.*

an end to a two-front war.

At the end of 1943 air attacks became increasingly heavier and Berlin was being badly hit. After a heavy raid on 22 November which set fire to much of Berlin, Goebbels, chain-smoking while listening to the disastrous news, commented: 'Another two or three such attacks and there will no longer be a Berlin.' Unlike Hitler, who never visited bombed-out cites, Goebbels frequently toured them to comfort the people. In those days Hitler would travel in armored trains so as not to see the ruins of his Reich. Goebbels often complained that neither Hitler nor any of the other leaders ever made an appearance at one of the damaged cities.

After the German defeats in Russia, North Africa and Italy were followed by the Allied invasion of France in June 1944, Goebbels knew that the final battle had begun. On 15 June the first rockets fell on London. Goebbels called them V-1 rockets, and the second version he called V-2. A staff member had suggested calling the weapon V-1. The V referred to *Vergeltung* (reprisal) and at the same time served as an antidote for the famed English 'V' for victory. These rockets had been developed by German scientists and were presented to the German people as 'wonder weapons' which would reverse the war. The population was not, however, informed that the rocket factory in Peenemünde had been badly damaged and that production would never be sufficient. The German war industry never recovered from the heavy blows inflicted by the American and British air forces. The end, for Germany, was clearly in view.

On 20 July 1944, Colonel Count Claus Schenk von Stauffenberg placed a time-bomb in the wood-paneled conference room of

Right: *Goebbels attends the opening of an art exhibition in Munich, 26 July 1941.*

Far right: *The Berlin Sportpalast, 1944: Goebbels attempts to rekindle the people's faith in Nazi victory.*

Hitler's headquarters at Rastenburg, East Prussia. At 1342 hours the bomb, which was to have ended the lives of Hitler and his most important general staff members, exploded. Hitler was only slightly wounded but Stauffenberg, who had fled from the headquarters to Berlin, was under the impression that he had been killed. In Berlin the other officers who had conspired with Stauffenberg to kill Hitler and seize power also believed the news of the Führer's death and started to execute their plan. One element in the conspiracy, *Valkyrie*, was the arrest of Goebbels at his ministry. However, Goebbels had been informed about the danger shortly before the arrival of Major Otto Remer, the officer who had been ordered to arrest him. When the major entered the minister's room, Goebbels faced one of the most difficult moments in his life.

As so often before, his silver tongue got him out of trouble. He reminded the young major of his oath to the Führer and said that Hitler was still alive – he had just spoken to him on the telephone. Whereupon he picked up the phone and asked urgently for a connection with Rastenburg. It was undoubtedly a mistake on the part of the conspirators not to have taken over the Berlin telephone exchange, for Goebbels got Hitler on the line and gave the call to the dumbfounded Remer. The Führer asked whether Remer recognized his voice. It was said that Remer sprang to attention. Hitler ordered him to suppress the rebellion and to follow orders from Goebbels and Himmler, who was on his way to Berlin. Moreover, Hitler promoted the major to colonel on the spot.

In the short time between Goebbels being informed of the assault and the arrival of Remer, he had managed to pass a radio message to the *Deutschlandsender* and at 0630 hours that evening the news that the attack on Hitler's life had been unsuccessful was broadcast to the world. The conspirators had also failed to take

over the *Rundfunkhaus* (German Broadcasting House). Goebbels' presence of mind had saved the day, while a complete lack of decisiveness on the part of the conspirators ensured that with each passing hour the chances of a successful *coup d'etat* lessened. Army and SS units loyal to the Führer managed to suppress the coup in Berlin and the commanders in chief on the two war fronts no longer dared to take action.

Hitler's revenge was terrible. The leaders of the coup were immediately executed, while thousands more were made to stand trial at a people's court before their death sentences were pronounced. Almost 5000 officers, members of the resistance, church leaders and other citizens were executed in this bloody purge. Goebbels started a hate campaign on the radio and in the press against the conspirators. Privately, however, he began to speak in a different tone about the Führer. He described Hitler's sickly appearance,

his trembling hands and his pallid skin. The boundless adoration of earlier years was giving way to a kind of disparaging pity. He also tolerated criticism about Hitler. When his close colleague Fritsche said to him that Hitler was offering up young German soldiers as cannon fodder, Goebbels did not respond. Encouraged, Fritsche said that the Führer ought to resign. Goebbels, who would have spoken of high treason only a few weeks before, maintained his silence. He did state that it was a miracle that Hitler had been spared. He was beginning to realize what kind of man his Führer actually was.

Goebbels had few illusions about the relationship between the Russians and the western Allies. In his article 'The Year 2000' he prophesied that the Allies would sooner or later wage war among themselves. 'Should the German people surrender, the Soviets will occupy the entire east and southeast of Europe, as well as a

Right: *Hitler meets with his Gauleiters at his headquarters shortly after the July Bomb Plot, 6 August 1944.*

Below right: *A clearly injured Hitler greets Goebbels and other leading Nazis on 20 July 1944.*

Below: *Goebbels gives the reading during the state funeral of SA chief Victor Lutze, 7 May 1943.*

large part of Germany. Along the border of this enormous country . . . a curtain of iron will fall . . . The rest of Europe will decline into political chaos which will only prepare the way for the coming of the Bolsheviks.'

On the afternoon of 22 April 1945 Goebbels, Magda and their six children left their official residence and moved to Hitler's bunker deep under the Reichs Chancellery. The bunker had two floors: the top floor had 12 rooms, of which four were used as a kitchen; the lower floor had 18 rooms.

On the night of 28/29 April, with the Russians barely 1000 meters from the Reichs Chancellery, Hitler married Eva Braun. The next day, a shot sounded throughout the bunker. Hitler had shot himself in the head. Next to him lay the body of Eva Braun, who had poisoned herself. The bodies were carried through an emergency exit to the garden of the Chancellery where they were set on fire. This had been the Führer's last order. When the flames flared up Goebbels, for the last time, raised his arm in the Nazi salute.

The first of May was spent on preparations for a mass evacuation of the bunker. However, Goebbels appeared to have taken a different decision. Magda gave her children a strong sedative with their supper. They were poisoned while sleeping. At 2045 hours Goebbels and his wife stepped out of their room arm-in-arm. Magda was very pale and clung heavily to her husband. Goebbels

seemed to be very calm when he said to those present: 'Everything is over. My wife and I are going to commit suicide. You shall burn our bodies.' His words were clear, almost overarticulated. He even raised a weak smile when he declared that they would go upstairs to spare their friends the trouble of carrying their bodies up. He then slowly put his gloves on, carefully smoothing out the fingers. He gave Magda his arm. Both turned and walked up the stairs without saying another word. After several minutes two shots were heard from above.

Early on the morning of 2 May, the Russians arrived. Very cautiously, they searched the bunker. Feeling their way forward, they moved from room to room finding nothing but corpses and garbage. Then they climbed up the stairs to the garden, where they found the badly burned remains of Joseph Goebbels at their feet. A hand, charred black and extended like a claw, stretched out as if greeting the victors. After identification, Goebbels was buried together with his wife in the torn up earth of Berlin. No one knows where he lies. Thus ended the life of a man who had always claimed: 'The essence of propaganda is winning people over to an idea in such a penetrating and all-encompassing way that they will accept the idea totally and will never be able to escape from its clutches.' His control of the minds of the German people had been absolute, now they would have to pay the price for their obedience to him.

HERMANN GÖRING

1893-1946

These pages: *Two formal portraits of the flamboyant Hermann Göring, as head of the Luftwaffe (far left) and as Hitler's Minister of the Interior (above).*

Nuremberg, 15 October 1946; time: 2245 hours. The 11 condemned war criminals of Hitler's Reich have only a few more hours to live. Two weeks have passed since the death penalties have been handed out. Strict security measures surround the condemned men. The cells stay lit all night and the guards are not allowed to let the prisoners out of their sight for a moment. The prisoner in cell number five is lying on his wooden bed, staring at the ceiling. In accordance with regulations, he lies with his hands outside the covers. The guard, continually watching through the spyhole, yawns. The man in the cell does not once look up at the spyhole.

Suddenly the guard notices something strange about the prisoner's behavior. His hands are convulsively clawing at the blanket, and his whole body starts to tremble. The prisoner's face contorts into a grimace. The legs under the blankets are now kicking, while the top half of his body is jerking to and fro. The guard gives a frightened shout. Iron bolts are thrown back and the guard rushes in. Within a few seconds, the duty officer and the Protestant minister are also in the cell. The convulsions decrease, the heavy body of the prisoner lies somewhat bent and his breathing is irregular.

The dying man's face is covered in sweat. Suddenly it turns blue, as if lit up by a sunlamp; the prisoner slumps backward, one more spasm and it is over. Hermann Wilhelm Göring, the Third Reich's second-in-command, prime minister, rebuilder and commander-in-chief of the Luftwaffe, Reichsminister for Air, Minister of the Interior, plenipotentiary for Hitler's Four-Year Plan, Reich Hunting Master, Chairman of the Council of Ministers for Reich Defense, and Chief of the Gestapo in Prussia is dead. By taking a cyanide capsule, which he had kept hidden in his riding boots, Göring had managed to escape the hangman.

Hermann Göring was one of the most intelligent and colorful men surrounding Hitler. Weighing about 220lb 'Fat Hermann' had, despite his jovial manner, a gangsterlike mentality which, combined with a disproportionate amount of power, proved to be disastrous for Europe. One of Hitler's veteran comrades-in-arms, Göring was able to secure for himself a large number of the many powerful offices, functions and honorary posts after the Nazis assumed power. He appropriated more than any other leader in Germany during the period 1933-45, an impressive number of offices with their accompanying honorariums, titles, uniforms and medals. His geniality, especially, won him a mixture of respect, admiration and affection from the German people during the period of the Third Reich. 'Iron fatty means well' was said of him when unpopular measures were taken. Furthermore, he was Hitler's chosen successor.

The following story went the rounds in the Ruhr area about a herring seller at a market singing the praises of his fish: *'Heuring, heuring so fass wie Göring'* (Herring, herring as fat as Göring). The man was arrested but set free again after several days. A week later

Above: *A youthful Hermann Göring pictured during his service with the famous Richthofen squadron in World War I.*

Right: *Aircraft engineer Antony Fokker (center) pictured with Göring who was, for a period, one of his test pilots.*

Far right: *Göring and Hitler in conversation with (from left to right) Gregor Strasser, Ernst Röhm and Bruckner, 1932.*

he was again loudly praising his wares: '*Heuring, heuring, genau so fasse wie letzte Woche!*' (Herring, herring as fat as last week!).

In the Berlin 'Cabaret of Comedians' Werner Finck frequently made the Nazis look ridiculous. Göring was one of his favorite targets. Finck was the first to suggest that the Reichsmarshal had rubber medals made for him so that he could wear them in the bath. The story about the baby elephant who saw Göring sitting in the first row at the circus and trumpeted 'Daddy, daddy' was also Finck's. Göring was proud of being the center of interest and never filed a complaint against Finck. Göring also won a good name for himself with the foreign press, mainly due to his many parties. He could be a very charming and attentive host when it suited him. But, like many Nazi leaders, Göring had several sides to him. It was

he who used the Luftwaffe as a weapon of mass destruction in the Blitzkrieg, mercilessly bombing defenseless cities such as Warsaw, Rotterdam and Belgrade.

He was also the one who set up the Gestapo and created the first concentration camps, which he handed over to a grateful Himmler in 1934. In that same year he actively took part in the purge of SA boss Röhm because, as he later said during his trial at Nuremberg, 'he stood in the way.' Göring was one of the initiators of the intrigues which led to the removal of two high-ranking Wehrmacht officers, Blomberg and Fritsch. He was also one of the five supreme commanders who participated in the notorious Hossbach conference in 1937 where Hitler announced his war plans. He announced the infamous Nuremberg racial laws on 15 September 1935 (more or less outlawing Jews) and with the 31 July regulation ordered Himmler and Heydrich to institute the '*Endlösung*' (final solution) of the Jewish problem within the German sphere of influence in Europe. He also used his authority in the execution of the Four-Year Plan, taking an active part in the plundering of the conquered territories.

Hermann Wilhelm Göring was born on 12 January 1893 in a sanatorium near Rosenheim south of Munich. His mother, Franziska, left the sanatorium after three months, returning to Haiti where her husband was consul-general. The doctor who had helped with the delivery was a Berliner named Ritter Hermann von Epenstein. He later became a close friend of the family and was to have a strong influence on the young Hermann Göring. The three-month-old baby was cared for by a family in Frith. He became a somewhat lonely child during the three year separation from his parents. 'The worst thing that can happen to a child is to be separated from his mother during the first years of his development,' wrote Hermann Göring in a memorandum during World War II in which he expressed his opposition to a proposal for providing crèches and calling on married women to work in factories.

After a successful career in the German colonies, Heinrich Göring retired in 1896 and returned with his wife and three children to Germany. For the first time in three years, they saw the young Hermann again. The family moved to Berlin where they lived in a modest house in one of the city's suburbs. Meanwhile

Page 38: *Three pictures of Hitler and Göring on the campaign trail in 1932. Here they arrive at Berlin's Tempelhof airport on 30 November after spreading their message throughout much of Germany.*

Below: *Göring peers into the crowd during a marchpast of the SA in 1931.*

Ritter von Epenstein, Hermann's godfather, started visiting them frequently. He had also retired from government service and lived the life of a typical *bon vivant*. He was well-to-do, a bachelor, and was regarded as a suitable match for the daughters of the lower aristocracy. At the same time he was a lover of several of their mothers. He dressed well and when he dropped in unexpectedly on the dull Göring household, he would be full of stories of his adventurous travels to places such as Cairo, Constantinople, Naples or St Petersburg.

In 1901 von Epenstein invited the Göring family to Austria, where he had acquired a castle in Mauterndorf. The castle was furnished in medieval splendor and magnificence. The servants were dressed in court uniforms from former days, meals were announced with bugles and a group of minstrels and musicians would sing and play music in the gallery of the main hall on festive occasions. This all made a deep impression on young Hermann. His obsessive interest in medieval tournaments and jousts, and his love of uniforms presumably stems from this period. When von Epenstein, of Jewish descent and having an affair with Hermann's mother, Franziska (they were lovers for 15 years), offered the Görings his Veldenstein castle near Nuremberg as a residence, the young Hermann began to see himself as a young aristocrat. The staff at Veldenstein treated the Görings with all due respect, as though they were the owners.

Hermann knew that one of his ancestors, Michael Christian Göring, had held an important economic post under Frederick the Great, a knowledge that filled him with pride and the ambition to obtain an important post for himself. When he was 12 he left Veldenstein and went to the military academy in Karlsruhe, which he left when he was 16 with good results. He then underwent officer-

cadet training in Lichtenfelde near Berlin. He passed his examinations *cum laude* when he was 19, joined the 112th Prince Wilhelm Regiment and was stationed at its headquarters in Mulhouse. When he visited his parents to show off his new uniform shortly before his transfer, he arrived in the middle of domestic troubles. Ritter von Epenstein had broken off his affair with Hermann's mother and had fallen in love with a 20-year-old woman, who was determined to marry the 62-year-old von Epenstein. Toward the end of 1913 von Epenstein evicted the Göring family from Veldenstein. They settled in Munich, where Hermann's father died shortly after their arrival.

At the outbreak of World War I Göring was 20 years old. There were few young men who longed for the war as he did. He saw the war as an exciting test of his courage, with a prize awaiting the strong, the brave and the chivalrous. Among the friends Göring had made in Mulhouse was a young officer called Bruno Loerzer. Their friendship lasted almost a lifetime.

Shortly after war broke out Loerzer received a place in a flying school, which filled the young Göring with envy. Göring wrote to his commander asking for a transfer to the air force, and when the answer was not forthcoming, he forged the papers assigning himself to the school in Freiburg. In the meantime he bought some flying gear and started practice as an observer in Loerzer's airplane. His transfer request was, however, rejected and he was ordered to report immediately to his regiment. Göring now saw not only his future at risk, but also his freedom, as his case had been handed over for court-martial. It was only due to the intervention of von Epenstein, who had received a desperate telegram from Göring, that matters were resolved. After quite some effort he managed to have Göring transferred to an air force unit, and out of the clutches of the military police.

Top: *Hitler and Göring with their cabinet, 1933.*

Above: *Göring in 1933.*

Right: *Göring attends the Reichstag opening ceremony, 21 March 1933.*

Göring and Loerzer made many flights over the front and fought numerous air battles. Göring soon earned the reputation of being a competent and fearless pilot and in 1917 he was appointed a commander of a newly-formed Jagdstaffel 27, which was based in Flanders. He was very successful in leading his squadron and received Germany's highest military honor, the *Pour la Mérite*. Pilots were normally given this medal only after having shot down more than 25 enemy aircraft; Göring had shot down only 15 and his final score was 22. In his case, however, the award was given as official recognition of his qualities as a leader and as a professional soldier. He was appointed commander of the famous von Richthofen squadron on 7 July 1918, following the recent death of its previous commander.

Despite heroic efforts Germany's defeat was inevitable. In his final speech to his fellow officers Göring promised them that 'the day will come when all who have betrayed Germany will be driven out. Prepare yourselves for that day. Arm yourselves for that day. Work towards that day.' After the German capitulation Göring hung aimlessly about Berlin for a time and then decided to visit his mother in Munich. He was wearing civilian clothing and no one suspected that the quiet young man was one of Germany's greatest fighter pilots, the victor of several of the war's most famous air battles and the proud bearer of Germany's highest distinction for bravery. 'That trip home was the most dreadful one in my life,' Göring would later say. 'I have never been so depressed.'

In Munich a Soviet-style republic had been proclaimed under Kurt Eisner but was crushed shortly after by volunteer corps. Chaos reigned – the King of Bavaria had fled, and there were raids and bloody purges. Göring had no definite prospects; he had no money, no job and could no longer make demands on his godfather who was somewhere in Austria.

The restrictions stipulated in the Treaty of Versailles did not include a ban on the production of airplanes and there were still several manufacturers in Germany building planes for, mainly, the foreign market. One of these was Dutchman Antony Fokker. Göring had the good fortune of being able to test the company's latest commercial model which was finished in the spring of 1919. The Fokker F7 was a monoplane and Göring did the tests in a very competent manner. He was then asked to take part in a flying demonstration in Denmark. His display of daring aerobatics was so

Above: *Hitler and Göring attend the 1933 Reichsparteitag.*

Right: *Long-standing party members including Hitler, Göring and Julius Streicher (third from left) march through Munich behind the 'Blood Flag' on 9 November 1933.*

breathtaking that Fokker decided to lend him the airplane permanently in the expectation that Göring would gain publicity for the F7. This led to the start of a successful period as a traveling pilot in Denmark and Sweden, where he would have himself introduced as the last commander of the famous von Richthofen squadron.

One of the ways he earned his living in those days was by using his airplane as a taxi. He made short tourist flights for pleasure-

seekers and also ran a charter service for businessmen wanting to fly anywhere in Scandinavia. It was through his charter service that he met Count Eric von Rosen, who had missed his train from Stockholm to his medieval castle in the middle of Sweden. It was the winter of 1920. Although three other pilots had refused the job because of bad weather, Göring was willing to take the risk. It was a terrible flight, but they eventually landed safely near the castle. He

Right: *President Hindenburg receives Adolf Hitler at a public ceremony in Berlin, early 1934. Göring and Admiral Raeder are in attendance.*

Below: *Hitler and members of his cabinet attend a ceremony at Berlin's State Opera commemorating the victims of World War I, 1933.*

Left: *Hitler and Göring take a closer look at a Mercedes during an automobile exhibition in Berlin, 1934.*

Below: *Hitler and Göring in the Schorfheide on 19 June 1934.*

was asked to stay the night and there he met Karin von Kantzow, sister to the mistress of the castle. Despite the fact that Karin was already married and had a nine-year-old son, it was love at first sight.

Later, in 1922, Göring decided that he wanted to study (among other subjects) economics at the University of Munich. Here, he came into contact with Hitler for the first time. He heard him speak on several occasions and became an enthusiastic admirer of the Führer and interested in the NSDAP. Göring was an important asset to Hitler. Not only would this great war hero boost the prestige of the party, but Göring also had energy, daring and an officer's education – qualities which would be very useful to the Nazis. Conversely, Göring found in Hitler a new Ritter von Epenstein, a new hero.

Hitler found Göring to be the ideal person to reorganize the *Sturmabteilung* (SA), basing it on military lines. Göring was appointed commander of the paramilitary organization which then totaled about 11,000 members. Göring worked hard and managed to give the SA discipline, coherence and drive. After only a few months, this motley crew of former soldiers, students, farm laborers, army officers and civil servants was transformed into a well-trained force with a strong *esprit de corps*. The Göring house in Munich (he had by now married the divorced Karin von Kantzow) soon became the meeting place for NSDAP leaders.

In January 1923, with the French Army occupying the Ruhr in protest against Germany's overdue war debt payments and with inflation increasing drastically, Hitler felt that the time was ripe for a bid to seize power. Hitler's 'putsch' took place on 8 November in Munich. It was however, a miserable fiasco for the NSDAP. The fighting in front of the Feldherrnhalle led to several deaths. It seemed as though National Socialism had committed political suicide as most of its leaders, including Hitler, were arrested and sentenced to several years of imprisonment.

Göring, who was seriously wounded in his side during the fighting, was smuggled across the border to Austria by his wife. The future looked very bleak. Not only was Göring taking large amounts of painkillers (which resulted in his later morphine addiction) but his wife's health was also declining and she was spending more and more time in bed. Illness, financial worries, concern for her husband and a desperate longing for her family in Sweden worsened her condition. The couple decided to move to Sweden, where they found a flat in Stockholm. Karin's health, not helped by unhappiness or concern for her husband, who was now showing signs of acute morphine addiction, continued to worsen.

Some time later Göring was admitted to a clinic. After he attacked a nurse he was examined by two doctors and officially declared insane. He was transferred to the Langro Institute for the Insane, where he received therapy for his morphine addiction. The consulting doctor described his patient as a 'sentimental individual lacking moral courage.' However, the therapy was a success and after several months of total abstinence he was declared cured. Göring's appearance had undergone a drastic change. He had gained a lot of weight, as his wound as well as his addiction had

This page: A series of formal pictures of Göring with other senior party figures (above right) and in conversation with one of his adjutants (below left).

Above, far right: Göring in the company of other senior military figures.

Far right: A poster announcing a Nazi meeting.

affected his glands. In 1927 Göring said goodbye to his wife and re-turned to a Germany which had changed drastically during his absence.

Germany, 1927. Hitler had been out of prison for two years and had built up the NSDAP to such an extent that its name was known throughout Germany. Many members were after high positions in the party and it was difficult to find something for Göring. His former position as commander of the SA had been taken over by Röhm. The outcome of two interviews Göring had with Hitler shortly after his return was disappointing. He (Göring) needed more 'empathy' with the party and should look for a job in the business world. 'And then we'll see,' Hitler said. Göring rebuffed, set out to find some form of gainful employment.

In early November Göring finally found a job with the Bavarian Motor Works (BMW). In the spring of 1928 he was able to bring his wife over from Sweden and she met up with her husband in Berlin. Slowly but surely Hitler became more willing to let Göring back into the inner circle of top Nazis. In 1928 Hitler offered him a safe seat in the Reichstag – the elections were to be held that same

year. Göring's campaign in Berlin was short, noisy and effective. The National Socialists won 12 seats in the elections and one of them was Göring's. Besides being a representative in the Reichstag, Göring was on the NSDAP payroll and traveled throughout Germany recruiting new members. He managed to sign up quite a number of prominent businessmen, manufacturers and bankers through his many connections in the German business world. In 1930 Göring became *Politischer Bevollmächtiger des Führers* (the Führer's authorized political agent).

However, his wife's health continued to deteriorate and she died, after a long period of suffering, on 17 October 1931. His many party activities left him hardly any time to mourn the death of his beloved wife. The elections of 1932 gave the National Socialists 230 seats out of those contested, with 38 percent of the votes. Göring's physical condition was excellent in 1932. He had vast amounts of energy, was very shrewd, almost crafty, and his enthusiasm overwhelmed most people. He was always on hand to cheer up the anxious and bad-tempered Hitler.

Thanks to his many friends in industry, banking, business and the nobility, he moved in the highest circles. Tirelessly, he would refute or soften the negative reports about the NSDAP, especially those referring to the rough street-fighters, the SA. Although his activities did not leave him much time for a private life, he was very charmed by the actress Emmy Sonnerman, whom he married in 1935.

On 30 January 1933 Hitler was appointed Reich Chancellor of Germany. Through various intrigues and bribes he had managed to force the hand of Reichspresident von Hindenburg. Upon hearing of the momentous appointment Göring hurried to Hitler to tell him the wonderful news. Goebbels wrote in his diary: 'This was certainly the finest moment in Göring's life. He had spent years smoothing the diplomatic and political path by means of exhaust-

Reichstagsabgeordneter Fliegerhauptmann a. D.

GOERING

der letzte Führer der Richthofen-Staffel   Berlin
spricht

Left: *Hitler and his government pose for the camera after announcing the reintroduction of general compulsory military service, 16 March 1935.*

Below: *Ernst Röhm greets Göring on the latter's fortieth birthday, 12 January 1934.*

Right: *Göring watches the proceedings on Reichsparteitag in Nuremberg, 1934.*

ing negotiations for the Führer. His nerves of steel and especially his strong character and loyalty toward Hitler were sincere and admirable.' Now, according to Goebbels, this 'sincere soldier with the heart of a child' had brought Hitler the 'greatest news' of his life.

On the evening of the 30th, a large torchlit procession passed the Reich Chancellery. Adolf Hitler stood at one of the windows and time after time gave the Nazi salute to the elated passers-by. The procession finally ended and the brownshirts and enthusiastic followers streamed into the pubs and beer gardens to celebrate. There was a reception in the Reich Chancellery and toward midnight Hitler and numerous prominent Nazis went to Crown Prince August Wilhelm's house where the Crown Prince had organized a double party in honor of Hitler's acceptance of office and of his own birthday. The imperial family, Hitler, the National Socialists and Germany were all toasted.

Göring was rewarded for his services with the important appointments of Reichsminister for Air, Prime Minister and Prussian Minister of the Interior. He saw as his first task the transformation of the Prussian state into the ideal National Socialist government: a model for all German states. He started by purging the Prussian police force. A number of important civil servants were personally sacked by Göring, among whom was the young lawyer Robert Kempner, head of the public prosecutor's office. Kempner had insisted on Hitler's arrest for high treason for turning a blind eye to Röhm's preparations for an armed uprising by the brownshirts in 1934. Göring fired Kempner on the spot. 'You're lucky that you aren't thrown in prison!' shouted Göring. 'Get out of my sight, I never want to see you again!' (Göring was to meet Robert Kempner again in 1945 in an Allied camp. Kempner by then had become an Allied interrogator and advisor and had acquired American nationality.)

After his purges, Göring was able to appoint his own people to key positions, and the SA and SS became official auxiliary police. In a speech given in Dortmund, Göring said: 'In future there will be but one man with power and responsibility in Prussia, and that man is myself. Those who do their duty in the service of the state, obey my orders and ruthlessly use their guns when attacked can

rely on my protection. Those, on the other hand, who act as cowards, have to realize that they will immediately be thrown out. A bullet fired by a policeman is a bullet that belongs to me. And if you say that it is murder, then I am the murderer. I know of only two types of people: those with us and those against us.'

A great deal of mystery shrouds the burning of the Reichstag on 27 February 1933. In spite of Göring's important role in the arrest of many communists (they were charged with arson), it is unlikely that he had prior knowledge of the fire since he had many personal

belongings in his office, particularly family heirlooms and portraits. The purges continued throughout March 1933. In a move legalized by an enabling act which rendered the constitution impotent, thousands of communists, social democrats and socialists were forced into the recently built concentration camps. In the spring of 1934 Göring handed the entire police force, the concentration camps and the Gestapo over to Himmler, although Göring did, cautiously, then organize his own personal police and espionage services. This *Ladespolizeigruppe* was to supply him with private information and a bodyguard.

One of the many offices he was given (or created for himself), was that of *Reichsjagermeister* (minister in charge of hunting) and in 1934 the office of *Reichsforstmeister* (minister in charge of forests) was added to this. Göring took these duties very seriously. His efforts in the area of environmental protection were beneficial. He restocked the forests of Schorfheide and Rominten with birds and animals, as wildlife had suffered harshly at the hands of hunters and poachers. He imported moose and bison from Sweden and Canada, wild ducks, swans and other wildlife from Poland and Spain. In 1934 he made German hunting laws more stringent and introduced planting schemes which created green areas around all the major cities. Less altruistically he managed to acquire 40,000 hectares of land on the Schorfheide for himself, where he had a palace-like villa built, naming it Karinhalle in memory of his first wife.

His most important function was that of Minister for Air. Göring was determined to create a powerful air force. He installed former comrades-in-arms and fellow pilots in key positions: Karl Boden-

schats became his adjutant; Erhard Milch his State Secretary. Milch held his position throughout the war, becoming a field marshal, despite the fact that he was Jewish. Göring's friend Bruno Loerzer was appointed head of the Air Sports Club, a cover for a secret training group for pilots. Also, Ernst Udet became advisor in the Air Ministry. The expansion of the Luftwaffe moved far too slowly for Göring, a situation which brought him into conflict with Schacht, the economics minister, when the latter appeared unwilling to reduce rations any further. 'I took from the German people what they allowed me to,' said Schacht. 'I have forbidden them to take money abroad. I have restricted imports so much that there are now hardly any. I have put the population on strict rations. All for the benefit of rearmament.'

Göring's answer to Schacht came in the form of a long speech in which he urged the nation to accept austerity. Göring said that 'rearmament is absolutely necessary. But rearmament is only the first step in our goal for the German people. Rearmament is not a goal in itself. I do not want rearmament for militaristic reasons, nor for the oppression of other peoples, but only to guarantee the freedom of Germany. What use is there in playing in an international orchestra if Germany is only allowed to play the triangle? I shall speak plainly. Some people outside Germany are hard of hearing. They only listen when they hear gun-shots. We shall get those guns. We have no butter my friends, but I ask you: what would you rather have, butter or guns? Should we import bacon or iron ore? I tell you, being prepared gives us our strength.' He gave his stomach a smack. 'Butter makes us fat.' His speech was effective and Schacht reluctantly gave in.

In 1935 Göring finally asked the actress Emmy Sonnerman to marry him. Their marriage ceremony was one of the 'grandest social occasions' of the Third Reich. Congratulatory telegrams and presents poured in from all over the world. Hermann and Emmy drove to the cathedral in an open carriage. Bells sounded and a formation of the latest German planes flew overhead. More than 30,000 members of the paramilitary organizations lined the streets. Göring's star was still rising, especially since Hitler had put him in charge of the second Four-Year Plan.

Above: *Göring and Emmy Sonnerman, his second wife, pictured at Obersalzberg, December 1934.*

Right: *Göring and his new wife Emmy leave the cathedral after their wedding ceremony, 10 April 1935.*

Above, center: *The marriage ceremony in Berlin. Reichs Bishop Muller conducts the proceedings.*

Above: *The Görings salute the large crowd that had gathered to view their marriage ceremony.*

Left: *The Görings and their best man, Hitler, at their wedding reception.*

To achieve the ultimate goal of National Socialism, a German empire in Europe, rearmament was considered a necessity. A serious obstruction to the development of the German economy was its dependence on foreign countries: 70 to 100 percent of the raw materials necessary for rearmament had to be imported from abroad. In order to protect Germany from a possible blockade which was not unlikely in the future, Hitler decided to introduce a program directed toward economic self-sufficiency. In the fall of 1936 Hitler announced the second Four-Year Plan. The main objective was to make Germany as independent as possible in the areas of food supply and raw material production. Göring was put in charge of the program.

The concept of autarky refers to a national economy that is largely independent of foreign countries. The autarky announced in the second Four-Year Plan was, for Hitler, more of a propaganda exercise than a practical plan, since he knew as well as Göring that Germany, with its territorial limitations, could not become self-reliant. Autarky was seen more as a long-term ideal. Hitler and his staff saw the best solution to the German raw material and food supply problems in the concept of *Lebensraum* (living space), involving the conquest of new territories in, especially, the East. When Germany finally created a powerful continental empire, then the *'Grossraumwirtschaft'* (great economy) of the state would be truly autarkic. Thus, Hitler saw the solution to the problem as a step-by-step development toward autarky, a progression to be achieved by a trade policy of controlling, politically and militarily, certain key countries.

The program began in 1933 with the first Four-Year Plan, which aimed to create work for six million people. This was followed in 1934 by the *'Neue Plan,'* which demanded the total submission of foreign trade to government policy. Finally, the domestic equivalent of the *Neue Plan*, the second Four-Year Plan, had as its focus the development of the synthetic raw materials industry and a higher level of food production. Both the *Neue Plan* and the two Four-Year Plans were intended as temporary transitional measures before the full development of *Lebensraum*: 'a definite solution by means of an increase of natural resources and food supplies for our people.'

The quest for autarky is expressed very clearly in Hitler's *Denkschrift zum Vierjahresplan* (*Thoughts on the Four-Year Plan*), from the summer of 1936. This can be regarded as a basic outline of the National Socialists' economic policies which were directed at short-term gains. Hitler concludes his memorandum as follows: 'In short, it is necessary that from now on an all-out effort be made in all possible areas toward 100 percent self-sufficiency. . . There has been time enough during the past four years to learn what we cannot achieve. In this regard I now make the following demands: The German Army must be ready in four years; the Germany economy must be ready for war in four years.'

Numerous state enterprises were set up as part of the second Four-Year Plan. The most important example was the Reichswerke Hermann Göring in Salzgitter, where ore with a low iron content was mined and processed. The underlying principles of the second Four-Year Plan had their origins in the war economy of 1914-18. During that period Germany was severely crippled by an economic blockade and from that period onward worked on the development of synthetic raw materials. The scientific and technical prerequisites for the production of *'Ersatzstoffen'* (synthetic

Left: *Ferdinand Porsche (third from left) shows off an early VW Beetle Volkswagen to a smiling Göring.*

Below: *Hitler and Göring view the latter's estate from Karinhalle, July 1935.*

materials) had been met long before the Nazis came to power and only the practical application of the scientific processes and finance still presented problems. However, the new synthetic materials were much more expensive than their natural counterparts. The price of synthetic rubber (BUMA) was originally seven times that of imported natural rubber. Manufacturing costs for synthetic petrol and synthetic coloring agents were also higher than for their natural equivalents.

In the case of certain vital raw materials Germany was far from self-sufficient by the end of the second Four-Year Plan. This was especially true of iron ore, oil and non-ferrous metals. The results of the second Four-Year Plan were, thus, patchy. However, one important goal was attained, namely, undesirable investments had been avoided, while desirable investments had been stimulated as much as possible. However, the German economy in 1939 was hardly less dependent on foreign countries than it had been before 1936. Nevertheless many foreign observers were impressed by the Nazis' economic progress.

10 September 1938: 'An insignificant strip of land in Europe is a nuisance to the entire human race. These wretched pygmies [the Czechs] are causing great trouble to a civilized people.' In spite of

Far left: *Blomberg, Göring, Fritsch and Hitler attending the Nuremberg rally of 1935.*

Left: *Nuremberg rally, 1935. Admiral Raeder joins Hitler, Göring, Blomberg and Fritsch on the podium.*

Göring's belligerent language at the time of the Czechoslovakian crisis, he was not in favor of war. He foresaw the dangers of escalation and believed that Germany could never win a lengthy conflict. However, when the German Army, without warning, invaded Poland Göring launched his Luftwaffe into battle, and not without success. Göring, now convinced of the effectiveness of his Luftwaffe, proposed attacking Britain as soon as possible. His plan was to destroy British aircraft and airfields, and paralyze British industry.

After the capitulation of France in June 1940, Göring urged Hitler to conquer Britain at once, but Hitler again refused. He still believed that the British would accept his peace proposals. According to Hitler, Britain was 'a factor in the balance between the world

powers.' Göring had, in the meantime, received the specially created rank of Reich Field Marshal of the Great German Empire for his notable contribution to the victories in Poland and the western countries.

During the Blitz, when the Luftwaffe carried out air attacks on England, radar towers along the English coast were also bombed. But because an English plane dropped several bombs on the suburbs of Berlin, a furious Hitler ordered an immediate retaliatory attack on English cities. The radar towers were left alone. If the Germans had carried on with their bombing of the radar posts they would have been able to cripple the English air defense system.

When Göring heard for the first time from Hitler that he wanted

Above: *Göring attending a function in the Italian Embassy accompanied by Italian Foreign Minister Count Ciano and German Foreign Minister von Neurath, 1936.*

Right: *Göring entertains a group of British dignitaries including Lord Halifax at the Schorfheide, 20 November 1937.*

Far right: *Hitler and Göring review a cavalcade from the balcony of the Reichs Chancellery, 16 March 1938.*

to attack Russia, he (Göring) returned to his former plan of first
neutralizing England. To this end he devised a new strategy which
would give Germany control over the entire Mediterranean Sea.
England would be cut off from its colonies and would have to
accept a peace settlement. A war on two fronts alarmed Göring,
however. He implored Hitler to think of Napoleon. Hitler replied
that Napoleon had not been in possession of the largest air fleet the
world had ever seen. Göring, however, maintained that a war
against Russia would be 'the worst thing we could do. It is econom-
ically wrong, politically wrong and militarily wrong. But von Ribbentrop wanted it and Goebbels wanted it and they persuaded the
Führer to want it too. I protested until I was blue in the face, but
they would not listen. Now, I wipe my hands of the entire matter –
the entire war. Do what you can. I can't worry any more about what
is going to happen.' Thus spoke Göring to one of his generals.

The German air force was indeed insufficiently prepared for a
war on two fronts. Adolf Galland, commanding officer of the German fliers, described the situation as follows: 'The unforeseen
continuation of the battle in the East threatened to upset the entire
strategy of the German supreme command. Hitler had only begun
a war on two fronts in the expectation of a quick and total victory in
the East. When the German offensive came to a standstill, Hitler's
plan to resume the raids on England after the quick termination of
the eastern campaign had, of course, to be dropped. This failure
could not be disguised by the largest and most far-reaching plans
for advancing in the direction of the Caucasus in the coming
spring.

'As supreme commander of the air force Göring should have
been the first to realize that he would never be able to regain air
supremacy in the West with an air force that had already reached its
limits during the fighting in the East. The German aeronautics industry [like the entire German economy] was no match for war on

such a large scale.' Göring knew only too well that Germany did not have sufficient raw materials to keep the vast war machine going, but he lacked the moral courage to clearly and frankly tell this to Hitler.

Seldom in modern history has anyone 'collected' art treasures as did Hermann Göring. He had the assistance of a team of art experts for his plundering and looting trips across occupied Europe, individuals like the young art connoisseur, Lohse, who was added to his staff and given a Luftwaffe uniform so that he could move freely in the occupied territories. In addition to these methods, Göring also 'bought' his treasures from *'Einsatzstab'* Rosenberg who did nothing other than confiscate the valuables of murdered Jews. Art treasures were brought by the wagon-load to Göring's mansions and country estates; he soon possessed the most valuable art collection in the world.

He had magnificent antique Gobelins, oriental carpets, alabaster vases and furniture – even a desk that had once belonged to Cardinal Mazarin. Göring's haul of paintings resembled a museum collection rather than a private one. The Reich Marshal

was in possession of as many as five portraits by Rembrandt, the *Infanta* by Velazquez, the *Resurrection of Lazarus* by Rubens, paintings by Frans Hals, van Dyck, Boucher, Goya, Cranach and 30 paintings from the fifteenth century Flemish school – a shortlist of the greatest and most famous works of art. Someone who had amassed such a collection was obviously not easily satisfied with mere trifles. Presents for Göring became increasingly larger and larger. Months before his birthday government, army and party officials would receive a questionnaire, to be filled in and returned, concerning the size of their planned gift to the Reich Marshal. There were even a number of organizations taxed with the coordination of present buying for Göring. One year, at the height of the war, the Berlin city council asked Goebbels if he agreed to them buying a painting for Göring worth 250,000 Reichsmarks on behalf of the citizens of the *'Reichshauptstadt.'* Goebbels is said to have replied irritably that a present worth 25,000 seemed quite sufficient.

It goes without saying that the various art dealers, who did good business with Göring, wanted to stay on good terms with him (for when he was not stealing his art treasures, he would buy them through art dealers with government money). The dealers would even bribe his servants for this purpose. Göring's manservant, Kropp, later said that he had once received a rather valuable painting from an art dealer in Amsterdam. He had said in passing that he found it quite beautiful. He later asked Göring whether he was allowed to keep it. 'Of course,' laughed Göring, 'it's yours.' However, after closer inspection the Reich Marshal decided he wanted it for himself. He forced Kropp into exchanging the painting for a larger, but worthless, one from the cellars of his castle Karinhalle. At Karinhalle Göring would dress with care when giving his guests a guided tour of his acquisitions. He would often wear velvet knickerbockers, gold-buckled shoes, a colored velvet jacket, a ruffled shirt and rings with enormous precious stones on his fingers.

Toward the end of the war, when the Reich began to shrink in size and Göring's country estates were falling one after the other into the hands of the advancing Allied Forces, he had his art treasures transferred to Berchtesgaden. The Americans discovered them in a rest home for the Luftwaffe. The stored treasures included the most important and famous works from Göring's collection: 14 rooms were filled with paintings and four with statues; there were several rooms with chinaware and Gobelins stacked in boxes up to the ceiling; and the chapel served as storage space for Renaissance furniture. An entire train had been needed to transport this collection to Berchtesgaden.

As the military situation worsened, with the Allied bombing of German cities and industrial centers becoming more severe, Hitler's confidence in Göring diminished. Hitler held him personally responsible for the failings of the Luftwaffe, particularly after the heavy bombing of Hamburg. Hitler exploded at Göring in the presence of other officers during the so-called 'Lagebesprechungen' (situation report) and shouted at him in a horrible and offensive manner. Göring retreated to one of his many estates, dejected and apathetic, leaving the conduct of the war to others. Only toward the end of the war would he again play a significant role.

Shortly before the siege of Berlin in the spring of 1945, Göring left the capital for Berchtesgaden. There he heard that the Führer had had a serious nervous breakdown. General Koller, Göring's Luftwaffe chief-of-staff, officially informed him of the Führer's last instructions: he intended to commit suicide in his Berlin bunker; if there were to be negotiations with the Allies, Göring would have to conduct them. This created a serious dilemma for Göring: should he intervene, or wait for developments in Berlin? He asked Koller for Hitler's decree of 29 June 1941 in which Hitler had named Göring his successor, and read the most important passage aloud: 'Should I be restricted in my freedom of action, or should I become incompetent in some other way, Field Marshal

Above, far left: *Göring, his daughter (on small bike) and a niece at Obersalzberg.*

Far left: *Göring's daughter Edda in front of a portrait of her mother Emmy.*

Above: *The opulent main hall at Göring's country retreat Karinhalle.*

Left: *The main courtyard at Karinhalle.*

Pages 60-61: *With Göring in the president's chair, Hitler speaks in the Reichstag, 11 December 1941.*

Right: *Martin Bormann (second from left) and Göring survey the effects of the bomb attempt on Hitler at Rastenburg, 20 July 1944.*

Below right: *Göring and Keitel attend a strategy planning meeting on the Führer's birthday, 20 April 1942.*

Above: *Hitler speaks at a Reichstag session in Berlin's Kroll Opera, 4 May 1941.*

Right: *Göring shows off a collection of old German manuscripts to the Japanese Foreign Minister Yosuke Matsuoka, Karinhalle, 29 March 1941.*

Göring shall be my successor regarding all services of state, party and Wehrmacht.' However, Göring still hesitated, mainly because he was terrified of Bormann. 'Bormann is my arch-enemy. He is just waiting for the moment he can get me. Should I enter negotiations, he will accuse me of treason; however if I don't, he will accuse me of having failed at the most difficult hour,' he later explained to Koller.

He finally decided to telegraph Hitler and, referring to his decision to remain in Berlin, ask whether he agreed to Göring's taking over the general leadership of the Reich with 'total freedom of action at home and abroad.' Koller: 'It was as though he had come to life again. He was full of plans and ideas on how to end the war.' However, Göring's fear of Bormann had not been unfounded. Hitler initially reacted very calmly to the telegram, but Bormann eventually managed to convince him that a *coup d'etat* was being planned. Speer, present in the Führer's bunker at the time, described the outburst of anger that followed: 'With a red contorted face and glassy eyes Hitler raged: "I knew this all along. I know that Göring is lazy and corrupt. He let the Luftwaffe go to ruin. He is corrupt, and through his example, corruption has spread in this country. Besides, he has been a drug addict for years. I've known that for a long time."'

The answer to his telegram was devastating. Göring was relieved of all posts, including the successorship and was to be immediately arrested for high treason. Furthermore, orders had been given to liquidate the 'traitor' upon the death of the Führer. On 27 April Göring and his family were taken to a castle in Austria by the SS. Shortly afterward he was freed by a unit from the Luftwaffe, but he was recaptured by the Americans several days later.

Together with the other important surviving war criminals, Göring ended up in the dock at Nuremberg. The process started in November 1945 and would last almost a year. Göring was found

guilty on all four counts of the indictment – conspiracy, crimes against peace, war crimes and crimes against humanity – on the basis of numerous documents and testimonies. At the end of the verdict the following was said: 'No mitigating circumstances can be put forward, for Göring was often, indeed, almost always, the moving spirit, only surpassed by his Führer. He was the main leader of most invasions, a political as well as military leader; he was in charge of the slave labor system and drew up the program for the oppression of the Jews and other races in Germany as well as in foreign countries.'

In spite of the magnitude of his crimes, which he openly admitted, Göring predicted during his trial that in 50 years time he

Left: *Göring (in sunglasses) and other surviving members of the Nazi hierarchy in the dock at Nuremberg.*

Top: *Göring delivers the funeral sermon for a fallen comrade killed in the July Bomb Plot.*

Above: *The last days of the Third Reich.*

would be spoken of as a great man, who had done everything within his power for the Reich. Furthermore, he succeeded in proving his ingenuity, intelligence and craftiness during the many months of that trial.

Göring did his utmost, despite his personal feelings, to act as one with the other prisoners. When he was asked why he had never stood up to Hitler and told him the truth, he answered: 'Show me one person who said "no" in Germany that is not fertilizing the daisies.' The British judge Sir Norman Birkett noted in regard to Göring: 'Göring is the man dominating the trial and that, surprisingly enough, without having said one word in public before sitting in the witness box. It is quite clear that someone with exceptional, possibly devilish, qualities is sitting in that box.' No one seemed to have expected such ability and knowledge. Birkett saw Göring as amiable, sharp, clever, competent and resourceful.

On 30 September 1946 at 1450 hours Göring hears the verdict: 'Accused Hermann Wilhelm Göring! In accordance with the counts in the indictment, of which you have been found guilty, the International Military Tribunal sentences you to death by hanging.' Calmly, Göring listens to the verdict. Then he removes his headphones, makes a quick military about-turn and leaves the room. The lift doors close quietly behind him. His request to be shot by a firing squad is rejected.

RUDOLF
HESS

1894-1987

Left: *Rudolf Hess, Hitler's
disgraced deputy, strikes an
heroic pose.*

Above: *Hess wearing the fulldress uniform of a Waffen-SS
member.*

Rudolf Hess, Hitler's former deputy, was the last prisoner in Spandau, and was fated to die there. The role Hess played in Nazi Germany and the influence he wielded as Hitler's right-hand man remains a controversial and complex affair, while his death in Spandau has never been fully explained. His political involvement came to a spectacular end in 1941 with his famous flight to Britain in an attempt to end the war between the two countries. Following his imprisonment in England for the duration of the war, he was tried before the International Tribunal at Nuremberg and was sentenced to life imprisonment.

On the morning of 17 August 1987, prisoner number seven was brought his breakfast. Rudolf Hess, by then 93 years old and a thin, weak man, was capable of only very limited effort. He had earlier suffered a slight stroke and in the 1980s a cerebral hemorrhage had weakened his eyesight in both eyes. His sense of balance had been seriously affected, partly because of his failing eyesight, but mainly due to arteriosclerosis of the blood vessels. After breakfast he was led, as usual, to the bleak prison garden where he went for his daily ration of fresh air.

The enormous prison in the Berlin suburb of Spandau, built to hold 600 inmates, was now inhabited by Hess, the only prisoner, together with 33 soldiers, 17 civil servants, four doctors, one chaplain and four prison governors. The former Allied powers (the United States, Great Britain, France and the Soviet Union) shared responsibility for his confinement, relieving each other every three months. Hess cost approximately 30,000 German marks per day to keep – the most expensive prisoner in the world.

After lunch on the 17th Hess took a nap. He woke up at 1430 hours, put on his jacket and was again taken to the garden. Shortly after 1430, the guard in Tower B (the main tower) saw him come outside, his bent body slowly shuffling along the main garden path,

R.P. Nürnberg 1927.

Above left: *A thoughtful Hess stares through the bars of a cell in Landsberg.*

Left: *Hess (far right) prepares to leave the prison of Landsberg.*

Above right: *Hess and Hitler at the 1927 rally in Nuremberg.*

Right: *Hitler and Hess with a group of early colleagues.*

led by his guard. The last specific entry made by the tower guard referring to Hess was at 1515 hours, when he saw the two men sitting on a small bench. Fifteen minutes later, Hess and his guard went to a small shed under a large tree, where the path forked and was out of sight from the tower. The shed, a small rectangular wooden building, was used by the gardener for work and storage space. It was as a special favour that Hess was allowed to go in and sit on a bench when it was raining outside, or if he felt tired.

The guard with Hess left him here alone when (according to his own statement) he was called back to the main building to answer a telephone call. On returning after a short absence, the guard found Hess in a state of collapse, half sitting, half lying on the floor. Around his neck was a piece of electrical cord, his face had turned dark blue. The guard could see immediately that Hess was dead. Resuscitation attempts were unsuccessful.

Rumors began to spread immediately: the prisoner had tried to hang himself, but the cord had broken and he fell to the ground; he had not tried to hang himself, but was able to strangle himself by tying a knot in the cord and pulling it tight; someone from outside

had gained entrance to the prison that day and helped him as soon as the guard was out of the way. Murder or suicide? The official statement – that Hess hanged himself – stands. Who was Hess, this man whose life and death are filled with so many mysteries and puzzles?

Rudolf Hess was born on 26 April 1894 at Alexandria, the eldest son of a businessman who had emigrated to Egypt and set up a flourishing business there. Rudolf remained in Egypt until his fourteenth year. The family lived in a lovely villa by the sea which was encircled by a beautiful garden. In his letters from Spandau to his mother, Hess wrote about the impressions that the Egyptian landscape made on him as a child, and which he had always remembered: 'the garden of Ibrahimieh with its flowers and fragrances, and the entire indescribable atmosphere: the horrible "Chamsin;" the cool, salty air; the winter storms when the sea would be covered with white foamy peaks out to the horizon; the crying of the seagulls and the listless rhythm of the waves whose melody we could hear until sleep overtook us. And then there were the long, balmy moonlit nights with the never-ending barking of the dogs out in the desert, their voices carrying clearly through the silence.

'How often did you have to sit with us children on a bench under the starlit heavens of Egypt, telling us about the great blinking stars and mentioning their names . . . our garden on the edge of the desert was a paradise. Do you remember how we used to pick violets together, and how marvelous they smelled? Every day we picked such a beautiful, large bunch of flowers. . . And it was wonderful on the beach in those days before the quays had been built. You were completely surrounded by a vast landscape where sea and desert met. The sea was mostly idyllically calm and we could wade to the rocks.'

Rudolf and his younger brother, Alfred, received a strict, traditional upbringing from their father. Meals were always at fixed times, and the children were only allowed to speak at the table if first spoken to. Rudolf's first years of education took place at a German school in Alexandria but in 1908 he was sent to the *Evangelische Pädagogium* at Godesberg-am-Rhein. His father had by then bought a country estate in Bavaria (Reichholdsgrün) where the family spent their summer holidays in the house he had built there. Hess came from an upper middle class background. Later, as various historians have noted, he was to become one of Hitler's 'gentlemen,' a welcome and useful contrast to the kind of rabble that mostly surrounded the Führer. Göring, also from a good background, filled a similar role. However, as Göring only regained Hitler's favor in 1928, after his return from abroad, Hess was Hitler's main spokesman in the upper echelons of society until that time.

At school Rudolf was a sociable and intelligent student with a pronounced preference for German history. He was good at maths and physics and very interested in astrology. Instead of entering university immediately after his secondary education, which was what he wanted to do, he attended a business training course to please his father. He first studied at a Swiss school (*Ecole Supérieure du Commerce*) in Neuchâtel and later worked as a trainee for a company in Hamburg.

On the outbreak of World War I, Hess immediately volunteered for action and was assigned to the 16th Bavarian Reserve Infantry Regiment with the rank of lieutenant. Hess was wounded three times, the third time seriously. On recovering he joined the Imperial Air Corps. In October 1918 he completed his pilot training, but the armistice was declared shortly after, and in December 1918 Hess was demobilized. After the war Hess threw himself into the work that was to keep him busy for the rest of his life: politics. The defeat of Germany provided fertile ground for young, ambitious politicians. The communist revolution in Russia had been in full swing for some time and many areas of Germany felt the effects of it. Although the threat of a communist takeover was soon dispelled, for those with right-wing leanings the danger was still real enough to warrant the creation of *Freikorpsen*, groups of volunteers who wanted to crush the local leftist movements. Hess was a member of the *Freikorps* between 1919 and 1920.

In May 1919 he was wounded for the fourth time during the Munich riots which put an end to the short-lived communist government in Bavaria. It is from this period that his fear of communism stems, particularly his fear of Russia which was later to become a political obsession. Beside the *Freikorps* Hess also joined the *Thule-Gesellschaft*, an organization that included such writers and intellectuals as Dietrich Eckhart and Alfred Rosenberg. The *Thule-Gesellschaft* mainly devoted itself to circulating anti-Semitic literature and to agitating against the 'Jewish revolutionaries' who were said to be 'hatching a worldwide plot against Germany.'

While the period of confusion and uncertainty carried on it seemed to Hess to be more advantageous to continue with his studies rather than to start a career. In 1920 he enrolled at the University of Munich to study history, economics (at the request of his father) and geopolitics. It was geopolitics that was to play a major role in his later life. The study of geopolitics is the influence of geography on the politics of a country. One of the professors in this subject was Karl Haushofer, appointed Professor at the University of Munich in 1921.

Haushofer was a man of amazing persuasiveness and unusual political ideas and theories. He had earned a certain name for himself as a general in the war and his students regarded him as a great authority in a period when all values and norms seemed to be faltering. His lectures were often peppered with references to the meaning of astrology and the supersensory, imperceptible side of German history. Haushofer believed that an end had come to the era of the great sea powers and that their place would be taken by

Above left: Hess maneuvers his aircraft into position before taking off from Frankfurt-am-Main, 1931.

Above right: Hess and Hitler are greeted by SA leader von Killinger, August 1932.

Right: Hitler and Hess attend the Reichsparteitag in the Luitpoldhalle, 1933.

land forces. It was his dream for Germany to take the initiative in creating a kind of United Europe. He believed that an Anglo-Saxon *Herrenvolk* would be able to rule the world if Britain and Germany could work together. If Germany could acquire *Lebensraum* the possibilities would be endless. Haushofer's theories would continue to influence Rudolf Hess.

Hess was also politically active during his student days. When he heard Hitler speak by chance he was so impressed that he joined the recently established National Socialist Workers' Party (NSDAP). His membership card was number 16. Although his name was not mentioned, Hess clearly had Hitler in mind when he wrote his prize-winning essay on the theme: 'What sort of man will lead Germany back to greatness?' 'If all authority has been lost,' he wrote, 'only a man of the people can restore it. It is popularity among the people that establishes authority. The closer the dictator identifies with the masses the better he will be able to influence them psychologically, the less the workers will distrust him, and the more followers he will win over from their ranks. If necessity demands, he does not shrink from bloodshed. Great issues have always been solved with the sword. His objective is solely and simply to achieve his goal, if necessary, at the cost of his best friends. . . and when necessary, he will use his boots to trample anything underfoot. We do not yet know when he will strike, this "chosen man." But he is coming, millions feel it.'

Hess already had close ties with Hitler in 1921. He talked with Hitler about politics, gave speeches for the party and fought alongside members of the SA. During a fight with communists on 4 November 1921 he was hit on the head by a beer mug that had been thrown at Hitler. The story goes that Hess saw it coming and tried to stop it. Hess also participated in Hitler's unsuccessful grab for power on 8 November 1923. The so-called putsch was quelled by the police in the center of Munich in front of the Feldherrnhalle with Hitler and most of his cronies being arrested. Hess fled to

Professor Haushofer in the Bavarian Alps, from where he later escaped to Austria.

Hitler, former General Ludendorff, Röhm (head of the SA), and seven others stood trial on 26 February 1924 for their part in the Nazi putsch. Hitler was sentenced to five years imprisonment for high treason but with the condition that he could be freed after six months for good behavior. In the end he only sat out eight and a half months of his sentence, and was set free on 20 December 1924. When Hess heard of Hitler's light sentence he returned from his exile in Austria and was sentenced to 18 months imprisonment. He was also sent to the prison in the small town of Landsberg in the valley of the River Lech.

The prisoners were allowed a great deal of freedom: they could walk in the prison garden as much as they wanted as well as receive visitors. Life in prison was pleasant and easy. Hess could now talk for hours with Hitler and he could read to keep up his university studies. He took good care of his health, practicing gymnastics daily, including high-jumping, in the prison garden. Hitler finally found the time during his stay in Lansberg to write the book that he had been thinking about so much: *Mein Kampf*. Hess acted as Hitler's assistant and private secretary.

Although there has always been an air of secrecy regarding Hess's cooperation, it is now accepted that Hess introduced Haushofer's ideas to Hitler. Haushofer was a frequent visitor to Landsberg and it is precisely those ideas of race and *Lebensraum* that are the essence of *Mein Kampf*. The close relationship between Hess and Hitler stems from their mutual imprisonment at Landsberg.

On his release from prison Hess was offered the position of assistant to Professor Haushofer at the University of Munich *Deutsche Akademie*. However, Hess preferred to continue his work as Hitler's private secretary, a function he was to fulfill until 1932. This position made Hess the administrative center of the seven-

Below left: Hitler, Hess and Himmler stand in front of the Feldherrnhalle in memory of fallen comrades, 9 November 1934.

Right: Hitler at the opening of the Nazi Party congress in Nuremberg's Luitpoldhalle, 1934. Also present are (from right to left): Julius Streicher, Hess, Lutze and Himmler.

year-long plot for the takeover of power. Hess always remained a devoted follower of Hitler but never became an intimate friend. In contrast to Röhm, for example, Hess preferred not to use the familiar pronoun form *'du'* when speaking to Hitler. Hitler would always remain 'the Führer' for Hess. He was even the first to address Hitler with this title, in imitation of Mussolini's title. Hitler often prepared and rehearsed his speeches and meetings in the presence of Hess.

Hess was present during a conversation between Hitler and Otto Strasser, Gregor's brother. The Strassers represented the left wing of the party and were in favor of nationalizing German industries. This meeting resulted in Otto Strasser being expelled from the NSDAP. The final confrontation with Gregor Strasser took place later. On 5 December 1932, following the disappointing elections in Thüringen, Gregor Strasser left the party conference after a violent argument and later wrote to Hitler complaining, in part, about the demagogic politics of the party which was being so disastrously influenced by Goebbels and Göring. Strasser prophesied disaster and ruin. The letter had a depressing effect on the party.

When Strasser went on holiday, leaving his followers isolated, Hitler struck. He immediately formulated a series of orders and summonses. Following the example of the solution to the crisis in the SA, he now took over the *Reichsorganisationsleitung* and appointed Robert Ley his chief-of-staff. He promoted Hess to head of a Central Party Commission to supervise and coordinate party policy throughout Germany (after 1933, assisted by Martin Bormann). Hess held his position until his flight to England in 1941. He was known as the 'Conscience of the Party' and there was hardly any aspect of public life that he was not involved with. His official work was so diverse that it is impossible to give a short summary of it. Hess controlled the party machinery which spread to the farthest corner of Germany.

Hess, a member of the Reichstag since the Nazi election success of 1933, was appointed the Führer's official deputy on 21 April of that year, several days before his 39th birthday. Hess had an impressive presence. Kurt Lüdecke, one of Hitler's earliest followers and a member of the NSDAP *Ausland Organisation*, met Hess in Berlin in 1933 and described him as follows: 'A man sat in front of me who was not easy to fathom. He had thick, dark hair above a forceful angular face; grey-green eyes and black, bushy eyebrows. Furthermore, he had a fleshy nose, a determined mouth and a firm, square jaw. He was tall and thin and looked Irish. One could sense a suppressed fanaticism in his eyes, but his behavior was controlled and calm. I remember him as a domineering personality, which is a compliment that you could give to only a few Nazi leaders. Hess made me feel uneasy. I could not place him and he did nothing to meet me half way. He was polite, too polite, very aloof; I could not break through his armor.'

Hess continued to rise in status during the course of the 1930s.

On 1 December 1933 he was appointed Reich minister without portfolio; on 4 February 1938 he became a member of the secret cabinet counsel (where aggressive policies were prepared during 1939 and 1940); finally, he was appointed to the Council of Ministers for the Defense of the Reich.

In theory the Führer's *Stellvertreter* (deputy) was responsible only for internal party matters but Hess was obliged to take over numerous official commitments from Hitler. In addition, he served as a kind of buffer between Hitler and other party leaders. However, his influence extended far beyond the party and he played an important role in the handling of state affairs. He formulated orders which were given to Hitler to sign and he had a deciding vote with regard to public appointments. He was authorized to take steps against people who had been found guilty of attacks on the party, the Führer or the state, and if he found the punishment too light he could overrule the court's sentence. And finally, he had the authority to formulate (or take the initiative in) new legislation. In other words, a bill could be drawn up and approved outside of the Reichstag by Hess. Hess's (and Bormann's) power rose as the Nazi Party and the state became increasingly synonymous over the years.

Public directives were published in a series of volumes called *Decrees from the Deputy Führer*. Hitler made a habit of governing by means of decrees and, as he had an aversion to most routine activities, Hess was given the task of translating the never-ending stream of decrees and Führer orders into official language. Hess dealt with many issues such as domestic party discipline using the SS and Gestapo, control of affiliated parties abroad, the appointment of civil servants, the passing of race laws, and, in connection with this, laws depriving Jews of their possessions and their place in society, and the eradication of every trace of Christian influence in the Nazi Party. In addition he signed important documents, such as those for the annexation of Austria (1938), the annexation of Danzig and other Polish areas (September and October 1939). He was also involved in issuing the decrees which brought a reign of terror to Poland. In the areas of education, he set up special offices for the control of teachers as well as university students. In March 1935 he signed the decree that introduced conscription.

In September 1935 the notorious law for the 'Protection of Blood and Honor' came into effect. This law forbade marriage and extra-marital sex between Jews and non-Jews with 'German or related blood.' In May 1938 he signed a decree disfranchising Jews and debarring them from all public offices. In July 1938 another followed, prohibiting clergymen from holding positions in the party and, also in July of that year, one which allowed Jewish doctors to treat only Jewish patients.

On 12 November 1938, following the pogrom on Crystal Night, Hess promulgated the infamous decree excluding Jews from German economic life. In a confidential order dated 14 December Hess reiterated the necessity for close cooperation between party officials and the Gestapo. In 1939 still more decrees were signed: Jews were denied the right to file complaints about maltreatment or other objections resulting from the previous year's pogroms; they could be mercilessly evicted by their landlords. The role that Hess played in Nazi Germany can certainly not be trivialized. The *National Zeitung* from 27 April 1941 – two weeks before his spectacular flight to England – stated: 'It is essential to the fulfilment of the obligations of the deputy Führer that there be only limited publicity about the activities of Rudolf Hess. Only a few know that many government measures, especially those to do with war economy and party organization, which often receive such a warm welcome when made public, have mainly been taken upon the initiative of the Führer's deputy.'

In 1927 Hess married Ilse Pröhl, one of the first female activists in the Nazi Party. After their marriage Hess forbade his wife to take an active part in politics. Ten years later, on 18 November 1937,

Left: *Hess and Hitler take the salute in Weimar, 1936.*

Above: *Hess attends a 'day of German arts,' 1936.*

their only son, Wolf Rüdiger, was born. Hess differed greatly in his private life from most of the other Nazi leaders, especially Göring and Goebbels. He, like Himmler, belonged to the more strict and puritan wing of the party hierarchy. He lived relatively modestly in a house on the Harthauserstrasse, a well-to-do neighborhood in Munich. A Mercedes sportscar was the only luxury he permitted himself. He chose a brown Mercedes so that he would be easily recognizable. He was interested in books and music.

Speer later wrote: 'He was crazy about chamber music and there were several strange but interesting types among his circle of acquaintances.' Hess's secretary described him as a courteous man to work for. Over the years he became more relaxed in manner at the office, and those who had known him for a long time could call him 'Mister Hess' instead of 'Mister Minister.' He was described by his close colleagues Heim and Klopfer as a quiet, extremely reserved man, sometimes strict and formal with strangers. They maintained that, although he had quite broad cultural interests, he was not especially intelligent. He had his own sense of humor which only those who knew him well understood.

A letter Hess wrote to his parents on 20 November 1927, one month before his marriage to Ilse Pröhl, demonstrates this remarkable sense of humor: 'I will tell you something about a marriage and a honeymoon while you perhaps did not even know that your eldest son was planning on marrying. Or did I not need to tell you? . . . I do not need to explain to you that she is an angel and why she is an angel. Or, to use a metaphor from Schopenhauer: "I do not need to explain to you why I am convinced that I have fished the only eel out of a bag full of snakes." I am certain that you will be happy to hear that the eel is six years younger than I. Moreover, we expect, the eel and I, no heaven on earth.'

Hess remained, in spite of his position, a quiet and modest man. He neither drank nor smoked. Like Hitler, he was vegetarian and very fussy about food. To the Führer's annoyance, he would bring his own food to the Chancellery or to the Berghof when invited to dine. Speer gave an example of this: 'About once every fortnight Hess showed up for lunch with Hitler, followed by his adjutant carrying a container of food to be warmed up in the Reich Chancellery kitchen. Hitler did not notice for quite some time that Hess was bringing his own vegetarian food with him. When he did hear about it he mentioned it to Hess during a meal and said somewhat irritatedly: "I have an excellent cook here. If your doctor has prescribed something special, she can certainly prepare it for you. One is not allowed to bring one's own food here." Hess stubbornly objected and tried to explain that his food contained biologically active ingredients. He was then told that if that indeed was the case, he had better take his meals at home. After this Hess was seldom present at lunches.'

Hess became increasingly eccentric in certain respects, and besides being fussy about food, was always concerned about his health. Like Himmler, he began to take refuge in special herbal medicines. Hess had had attacks of abdominal pain since 1933, and when he thought the conventional doctors were not doing enough for him, he turned more and more to those practicing natural medicine. There was something else special about Hess – his interest, apparently since the beginning of the war, in horoscopes and semi-occult practices. He attached high value to the influence of the stars, and on the charts that were made for him by an elderly fortune-teller. It was claimed that Hess made his flight to England because of astrological predictions. Although this was later denied, the Nazis did partially blame the astrologers for the flight of the deputy to the Führer.

All is quiet at the Berghof. Suddenly the peaceful silence is broken by a car racing up the road to the building. The car brakes to a stop. A man in uniform jumps out. It is Pintsch, Rudolf Hess's adjutant. It is Sunday morning, 11 May 1941. Once in the Berghof hall, Pintsch tells one of Hitler's adjutants that he has a most urgent message for the Führer. Hitler is woken by his manservant, Heinz Linge. Minutes later, and in dress uniform, Hitler enters the main hall, where Pintsch is still waiting for him. Hitler grabs a letter out of Pintsch's hands. Hess writes that he has flown to England on his own initiative to try to convince that country to make peace with Germany; the Reich would then be able to direct all its energy toward the Soviet Union. 'And if this plan misfires, and I must admit that it has but small chance of success, and fate turns against me, it will be a disaster neither for you nor for Germany; you can always deny all responsibility. You only have to say that I went mad.'

Hitler hisses at Pintsch: 'Do you know the contents of this?' When Pintsch answers in the affirmative Hitler has him immediately arrested by one of the guards. 'It was as though a bomb had exploded,' wrote Hitler's interpreter. Speer was also witness to this dramatic event: 'I suddenly heard an inarticulate, almost animal-like cry, immediately followed by: "Where is Bormann?" When Bormann arrived later, Hitler shouted at him to immediately contact Göring, von Ribbentrop, Goebbels and Himmler.'

According to General Keitel, Hitler stalked back and forth, tapping his forehead while mumbling to himself: 'Hess has gone mad, gone mad. I don't recognize him anymore. He must have been unbalanced. . . It is somebody else. Hess. . . was very sensitive.' For Hitler, Hess's flight meant a serious setback, at least that was the impression he gave. In an attempt to prevent the British from turning the flight into a propaganda coup Hitler acted immediately. Otto Dietrich, Hitler's press chief, wrote the announcement that was broadcast by Munich radio on Monday evening, 12 May: 'The National Socialist Party officially declares that party member Rudolf Hess, who due to illness was barred from flying, disobeyed his orders and managed to take possession of an airplane. Hess flew off on Saturday, 10 May, and has not yet returned.

'A letter which he left behind shows, unfortunately, by its incoherent tone, signs of mental illness. It is feared that he has become the victim of his hallucinations. The Führer immediately had the adjutants of party member Hess arrested since although knowing of his ban on flying they neither prohibited nor reported it. Under the circumstances, it must be assumed that party member Hess has either jumped out of the airplane or has had an accident.' Bormann was appointed head of the Party Chancellery that very

Left: *Hess pictured at the Reichsparteitag, Nuremberg 1936.*

Left: *Hess leaves a meeting in the wake of Göring, Mussolini, Hitler and Ciano.*

same day.

With the outbreak of war Hess very much wanted to fly again, and he asked Hitler for permission to join the air force in September 1939. Hitler, however, refused his request and Hess had to promise that he would not fly for one year. He seems to have kept his promise. The 12 months were hardly over (Autumn 1940) before he started a series of training flights. According to Willi Messerschmitt, the famous aeronautical engineer for whom Hess had flown as a test pilots in the thirties, Hess had made about 20 training flights between October 1940 and May 1941. It is hard to believe that Hitler did not know about his training program.

Is it true that Hitler wanted peace with Britain before invading the Soviet Union, and sent Hess to make it clear to the British that he was serious? Hitler had often spoken of wanting to maintain good relations with Britain and Britain's declaration of war after the German invasion of Poland had surprised and even dismayed him. As Hess would later explain in England: 'The Führer had never wanted war with England. He had a high regard for the English people, for their culture, for the British Empire and for the civilization they had spread throughout the world.' Had the Führer not consciously silenced his tanks in 1940 so that the British Expeditionary Force could escape from Dunkirk? Did this not demonstrate the Führer's peaceful intentions toward Britain? In July 1940 Hitler recalled his previous desire for good relations between the two countries: 'Mister Churchill will now finally have to understand that a great empire shall be destroyed – an empire that I actually never wanted to destroy or to harm.'

Hess knew of Hitler's plans to invade the Soviet Union in the first half of 1941. Speer: 'Hess must have been well informed. It was indeed top secret – I knew nothing of it – but the entire Soviet Empire had already been divided up into a number of political districts. It was even known which party members would be appointed commissioner of which districts. It would have been absolutely impossible without Hess's knowledge, the highest ranking party leader after Hitler, to plan. . . . I am convinced that Hitler never intended to conquer England. Germany was to be a continental empire on the European mainland, guaranteed by England while England was to be the most important sea power in the world with

Right: *Hess exchanges greetings with Soviet Commissar for Foreign Affairs Molotov during late 1939.*

Right: *Hess pays a visit to the Western Front during the period of the Phony War, 5 February 1940.*

Below right: *The 'Brown House,' the Nazi Party's headquarters in Munich.*

German guarantees for the preservation of her Empire. That was Hitler's intention. The English would then have to give Hitler a free hand in the East so that Germany would be spared a war on two fronts. If Hess had been successful in inducing England into settling for peace, then Hess would have returned a great hero.'

Linge was convinced that Hitler was fully aware of Hess's plan to fly to England. When he knocked on Hitler's door to report that one of Hess's adjutants had an important message for him, Hitler came fully dressed to his bedroom door within a minute. It was still only 0930 hours, while Hitler had ordered Linge not to wake him before noon. 'It flashed through my mind that he had already known. There was no other explanation for his already being dressed, shaved and waiting in his bedroom. In all the years, I had never seen that before.'

Linge thought he noticed that Hitler was acting as though he was shocked and painfully surprised: 'When Göring phoned, Hitler said to him in a dramatic tone of voice: "Göring, something terrible has happened." Everyone tried to stay out of the chief's way. I couldn't avoid him though, and to my own surprise I noticed that he only showed surprise, anger or bewilderment in the presence of others. Perhaps he had known the exact moment that Hess had left. I could not help thinking about the more than four-hour meeting that Hitler and Hess had had on the Obersalzberg several days before the flight. The two of them had not had such a long meeting since before the war.'

The US magazine *The American Mercury* also doubted Hitler's ignorance regarding Hess's flight. An article entitled 'The Inside Story of the Hess Flight' (May 1943) reported that the British secret service were well informed about the flight, and on entering British airspace, Hess was escorted by the RAF. Hitler sent his deputy to make perfectly clear that he was serious. The article also reported the proposals for a peace settlement that Hess took with him to Britain: France, with the exception of Alsace-Lorraine, would be relinquished as would the Netherlands, Belgium, Norway and Denmark; Luxembourg would remain in German hands. In exchange, Britain would have to adopt a neutrality favorable

toward Germany. Moreover, the Führer was prepared to withdraw his troops from Greece and Yugoslavia and to mediate in the conflict between Britain and Italy, on condition that he be given a free hand in his battle against Bolshevism.

Hitler officially denied the rumor in a speech given to 60 to 70 top officials, including ministers and gauleiters, who had assembled at the Berghof on 13 June 1941. Paul Jordan, former gauleiter and governor: 'I received a telex informing me that I, along with other Reich gauleiters, was to present myself at the Berghof that evening. I had been to the theater where I had heard the report of Hess's flight to Britain. I had my doubts about the announcement that party member Hess "was not right in his mind." Someone in a state of insanity and mental imbalance can certainly not start, fly and carry out a successful emergency landing.

'We nervously entered the Berghof main hall, where we were received by Bormann. When Hitler entered shortly after we saw from his face that the event had deeply affected him. He had a letter from Hess in his hand which, after a short while, he began to read to us. In his letter Hess summed up a number of points which, to him, stood in the way of a successful war against Bolshevism. He emphasized the importance of German-British relations which, via the normal political and diplomatic channels, had come to a full stop. Only an extraordinary action could still bring Britain around to another viewpoint.

'The letter made a deep impression on us even had Hitler not showered Hess with blame in his shrill voice. Hitler began to talk even louder: "Party members, Hess has deserted me at a time when our divisions on the eastern front have been put on alert. The commanders could receive the order at any hour for the most difficult military operation yet." With this he announced an event which silenced us all.' (Hitler was referring to the invasion of the Soviet Union planned for June 1941.) Rumors about all sorts of strange conduct by Hess continued for a time, in part spread by Goebbels, although his flight would soon be forgotten due to the rapidly changing military situation. However, Speer later maintained that Hitler never completely recovered from his deputy's disloyalty.

Left: *Hess enjoys a thick stew cooked in a field kitchen on the Western Front, 2 May 1940.*

Right: *Hess inspects a defensive position, possibly part of the Siegfried Line, 5 February 1940.*

On Saturday evening, 10 May 1941, a German parachutist landed in Scotland. His first encounter was with a farmer, Davis MacLean, who had heard the plane descending and a dull explosion when it crashed. MacLean helped Hess to stand up, and although Hess had an injured ankle, he was able to walk. Hess introduced himself as Alfred Horn and asked for the home of the Duke of Hamilton. After a short time Robert Williamson, an auxiliary policeman and Clark, a neighbor of Williamson and a Home Guardsman, arrived. They arrested Hess and took him to the barracks. Higher authorities were informed of the arrest and of Hess's statement that he had come to Britain on a 'special mission' and wished to speak to the Duke of Hamilton. Hamilton arrived the next day and Hess identified himself, mentioning that they had met in Berlin during the 1936 Olympic Games. Hess went on to say he was the Reich minister and had flown to England to show how serious Germany was in its quest for peace.

Hamilton telephoned Winston Churchill the same evening. Churchill gave precise instructions that Hess was to be regarded as a prisoner of war, that he was to be completely isolated in a comfortable house near London and given books, good food, writing materials and the necessary peace. He must, however, have no contact with the outside world and was not to receive visitors. The Hess case was handled during the Monday morning Cabinet session. It was decided to send Ivone Kirkpatrick, head of the BBC European section and First Secretarty at the Berlin embassy from 1935 to 1938, to ascertain whether they really were dealing with Rudolf Hess, deputy to the Führer.

Kirkpatrick visited Hess at Buchanan Castle and verified that he was, indeed, Rudolf Hess. Hess again explained in detail his reasons for coming to Britain. The final interrogation took place on 15 May, after which he was transferred to the Tower of London. He was, however, soon moved to Mytchett Place, a Victorian country house near Farnborough, where he stayed for almost 13 months. A visit to Hess by Lord Chancellor Sir John Simon on 10 June brought about no progress and Hess soon slipped into obscurity until his reappearance at Nuremberg.

Hess was under psychiatric treatment for the entire period that he was in England (and in Nuremberg). According to some, he decided to display symptoms of mental instability as a means of obtaining early repatriation (through exchange of sick prisoners of war) and, partly, to avoid accepting responsibility for the war. It could be said that his simulated madness was, to a certain extent, the result of his psychological makeup which somewhat supports the theories of those psychiatrists who found him disturbed but not, in a technical sense, insane.

Some manifestations of his disturbed character were undoubtedly real: he suffered strongly from 'prison psychosis' and the paranoia that goes with it. His amnesia (Hess began to complain about amnesia toward the end of 1941, eventually stating that he was suffering from total amnesia) was found by many to be real, although Hess later wrote in a letter to his wife that, to put it mildly, he had been exaggerating. Hess was, in any case, suffering from depression (he seemed to be totally unable to cope with the unsuccessful result of his mission) and a persecution complex. He made two suicide attempts during his internment in England.

In June 1942 it was decided to transfer him to the Maindiff Hospital at Abergavenny in Wales, a quieter and more remote place of detention. Here he received the first letters from his family. One letter he wrote in September 1943 typified his attitude to Hitler, an attitude that would not change for the rest of his life. He wrote: 'I am feeling very happy to note again and again from your letters that your feelings have changed as little as mine with regards to the man with whom we have shared so many ups and downs for more than 20 years. You must not forget that he is going through a period of heavy mental strain and because of the tension could perhaps make decisions that he would not make during more normal times.'

Hess recovered his memory in February 1945. Hess stated that he had an important announcement to make to the world: 'The Jews possessed a secret power. They were able to hypnotize people. They hypnotized Winston Churchill, those who designed the assault on Hitler, the King of Italy, his doctors and guards.'

Hess was flown to Nuremberg on 10 October 1945 to stand trial along with the other war criminals. Initially, Hess pleaded amnesia (or actually did suffer from amnesia; there was no consensus on this). Three Russian, one French, three British and three American psychiatrists finally agreed that the basic structure of Hess's personality was 'hysterical and paranoid.' Hess would later state, under cross-examination, that his amnesia had merely been a tactical position. This was, however, according to the psychologist Kelley, a typical, dramatic and hysterical gesture which only sup-

ported his position and that of his colleagues that people suffering from amnesia often deny it.

The trial began on 20 November. Replying to the indictment read out by the prosecutor, Hess asserted his innocence with a simple 'Nein.' Taking into account his mental condition, it had initially been decided that he was in no state to defend himself, but after his statement about amnesia this decision was reversed. Hess often appeared aloof during the sittings, frequently reading a book or turning off his headphones. Hess was initially defended by Dr Gunther von Rohrscheidt, later by Dr Stahmer. Stahmer was in turn replaced by Dr Alfred Seidl, who also represented Frank.

One of the prosecutors, the English jurist Lieutenant-Colonel JMG Griffith-Jones, covered Hess's career in detail and the positions he had held. He emphasized his close relationship with Hitler, his part in drawing up and signing decrees and laws, citing excerpts from his speeches and referring in detail to a number of decrees which Hess had contributed to. He also referred to Hess's part in Nazi foreign policies. He also proved Hess's involvement in the Austrian Anschluss, his part in stirring up pro-Nazi feelings among the Sudeten Germans and his role in the Polish affair. He also covered the flight to Britain in depth and the fact that Hess must have known about the planned invasion of Russia.

Dr Seidl, counsel for Hess, stated that Hess accepted total responsibility for the laws and decrees signed by him; he did, however, argue that Hess was often not present when important decisions were taken, therefore having no more than an administrative role. He tried to minimize Hess's role in foreign affairs, as well as his involvement in the invasion of Poland. Regarding his flight to Britain, Seidl pointed to the peace offering, stating that Hess was one of the few who had Hitler's complete trust. Seidl caused quite a stir during his address by stating that the Soviet Union had already made a secret agreement with Hitler before the invasion of Poland regarding the spheres of influence of both countries with that region. As proof, Seidl produced an affadavit from the former ambassador to support his case. The tribunal did not, however, recognize it as sufficient proof to be admitted as evi-

dence. The Russian prosecutor, General Rudenko, paid the most attention to Hess, holding him guilty on all counts and even finding him 'extra' guilty because he had tried to avoid punishment by 'declaring himself mad.'

Hess, like the others, was given the opportunity to make a closing statement. He spoke incoherently about, among other things, his Jewish theories and the influence of their hypnosis on his guards. He ended his address with the following, for him, characteristic words: 'I have had the privilege of working for many years of my life under the greatest son brought forth among my people in the thousand years of their history. Even if I were able to I would not be willing to erase this period of my life. . . I regret nothing. If I had to begin anew, I would behave as I have behaved, even if I knew that I would be burned at the stake in the end. Whatever is done with me by man, I know that I shall appear before the tribunal of the Almighty. I shall have to answer to Him and I know that He will absolve me.' The International Tribunal at Nuremberg sentenced Rudolf Hess to life imprisonment. Hess had expected the death penalty.

After the sentences of those condemned to death were carried out, those given prison sentences remained in Nuremberg prison until July 1947, when they were transferred to Spandau in Berlin. The regulations were strict in the beginning. The prisoners had to rise at 0600 hours and wash by twos (talking was not allowed); breakfast was at 0645; at 0700 they cleaned their cells and made their beds; at 0800 they began all sorts of chores, such as cleaning the prison and working in the garden. Noon was meal time. After the midday meal they rested for a time before continuing their chores and then worked again until 1645. The evening meal was at 1900 and lights out at 2200. Each cell was searched regularly twice a day, the prisoners shaved three times a week and, in the beginning, bathed once a week.

Hess spent most of his free time reading books, finding history and science the most interesting topics. He later became an avid reader of space stories. Hess refused to see any members of his family; Dr Seidl was the only person from his close circle who

Strasbourg; it was rejected. The number of visits to Hess reached a high point after the release of Schirach and Speer. The fact that an enormous prison was being kept open at considerable expense for one old man certainly played a role in this. It had been clear for some time, however, that Hess's continued incarceration had, especially for the Russians, taken on a symbolic, political importance. As Hitler's former deputy he, much more than the others imprisoned in Spandau, represented the completeness of the Russian victory over Nazism.

A high-ranking officer from the Soviet Union, who was also concerned with guarding Hess, reaffirmed this later to Eugene K Bird, former United States commander of Spandau Prison: 'The steps taken by the English for the release of Hess will come to nothing. He must die in prison. He is the last symbol of the Nazi Party, and the Nuremberg Tribunal sentenced him to life imprisonment. No one has the right to change that decision. You would not be able to convince a single Russian that Hess knew nothing of the planned invasion of the Soviet Union when he made his flight to Scotland. He did not fly there to restore world peace but, rather, to neutralize the British, giving the Germans a free hand in the East to invade Russia. I do not believe that my country will ever agree to the release of Hess.'

Seidl made a fourth appeal on 18 May 1966, directed this time to the Queen of England, the Presidents of France and the United States and the Chairman of the Soviet Union. The appeal was rejected by a veto from the Soviet government. Hess's health deteriorated toward the end of 1969 to such an extent that he was transferred to the British Military Hospital in West Berlin. Hess, by then 75 years old, for the first time agreed to visits from his family, although under very restrictive conditions. Numerous articles again appeared, especially in Britain, pleading for his release. However, after his recovery Hess was sent back to Spandau. Subsequent appeals for his release had no effect and Hess remained the sole prisoner in Spandau until he died in mysterious circumstances in 1987.

The events surrounding Rudolf Hess, those associated with his flight to Scotland, as well as those associated with his death, still remain one of the puzzles of World War II. The final story of Rudolf Hess, Adolf Hitler's enigmatic and disgraced former colleague and deputy, has yet to be written.

visited him before 1969. Both Schirach and Speer said that Hess was a difficult prisoner. He regularly called out to the guards in the middle of the night and they would have to fetch the doctors because he had stomach pains and thought he had been poisoned. He often woke up the others with his shouting and cries of pain. Neurath, Raeder, Dönitz and Funk were released from Spandau in the 1950s; Speer and Schirach both regained their freedom in 1966. Only Hess remained, paying the penalty for the important position he had held in the Third Reich. A reduction of his sentence was rejected several times, the Russians always rejecting all attempts to have him freed.

In 1947 Seidl submitted his first appeal for the release of Hess. He based it to a large extent on Hess's bad health and other humanitarian grounds. An appeal made in 1956 to the United Nations was equally unsuccessful. The third appeal, made in 1957, was directed to the European Commission for the Rights of Man at

Above left: Hitler addresses a group of leading Nazis in 1941 including Goebbels, Ley, Himmler, Hess, Raeder, von Brauchitsch, and Keitel.

Above: A British officer inspects the remains of the aircraft used by Hess during his flight to Scotland.

Right: Hess in the dock at Nuremberg.

MARTIN
BORMANN

1900-1945

Left: *Martin Bormann, the
Third Reich's arch bureaucrat.*

Above: *Bormann enjoys the
view from the terrace of a house
on the Obersalzberg.*

Berlin, 2 May 1945, 0130 hours. A small group of people are cautiously leaving the garden of the burning Reich Chancellery. The screeching of shells is deafening. Suddenly, they hear a dull rumble behind them. Then, after a few minutes, flames shoot out from what had once been Hitler's bunker, from where he had formulated his mad plans and commands. One of the members of this group was a small, stocky man with an ever-present briefcase under his arm. His name: Martin Bormann. With his Führer's testament in his briefcase he tries to get through the Russian lines, now very close to the Chancellery. 'Hitler's shadow,' also called 'the brown eminence,' realizes that with the death of his Führer he has lost his power and that the game is over. Dodging between the fires and explosions, the small group, with Bormann among them, suddenly goes underground in an attempt to escape.

After the National Socialists had come to power in Germany on 30 January 1933, Nazi propaganda declared that a 'new Germany' had arisen due to 'the genius of the Führer' and the 'driving force of the NSDAP.' The assumption of power was quickly followed by the abolition of parliament, the creation of a united German state, the prohibition of all political parties other than the NSDAP and the Nazification of the trade unions. These moves signified an absolute authoritarian regime which exercised control through strong leadership, an all-pervasive government machine and the sole political party – the NSDAP. Using the concept of *Führerprinzip*, strict obedience was demanded from both the government and the party.

In practice, however, the structure and organization of the National Socialist regime, with its pyramidal hierarchy, was less efficient and effective than it outwardly seemed. Certainly a consciously monocratic and centrally led economic plan was out of the question. Within this framework one may rightfully speak of a number of small, independently acting power groups which existed at all levels and throughout all state authorities and agencies, and which fought among themselves on all manner of issues. Because of this, Hitler's Third Reich can also be termed an 'authoritarian governed anarchy'.

One of the main reasons for the chaotic government structure was the strict separation between state and party. Each government department was mirrored by a corresponding party department, a situation which resulted in a plethora of rival bodies, all competing in areas such as, for example, foreign intelligence, political and legislative affairs. This dichotomy was to a large extent a reflection of the sweeping radicalism that lay behind the rise of National Socialism. Such a totalitarian movement does not see itself as a democratic political party, or part of an accepted order which it, to a degree, represents, but rather regards itself as a movement for change which puts the past behind it and aims for domination.

Once the party gained power, the government degenerated into a purely technical apparatus with exclusively executive tasks. The state departments were, in reality, purely formal bodies and true power was exerted behind the scenes. Study of this type of structure has led to the theory that in a totalitarian system the actual power and the hidden power are one, and that this is the only certainty in such a state. If holding an official function in such a system signifies anything then Martin Bormann, whose career and leading role in Nazi Germany perfectly fulfills this principle, must have been an extremely powerful man. It will also become apparent that he was continually expanding his power in a very clever and very subtle way.

At the end of Hitler's life Bormann received an honor which meant more to him than any other tribute, namely, a statement describing him as 'my most loyal party member, Martin Bormann,' given when Hitler appointed him executor of his testament. Bormann had achieved his ultimate goal: total identification with the central will of the Nazi power structure. Austere, cunning, industrious and always at his Führer's side, he had constantly thirsted after power, never after the accompanying rewards.

He achieved his goal gradually during the years 1933-45. Despite unrevealing titles such as 'Head of the Party Chancellery' and 'Secretary to the Führer,' there was no one more powerful than Bormann in the last years of the war. He was a true bureaucrat, someone whom Hitler relied on in most matters. He stood in the background, but was always ready to strike; a small, thick-set man with a bull's neck. He had everything Hitler said put down on paper to be used later, if necessary, for the so-called 'Führerbevelen,' and in some respects was more powerful than Hitler himself. All letters, reports, telegrams, telephone calls (and later all visitors) went to Bormann and he decided what or who was presented to Hitler.

Whatever Hitler proposed, Bormann carried out quickly and efficiently. One incident will illustrate this. It was Hitler's habit when he stayed at the Berghof, his country residence on the Obersalzberg, to greet parading *Volksgenossen*. On one such occasion he stood for hours in the direct sun waving at the passing crowd. Afterward he told Bormann that he was shattered from having stood in the sun so long. When Hitler went to his regular place the following day he found that a huge shady tree had been planted there. Bormann even had all of Hitler's *Tischgespräche* (table conversation) recorded, down to unimportant comments and asides. When it suited him he changed dramatically the character of the Führer's most inconsequential remarks.

Bormann had an elephantine memory. Hitler had an aversion to routine administrative work which Bormann took advantage of. As he was an avid organizer and bureaucrat he gladly relieved Hitler of these unpleasant tasks. He sent generals away who were unhappy about the course of the war in Russia; he kept silent about the situation in the bombed out German cities. The Führer's 'creative work' was not to be disturbed by such 'futilities.'

Hitler regarded Bormann as the only close staff member who was capable of formulating his opinions and ideas in clear language. Bormann could shorten entire books, thick reports or mem-

Above left: Bormann and Hitler study architectural plans for the development of the Nuremberg arena.

Above: The power behind the throne. Bormann takes the salute behind his Führer, Munich, 1934.

oranda to a few sentences. The long-winded German style was foreign to him. Hitler frequently sang the praises of his 'brown eminence': '. . .his reports are so perfectly detailed that I only have to sign them. With Bormann I can work through a pile of dossiers in 10 minutes that would take hours with others. When I say to him in the course of a conversation: "Remind me in six months of such and such an issue," I can be sure he will do so on the appointed day.'

Bormann was hated by nearly all the leading party figures. During his trial in Nuremberg Hans Frank, Governor-General of Poland, called him an arch-villain and then remarked that the word 'hatred' was too weak to describe their relationship. According to Speer, a few critical remarks from Hitler would have been sufficient for Bormann's enemies to go for his throat. However, Hitler always supported Bormann, and when complaints reached Hitler, he would always say: 'I know that Bormann is a brute. But everything I charge him with he carries out with remarkable preciseness; everything he does shows common sense.' Bormann's competence, which he undoubtedly possessed, was greatly underestimated by his rivals. It was, after all, Bormann who won the power struggle in the end.

Many of Hitler's 'veterans' were not capable of running a country, lacking the necessary 'desk experience,' whereas Bormann was a typical representative of the 'second generation.' He had been weaned off patriotism and all ideological values. 'Bormann is not a man of the people,' Goebbels noted. 'He is always involved in administrative and governmental affairs, missing true leadership because of it.' This opinion was typical of a representa-

tive of the 'first generation.' But for how long could the 'true' leaders, men of the people, hold on to power before it slowly but surely passed into the hands of those who had thoroughly mastered the techniques of organization and control?

Martin Bormann derived his power solely from his position. He was not a compelling personality; he had done nothing particularly creditable for the party during the years of struggle. He had no friends and should he have lost Hitler's confidence he would have had nothing to fall back on. It was precisely because of this lack of background and lack of personality that he was a very useful instrument in the hands of those who used him. He was the prototype of the obedient supporter. He had no hobbies, did not smoke, did not drink much, was a moderate eater and had only one passion: to serve his Führer and to serve him in such a way that he would become indispensable. Keeping the gigantic party machine running was his forte.

Martin Bormann was born on 17 June 1900 in the small town of Halberstadt in Lower Saxony. His father, a trumpet player in a military brass band, died when Martin was four years old. His mother remarried a banker. Toward the end of World War I Bormann was drafted as a gunner; he did not, however, see action. After the war and following a short period without work, he found himself employment as a steward on an estate. He also joined the *Freikorps*, a group of armed volunteers secretly supported by the German Army which was unable to accept the terms of the Treaty of Versailles.

Bormann's life can be divided into five stages. The first phase of his development started in 1920 when he began to train himself ideologically and studied. He joined the NSDAP in 1925, working first as head of the press service in the *Gaue* of Thuringen, before transferring to the staff of the supreme SA leader toward the end of 1928. Bormann quickly worked his way up the ladder, gaining a clear insight into the workings of the party along the way. This period ended in July 1933 with his appointment as *Stableiter* for Rudolf Hess, the Führer's deputy. His second phase of development ended on 10 May 1941 – the day Hess flew to Britain. On Hitler's command Hess's office was renamed *Parteikanzlei*. Bormann was promoted to head of the *Parteikanzlei* and to chief-of-staff to the Führer's deputy. He also became a member of the Council of Ministers for the Defense of the Reich. The third phase can be seen as the period from May 1941 until 12 April 1943, when he received the title of Secretary to the Führer. This was followed by the period from April 1943 to the end of 1944, the point at which the last German offensive in the West came to a standstill in the Ardennes. The fifth phase embraces the period from January 1945 to April 1945 and the moment of Hitler's suicide.

In September 1929 Bormann married the daughter of the President of the Party Court. The speed at which his career had pro-

gressed can best be illustrated by the fact that Hitler acted as witness at his wedding. It was a marriage based on true National Socialist principles. Gerda Bormann-Bach was, if possible, even more fanatical in her beliefs than her husband. She was a zealous follower of Julius Streicher who preached that the Jews were the cause of Germany's misfortune. His speeches and obscene writings served as a theoretical basis for the policy geared toward the total extermination of the Jewish people.

The notion that German women, being good National Socialists, should have as many Aryan children as possible found ample favor with Mrs Bormann (she bore her husband 10), as the following correspondence from Bormann to his wife (sweet mummygirl), dated 21 January 1944, shows: 'You said that M [his mistress Maja Berhens] must be an amazing girl because she was able to convince me of the vices of magnesia. But, sweetheart, she is not the amazing girl, I am the amazing man! You know that in the beginning there was nothing between M and me. I only found her attractive because she had put me off. When I saw her again in October after years I was overjoyed, yes beside myself with happiness. You cannot imagine how delighted I was. She attracted me immensely. I kissed her without further ado and set her afire with my burning happiness. I fell madly in love with her! I arranged it so that I met her again many times and then I took her in spite of her protests. You know my willpower, against which M was of course no match. She is now mine and I – lucky fellow – am now, or rather, I feel doubly and happily married. O, dearest, you cannot imagine how happy I feel with the two of you!'

Mrs Bormann replied to her husband's letter by return post (my sweetest and dearest daddy): 'I love M so much that I simply cannot be angry with you. The children also love her very much. You must make sure that M has a child one year and I the next. Only one thing sweetheart, you must be very careful with her and care-

Right: *Bormann, Göring and Himmler confer at Nuremberg during the 1936 Reichsparteitag.*

Below: *Bormann and Hitler study an architectural model depicting the planned development of Kassel, 1936.*

Right: *Hitler surrounded by his entourage, including Bormann (second from right) and his brother Albert (to Hitler's right), in Munich, 22 May 1938.*

Below right: *Bormann and his brother accompany Hitler during a visit to Danzig in 1939.*

fully educate her. Although she does not go to church she cannot bear it when you attack Christianity, for then she gets very angry. Enlighten her carefully and she will in time come to the right conclusions. . . It would be good if at the end of this war, like at the end of the Thirty Years War, a law was enacted allowing healthy, worthy men to have two wives. . . .' Bormann added the comment: 'The Führer fosters the same thoughts.'

And, in a letter dated 10 February 1944 Gerda writes in part: 'The state must acknowledge these commitments [a husband taking on a second wife] and guarantee that the second wife has equal rights under the same conditions as the first wife. Experience teaches us that these relationships are often very happy. The husband, freed from the minor daily irritations, would have a better temperament. Such relationships should be formalized by the civil authorities and regarded as a legal marriage. It could be done according to the following rules:

'"I, Martin Bormann, born on 17 June 1900, declare that I, with the knowledge and approval of my wife Gerda, born on 23 October 1909, wish to conclude a national marriage of necessity with M. This marriage shall have the same legitimacy under the law as my first marriage."'

And the wife would make the following declaration to the civil authorities: 'I, Gerda Bormann, born Bach, express my approval of the marriage of necessity between my husband and M, and am in agreement that this union shall have the same legitimacy as the bonds which bind us.' The letter closes with the question: 'What do you think of this?'

It may seem surprising that this not very talented, coarse man managed to work his way to the top, but by 1937 Bormann belonged to Hitler's intimate circle, and in time would become indispensable to the Führer. Bormann cunningly manipulated Hitler and was a master at camouflaging his own thirst for power. Whenever Hitler asked a question or remarked on something, Bormann

would be ready after several minutes with a detailed answer. His art lay in presenting matters in such a way that, knowing Hitler, could only allow for one reaction – the reaction Bormann wanted. It was Bormann who in fact controlled the millions of marks in the *Adolf Hitler den Deutschen Industrie* fund which had been set up as a joint venture between German trade and industry. A good part of the money was used to extend Hitler's summer residence on the Obersalzberg. Hitler often spent months at his country estate there and it seemed self-evident that his loyal supporter Bormann should also have a house as well.

The *Reichsleiter* laid claim to the former children's sanatorium several hundred meters from the Berghof. It cost a fortune to convert this solid, two-storey villa into a luxury country house. Its splendor was hardly less than that of the Berghof. The house was equipped with all the latest household gadgets, although judging from the rather ordinary wooden exterior one would not have expected the interior to be so splendid. Nowhere on the mountain could such magnificent furniture, appliances, light fittings and bathrooms be found. The children's bedrooms were lavish: they had their own bathroom with an expensive marble bath. Even late into the war Bormann had specially designed hand-knotted, heavy carpets made. The house possessed an ambience of extreme luxury from the cellars to the attic.

The entire area around the Obersalzberg became *Hoheitsgebiet* (sovereign territory) so that the Führer could make his greatest decisions in a restful environment. Bormann became the *Bauherr* and the Obersalzberg was, over the years, expanded to include barracks, guest houses, kilometers of underground tunnels, telephone exchanges, telex installations, a gigantic model farm, a stud farm, garages and living quarters for the hundreds of employees.

Once Bormann was held in high regard by Hitler, he started systematically filling all the important staff positions with his own people. With Machiavellian cleverness he managed to worm his way into every area and there were few staff members working directly with Hitler who were not part of his network. During the

final war years Reichsleiter Bormann reigned as the undisputed ruler of Hitler's headquarters. He slowly but surely built a wall around Hitler, with entrance only granted to those in Bormann's favor.

Bormann would often blow up unimportant incidents to such proportions that severe consequences for the parties involved would ensue. One day the *Deutsches Nachrichten* bureau published an article about a farmer who had been sentenced to two months imprisonment for holding back a liter of milk per day for his own consumption. Hitler's official photographer and close friend, Heinrich Hoffmann, also a farm owner, let slip that in such a case he would have been sentenced to years of imprisonment because every time he visited his farm he took away five liters of milk. Bormann heard of this remark from one of his spies and immediately wrote to the Führer that, according to the law, Hoffmann too had a right to only half a liter of milk per day.

Sometime later Hoffmann received a telephone call from Bormann. Bormann's intelligence service suspected that Hoffmann was a paratyphoid carrier so that further visits to the Führer were out of the question. Hoffmann, very shaken by this, put himself under medical observation with the best specialists for six months. No paratyphoid was found but when Hoffmann accidentally met Hitler again in 1945 he was given an extremely cool reception. With a threatening note in his voice Hitler asked Hoffmann if he was now cured. Hoffmann told Hitler of the results of his thorough medical examination. However Hitler still avoided him. One of Hitler's secretaries later heard that Bormann had insinuated that Hoffmann had sent his son of the same name to the medical specialists. The certificate stating that Hoffmann had never been a paratyphoid carrier had been, according to Bormann, for his son.

In July 1933 Bormann was appointed *Reichsleiter* and chief of staff to the Führer's deputy, Rudolf Hess. Hess's chancellery handled all party matters. The party was, in reality, the collective

Above, far left: *A view of Bormann's Party Chancellery at the Eagle's Nest.*

Below left: *Many of the buildings at Obersalzberg; Bormann was in charge of new building projects at the complex.*

Above: *A panoramic view of the Eagle's Nest with mountains beyond.*

thoughts of the Führer and the chancellery had to sort out these thoughts and transform them into decrees and laws. As Hess did not much concern himself with such matters – his interests lay more in astrology, spiritualism, flying, skiing and driving – Bormann was soon the one who kept the machine going.

An interview with Bormann conducted several years before World War II made clear which important functions the party fulfilled and how far its power extended. Hannah Ahrendt wrote thus: 'Rudolf Hess is deputy Führer for the NSDAP; and as such stands at the head of the entire party and party organization, including its branches and affiliated institutions. He is in this capacity also the Reich minister expressing the party's will in the political sphere and guaranteeing that this will is fully realized. One of his tasks is the safeguarding of party and state unity. The most important powers granted to him by the Führer enabling him to realize this, lie in the stipulation that he participate in the preparatory stages of all laws and regulations in so far as they are made public in the state newspaper and require his approval. The deputy Führer also takes an active part in the appointment and promotion of civil servants.

'As chief of staff to the deputy Führer, with the knowledge and will of the Führer in mind, it is Bormann's task to select staff members, organize the structure of this department and to supervise the work. Bormann has held this function since 1933. There are already hundreds of party members working in this organization.

Left: *Hitler and Bormann pay a visit to the Polish front, 1939.*

Right: *Hitler visits the Austrian town of Marburg in 1941 accompanied by Bormann.*

Below: *A photograph taken on Hitler's fifty-first birthday at Obersalzberg. Also present are Eva and Margarethe Braun (to the left and right of Hitler) and Bormann (second row, third from right).*

There are countless items that have to be read and investigated – more than a thousand letters each day. Everything has to be looked and decided upon in the spirit of the Führer.

'Only those – such as Rudolf Hess and Martin Bormann – who, after years of close cooperation with the Führer thoroughly understand his way of thinking, are capable of determining which criteria to apply to research and decisions. Since both possess this knowledge, Martin Bormann is able to relieve the deputy Führer of a large proportion of his work load. He can act for him, for he knows how he should act in a certain situation. He can prepare decisions, action important matters and give advice.'

Bormann managed to lighten Hess's load in such a way that he was able to deal with matters such as promotion for all senior civil servants and party members entirely by himself. Bormann was deputy to the Führer's deputy and also at the head of all *Gauleiters*, the local party representatives who were true 'kings' in their *Gaue*. Most of his instructions were given in the form of circulars sometimes detailed to the point of absurdity. For example, a circular dated 20 November 1933 read: 'It has come to the attention of the deputy Führer that in certain towns and villages discord exists as to whether the NSDAP salute is "Heil" or "Heil Hitler".' Several people had already been arrested for having the audacity to shout a mere 'Heil.' Bormann now made it known that the 'Heil' salute had never officially been replaced by 'Heil Hitler.' Thus both forms were acceptable.

The party machinery and Bormann's power grew in proportion to Nazi Germany's territorial expansion. Two very important bodies in the Third Reich were undoubtedly the party itself and the SS. Bormann made sure that he stayed on good terms with the SS. As a token of thanks Reichsführer-SS Himmler appointed Bormann SS-General on 30 January 1937.

After Hess flew to Britain, Bormann succeeded to his position as head of the party chancery and also became a member of the Reich government. When he was given authorization, on 16 January 1942, via a *Führerlas* for full participation in the preparation of government laws or regulations, including those of the Council of Ministers for Reich Defense, he was in fact given responsibility for the supervision of government policy. On 29 April Hitler acquired the right to reverse all court decisions – an action which unquestionably broadened Bormann's powers. And, from 21 November all decisions made by the highest party court, of which Bormann's father-in-law was president, had to be ratified personally by Bormann.

The crowning touch to Bormann's intrigues was his appointment, on 12 April 1943, to the position of Secretary to the Führer. His authority included: settling the Führer's personal affairs, participating in meetings, reporting to the Führer on all incoming messages (telegrams, memoranda, letters) relating to military, political, social and economic spheres; passing on the Führer's decisions and opinions to ministers and other high-ranking Reich authorities or services; settling differences of opinion between Reich ministers and other high-ranking civil and party officials; finalizing matters connected with assignments in Linz, such as the large Adolf Hitler museum there and the monuments still to be built; and the supervision of the secretaries working at the Führer's headquarters.

Many government and party officials suddenly recognized the enormous amount of influence Bormann had acquired. He had the authority to send 'Führer orders' to all military and state institutions without their origins being ratified. Bormann had become an uncontrollable, anonymous force with unlimited powers. In the name of Hitler, he sent orders to the *Oberkommando der Wehrmacht*, the SD, the SS and to Himmler, Göring, Goebbels and Speer. Only one man was free from Bormann's insatiable hunger for power – Adolf Hitler. Bormann needed Hitler; without him he had no authority at all.

Hitler's most loyal Party member acted as witness at the marriage of the Führer and Eva Braun. The following day Bormann, together with Goebbels, General Burgdorf and several faithful followers, stood looking at the two charred bodies in the garden of the largely destroyed chancellery. In the afternoon of 30 April 1945 at 1630 hours the newly-weds had committed suicide. One of the Führer's final instructions had been that their bodies were to be burnt. As mentioned, those still present in the bunker, among them Bormann, then tried to get through the Russian defenses during the night of 1/2 May.

At that moment Bormann disappeared. His trail comes to an end, surrounded by darkness between the Weidammer bridge and Lehrter station. Directly after the war all sorts of stories were circulated: he had been seen in South America, Egypt, Italy, and Spain. Nevertheless, it is likely that Bormann was killed while attempting to escape.

On 7 December 1972 two skeletons were found in the vicinity of the Lehrter station in Berlin during work on a building site. They were believed to be the skeletons of Bormann and Dr Stumpfegger, Hitler's personal physician. Work on the identification of the skeletons began – for Stumpfegger this was relatively easy as X-rays of his teeth were in existence. However, the experts only had the drawings of Bormann's teeth which had been made by Professor Blaschke (Hitler's dentist) during his imprisonment by the Americans. Other leads were also checked out during the investigation: the traces of a collar bone fracture and the remains of a cyanide capsule. A very important piece of evidence was still missing – Bormann's dental bridgework. However, in early March 1973, a bridge perfectly fitting the second skeleton was found nearby. A plastic reconstruction was made and the results bore a striking resemblance to Bormann's photographs. In January Martin Bormann's death was finally and officially recorded at the Registry Office.

Bormann, still missing at the time of the Nuremberg trial, was prosecuted in absentia. The American prosecutor, Thomas F Lambert, summarized Bormann's guilt as follows: 'My Lords, any child knows that Hitler was an evil man. The public prosecutor

Left: *Hitler, Bormann and senior military figures pose for a publicity photograph during the Blitzkrieg attack of 1940.*

Right: *Bormann (second from left), Mussolini, Dönitz and Göring meet with Hitler following the Bomb Plot, 20 July 1944.*

would like to point out, however, that Hitler would never have been capable of attaining and holding total power without followers such as Bormann. Bormann was an evil archangel on the side of Hitler.'

On 1 October 1946 the International Tribunal sentenced Martin Bormann to death. He was charged with war crimes and crimes against humanity. The sentence read as follows: 'Martin Bormann was a member of the NSDAP, a member of the Reichstag, a staff member of the highest SA leadership, founder and administrator of the *Hilfskasse* of the NSDAP, head of the *Parteikanzlei*, leader of the Party Court, Secretary to the Führer, member of the Council of Ministers for the Defense of the Reich, organizer and leader of the *Volkssturm*, general of the SS, and general of the SA.'

As the successor of Hess, Bormann had control over all of Hitler's legal measures and guidelines. When the *Gauleiters* who were directly responsible to him were made Reich Defense Com-

missioners, Bormann gained absolute authority over the exploitation of subjected peoples. He contributed to the persecution of the Jews, not only in Germany but also in the conquered territories. He also helped, with the forced labor program, in carrying out the policies. He ordered that foreign workers should come under the authority of the SS and gave his *Gaue* leaders instructions to report cases of mild treatment. He handed prisoners of war over to the SS; Bormann was responsible for the lynching of Allied pilots. Since his death had not been confirmed by evidence, the tribunal had decided to sentence him to death by hanging.

The Nuremberg Tribunal added the following provision to Bormann's sentence: 'Should Martin Bormann be still alive and be arrested later, then, in accordance with Article 29 of the Statutes, it would be left to the German control council to take mitigating circumstances into consideration, and if these are deemed applicable

Right: *Bormann accompanies Hitler and Foreign Minister Joachim von Ribbentrop on a walk through the compound of the Führer's headquarters.*

to change or reduce the sentence.' In view of later developments, in particular with regard to the skeleton excavated near Lehrter station, it may be confidently predicted that this additional provision will never be applied. For all of the alleged sightings of Bormann since the end of World War II, it seems unlikely that he escaped from Berlin in 1945.

With the care of a meticulous bookkeeper Martin Bormann fulfilled his role in the shadow of his Führer. The disastrous years of National Socialism which led the German people and the larger part of Europe to the brink of the abyss should make us reflect on just how dangerous the role was of those loyal civil servants who, in reality, embodied the plans and ideas of an expansion policy which, at first, seemed so unrealistic. When Alfred Rosenberg, the party ideologue, announced that National Socialism had set itself to attain the unattainable, he was not far from the truth, for he knew how National Socialism would operate. Thus, the question as to whether Bormann is still alive or not is irrelevant. He is a terrible shadow from the past, but with a view to the future we must make certain that the Bormanns, or whatever their names may be, will never get another chance. To this end our democratic system still offers the best guarantee against the creation of another totalitarian regime similar to the Third Reich.

HEINRICH HIMMLER

1900-1945

Left: *Heinrich Himmler, the brutal, calculating head of the SS and its associated state security forces.*

Above: *Himmler in the uniform of the Reichsführer-SS.*

Left: *Himmler (standing at right) pictured with his immediate family.*

They wore black uniforms with a skeleton's head on their hats and were feared by an entire nation. They had sworn eternal faith to their Führer and wore the motto '*Unsere Ehre heisst Treue*' on their belts. The double S-rune (SS) was their symbol. They controlled the entire German police force, including the secret services, guarded Hitler's Reich Chancellery and his residence on the Obersalzberg, and had complete power over all concentration camps, work camps and, later, the extermination camps. During the war they followed in the wake of the Wehrmacht, establishing a reign of terror in the newly subjugated territories. They held key positions in the national economy, in the health service, in the political world and in the scientific sector. Every piece of information from universities, businesses, farms, and public institutions was analyzed at their central base in Berlin. This many-armed monster kept an eye on the *Volksgenossen* (and later also the inhabitants of the occupied territories), registered all traceable anti-Nazi movements and terrorized suspected or actual adversaries of the regime in the concentration or related work camps.

Only after the collapse of the Third Reich could a count be made of the reign of terror carried out by this odorous organization: four to five million Jews murdered, two-and-a-half million Poles liquidated, 520,000 gypsies murdered, 473,000 Russian prisoners of war executed, 100,000 incurably ill gassed under the euthanasia policy – numbers so large that they almost become cold statistical ciphers. The body responsible for all this horror was the SS.

The origins of the SS are found in the establishment of a small group of trusted SA (*Sturmabteilung*) men in March 1923, initially intended as a sort of bodyguard (*Stabswache*) for Hitler. With the failure of Hitler's putsch, the SS together with the SA and the NSDAP were banned. One of the first measures Hitler took after his release from prison in 1924 was the re-establishment of the *Stabswache*. Similar groups were also formed in other places, now under the name of *Schutzstaffeln* (SS). These small groups were set up mainly for the protection of party officials and meetings against political opponents and, if necessary, against party dissidents and rebels. The *Schutzstaffeln* were intentionally kept small, with members being recruited from the most reliable, the most fanatical, the most devoted followers of Hitler.

The SS had no pretensions in those early years. The organization was quantitatively and qualitatively weak. Although the SS was fairly autonomous, the national leader (Reichsführer der SS) was subordinate to the head of the SA. There was, however, a definite feeling of elitism even if only because the members knew they were the most dedicated and trusted of Hitler's followers. Hitler made great use of that devotion. For example, on the Party Day in 1926, he ceremoniously handed over the Nazi flag which had been carried in the unsuccessful putsch three years earlier, thereby making explicit his trust in the SS. This sort of symbolic 'reward', even though materially rather meager, bound the SS ever closer to Hitler. Hitler's continual demand for blind faith and sacrifice would soon give the SS man the feeling that he was someone special, that he was certainly better than the ordinary SA member.

Turning the SS into an almost mystical political, racial and spiritual elite was, for the most part, the work of the man appointed by Hitler as Reichsführer-SS in 1929, a man whose name is synonymous with mass murder: Heinrich Himmler. Under Hitler's orders Himmler tried, not without success, to mold the SS into an elite unit. The SS had to become more than just a horde of reliable, violent assistants. They also had to be sharp, obedient and physically perfect. Intellectual capacities were not included in the original selection criteria, until it was later realized that intelligence could not be totally ignored. Other demands, especially racial purity, were already of key importance. National Socialism was for them not a 'doctrine' but a world philosophy, a way of being.

Himmler's idea was that the SS should be an order, a closed community, with the attraction of a closed society. Members had to be bound together by a communal pattern of behavior, a communal ethos, and communal traditions which were yet to be formed. Those who had to protect the Führer and the party from all internal and external attacks had a special and privileged position in the Reich. The SS was, certainly after the takeover of power in 1933, developing into the backbone of the Reich, executer of the most delicate commissions, and the conscience of the party; at the same time it was a state-sponsored murder machine.

Heinrich Himmler was Reichsführer-SS, head of the entire German police force including the infamous *Sicherheitsdienst* (SD) and the Gestapo (*Geheime Staatspolizei*), Minister of the Interior,

Left: *Himmler (front row, second from left) during his time at an agricultural college in Munich, 1919.*

Below: *Manning the barricades during the 1923 putsch in Munich. Himmler carries the flag, standing fourth from left.*

and commander of the Waffen SS and the Home Army – a man whose name became synonymous with diabolical maliciousness during his lifetime. One of the most sinister figures of the Third Reich, his name is linked with the concentration camps, with death and with extermination. He was a man who sincerely believed in his Führer and in the missionary task of National Socialism to cleanse the entire European continent of 'non-Aryan impurities' and refurbish the gene pool with carefully selected blond, blue-eyed '*Edelgermanen*' (noble Germans).

As more information about Himmler became available after the war, the picture of a bloodthirsty sadist, of an angry devil with hardly any human characteristics seemed not to agree with the facts. A different picture of Himmler emerges from the mountain of raw data: a shy, almost unsocial man, who avoided all publicity and whose favorite activities were clearing his workload and busying himself with his 'beloved' dossiers of which he could not get enough. He was a man who was, in general, valued by his subordinates because he kept his word and could listen; a police official who chose a light sunny interior for his office, showing a preference for white; and a man who believed in reincarnation and the pagan myths and sagas of German legend. Himmler was also a functionary who would do nothing without first receiving an explicit directive from his Führer; a man who spontaneously protested when someone talked of the joys of hunting and felt faint when present at an execution; a typical clerk who made his masseur Felix Kersten, who had brought back a watch from Sweden costing 150 Reichsmarks, pay for his dishonesty. He was a ridiculously conscientious bookkeeper, who with painful precision would keep a very detailed filing system of those who had given him presents, and a man who strongly protested when he was reproached for crudeness and felt honored when amicably called 'Reichs-Heini.'

This small-minded clerk, with the appearance of a country

headmaster was, however, the leader of the SS and, as the war progressed, undoubtedly the most powerful man after Hitler. He was responsible for the concentration camps and the murder of millions of people; the chief exponent of a racist morality; the authority who ordered mass executions; and the man who personally gave the order for human experimentation.

There is no indication that he benefited from his crimes or derived pleasure from his perfidious practices; neither did he brag about his success with the mass extermination policies. On the contrary, his endless hesitations, his indecision, his constant attempts to shift responsibility for his own deeds to Hitler, all help to explain his indignation when his masseur and confidant Kersten accused him of having murdered more people than he was aware of. With Himmler we are not dealing with a cold intellect who, with

Below: Himmler and other leading Nazis view a marchpast by the SA in Berlin; their leader, Röhm, stands on the extreme right.

Right: Himmler and Röhm in Gera on 8 September 1931. They were soon to fight for control of the Nazi security service.

Right: *Himmler with his wife
Margarethe and daughter
Gudrun.*

Below: *An informal picture
taken shortly after Hitler was
announced as the new Reichs
Chancellor. Also present:
Goebbels, Röhm, Göring,
Himmler and Hess.*

a total lack of scruples, schemed to satisfy his hunger for power.

Himmler definitely had something in common with his Napoleonic counterpart Joseph Fouché: the preference to remain in the background, to pull the strings but avoid the limelight. Still, he lacked Fouché's craving for wealth. Himmler did, by means of his SS bureaus, spend millions of Reichsmarks on satisfying his hobbies such as research into the origin of the Aryans and for attempts at deciphering runic writing. In his private life he was extremely sober and at his headquarters he tolerated no extravagances. His yearly wage was only 24,000 Reichsmarks and the Reichsführer-SS would often have to scrimp to make ends meet at the end of the month.

He always, no matter what, fulfilled his duty and carried out the Führer's orders. Yet, he was so totally convinced of his innocence that he thought himself the most suitable person to negotiate on the capitulation of Germany with the Allies. If there is something puzzling about Himmler, then it is the fact that this unstable, half-hearted figure managed to survive in the center of a merciless system.

This man, who would bear the responsibility for one of the most heinous crimes in world history, was born in Munich on 7 October 1900. He grew up in a well-to-do Catholic Bavarian family. His father was tutor to the Bavarian Prince Heinrich von Wittelsbach, after whom he was named. He had a close relationship with his parents and two brothers.

When his mother died, Himmler, though ill himself, held a night-long vigil, and at the funeral he reached out over the casket to his two brothers and swore with pathetic weightiness: 'We shall always be together.' He always thought of himself as the family's protector and, even when still young, he tried to fulfill this role. As

a 21-year-old student he wrote to his 'dear little mother': 'Really, dad shouldn't work so hard, but should go walking more often during the week otherwise he will tire himself out.' His brothers did not always escape Heinrich's schoolmasterly pedantry. 'I am very happy with your good school report. But don't let it give you a big head,' one of his brothers was to hear from the barely five-year-older Heinrich. 'For the rest, I expect you to start working on your history. You really mustn't become one-sided. And be always good and well-behaved and don't annoy mom and dad.'

At the end of 1917 he was accepted for officer training in the Bavarian 11th Infantry Regiment, but never saw action. After World War I his father was able to convince him to leave the army and in October 1919 Himmler signed up as an agricultural student at the technical institute in Munich. Agriculture had always interested him; as a boy he already had a sizeable collection of plants, and concentration camp prisoners would later learn to fear his predilection for small herb gardens. On the order of the Reichsführer-SS, every concentration camp had to lay out a selection of herbs. Himmler expected better healing results from his herbs than from the medicines produced by the more usual pharmaceutical companies.

Perhaps here lie the roots of his fanaticism for the NSDAP '*Blut und Boden,*' (literally, blood and soil) idea, whereby '*edelgermaanse Wehrbauern*' (armed farmers of pure German stock) would cultivate the fertile (conquered) lands in the East for the Reich. But, no one then could see in this friendly, obliging and rather boring student, who went to a masked ball in Munich as the Turkish Sultan Abdoel Hamis and entertained an unhappy love for a certain young woman (Maja Loritz), the future head of the notorious SS. In 1920 he met, more or less by accident, one of Hitler's closest

Left: *Nuremberg, 13 August 1933. Himmler, Röhm and Seidel survey the crowd.*

Right: *Himmler in fulldress uniform in the 1930s.*

cronies, Captain Ernst Röhm, a man who managed to bend Himmler to his will completely and brought him into contact with Adolf Hitler.

In 1923 Himmler, who had by then successfully completed his examinations and was working as an assistant agriculturist at the Stickstoffland (plc) in Schliessheim, took part in Hitler's un-

successful putsch. After the putsch he became secretary to Gregor Strasser, one of Hitler's close colleagues. Strasser was in charge of party propaganda in lower Bavaria. Himmler's job was to keep contact with the more remote departments of the NSDAP, visiting them regularly on his scooter.

In 1928 he married the eight-years-older Margarethe Boden,

daughter of a large landowner in West Prussia. The wage that Himmler received as a party official was far from adequate and the young couple prepared themselves for an austere farming life together. They bought a small piece of land near Waltrudering in the vicinity of Munich and had a small wooden house built on it. Himmler built a chicken coop himself. The couple purchased 50 breeding hens, but their farming plans came to nothing due to money problems and Heinrich's party career which was taking up more of his time. His wage of 200 Reichsmarks as a party official was insufficient to get the chicken farm off the ground.

Marga sent her husband a letter (Himmler was then in Berlin) lamenting their situation on 26 May 1929: 'The chickens are laying terribly poorly, only two eggs a day. I am furious, how are we supposed to live on that and then even save for Whitsunday. Always bad luck. Always more money problems.' A marriage crisis, which had come about sooner than either had expected, added to their troubles. The Himmlers separated after the birth of their only daughter, Gudrun. On 6 January 1929 Himmler was appointed head of a small group within the larger SA whose task was to act as Hitler's bodyguard, namely, the SS. Membership then totaled 280, but due to Himmler's inexhaustible enthusiasm the SS rapidly grew and by 1933 had about 50,000 members. Aided by his alter-ego, the malignant, brutal and cynical Reinhard Heydrich, Himmler worked with tenacity and tireless patience to expand the SS.

The so-called 'Röhm Putsch' of June 1934 was an important boost to Himmler's career. By taking advantage of the rivalry between the SA and the army Himmler was able to come out of the conflict with his SS greatly in favor. The SS with all its departments soon grew into one of the most influential organizations in the Third Reich. By 1936 Himmler was head of the entire German police force and was given the title of Reichsführer-SS.

Left: *Himmler discusses the filming of the 'Triumph of the Will' with its director Leni Riefenstahl during the 1934 Reichsparteitag at Nuremberg's Luitpold arena.*

Below left: *Reichsparteitag, Nuremberg, 1934. Hitler with Himmler (left) and Victor Lutze (right) salute a Nazi memorial.*

Right: *Himmler in conversation with a Wehrmacht officer; Reinhard Heydrich, the Reichsführer-SS's chosen successor is to the right of his master.*

Below: *Himmler inspects recruits to the SS, 8 May 1936.*

Left: *Himmler and Hess (right) inspect Dachau concentration camp near Munich, 8 May 1936.*

Above right: *Hitler salutes his personal bodyguard, the Leibstandarte Adolf Hitler as they goosestep down Berlin's Wilhelmstrasse, 30 January 1938. Also present are Hess, Sepp Dietrich and Himmler.*

Right: *An honor guard of the Leibstandarte Adolf Hitler awaits the arrival of the Führer.*

After the war it became clear that the Third Reich was not as soundly and rigidly organized as many, both in and outside Germany, had assumed. The totalitarian system in Germany was, in actual fact, a muddle of privileges and power struggles. Germany was governed solely by the will of the Führer, with his 'Führer decrees' and his 'Führer orders.' Insofar as the aims of the Führer were acted upon, the SS, as the most pervasive force in the dictatorship, had absolute power. Hitler did not want to be reliant on any single group, thus he delegated his orders to as many departments as possible.

A system was created wherein the state was reduced to a non-political administrative machine, a façade behind which leaders fought for personal prestige. There was no way that in this chaos of self-centered money-grabbers, private armies, and private espionage services that the SS could enjoy absolute, uncontested power. Also, just as with the feudal monarchs of past centuries, the despots of Hitler's regime formed coalitions, fought each other and

became reconciled again. The SS did hold many positions of power which were used to keep the civilian population under close control, but two important power sources evaded them: the party and the armed forces. There was, however, a totally helpless group of people in the Third Reich, the Jews, victims of the only SS state that actually existed: the closed world of the concentration camps, where the prisoners were handed over to (mainly) criminal, sadistic SS guards to face an iniquitous fate.

History has taught us that there were a few men, some party brownshirts, some prominent SS members, who did try to undermine Himmler's extermination program. For example, the former Gauleiter Kube, Commissar-General for White Ukraine, who made charges against police officers for the maltreatment of Jews, brought Jews transported to Minsk for extermination under his protection and carried out a one-man crusade against the SS, SD and Gestapo until he was killed by a Russian partisan bomb. There was Obergruppenführer Dr Best, who helped thousands of Jews to

Above: *Various categories of prisoners are marched out of Dachau on a work party, May 1938.*

Right: *SS recruits head out of their training school on an early morning run.*

escape to neutral Sweden. And finally, Felix Kersten, Himmler's masseur and personal physician (Himmler: 'my only friend, my Buddha') who, while treating Himmler for his stomach pains, was also able to save human lives. Kersten, of Finnish origin, wrote an account of his five years with Himmler based on his detailed diaries from that period.

Dr Kersten, who was for many years the personal physician of Prince Hendrick, tried to save Dutch people from deportation and execution, and to free them from the concentration camps whenever possible. On 8 December 1944 Himmler promised to free 1000 Dutch women from the concentration camps; at the same time he gave Kersten permission to free 50 Norwegian students and 50 Danish policemen. It was also Kersten who convinced Himmler to rescind the orders for blowing up the Clingendael 'fortress' in Den Haag and for cutting the sea dikes. He was also able to stop the transport of art treasures from the Netherlands planned for March 1943. This man who had been of such invaluable service to the Netherlands was rewarded in 1950 when he re-

ceived the country's highest decoration, the '*Grootofficier in de orde of Oranje-Nassau*,' from Prince Bernhard. Also, the Swedish department of the World Jewish Congress thanked him, describing in detail his services to the Jewish people: 'In particular we think of your efforts during the tragic war years when you were successful in freeing approximately 3500 Jews from German concentration camps and having them transferred to Sweden. The Jews of all countries, whose fellow Jews have been saved by your hands, shall always remain grateful to you.' The World Jewish Council states in a memorandum that it was Kersten who had talked Himmler out of his diabolical plan to exterminate all the remaining concentration camp prisoners and their guards in the face of the Allied advance. 'With this,' reads the memorandum, 'hundreds-of-thousands were saved, among them 60,000 Jews.'

In Kersten's report on his patient, Himmler is shown as a perfect German. He had a kind-hearted manner and was somewhat sentimental. A primitive German work ethic reigned at Himmler's headquarters, a work ethic that fitted in perfectly with Himmler's

Right and above: *Two views of one of the many Nazi death camps.*

ideas about loyalty. Fidelity to one's given word was of the greatest importance to Himmler, irrespective of the (horrific) consequences to which it might lead. Kersten's report also reveals that Himmler's ideas took on a more grotesque form as the years passed. He expounded macabre fantasies about the 'new Europe,' free of all non-Aryan impurities and ruled by blond, blue-eyed noble Germans.

The combination of unreal fantasy with rational planning was one of the most striking characteristics of this generally colorless figure. In one of the most frightening speeches given during World War II, on 4 October 1943 at Posnan, Himmler explained his views to his SS generals: 'What happens to the Russians doesn't interest me; what happens to the Czechs, I find unimportant. That people are living in hunger and misery is only of importance to me to the extent that we need them as slaves for our culture. If 10,000 Russian women were to die of exhaustion while digging a tank ditch, it would be of interest to me only insofar as whether the tank ditch would be finished for Germany.

'I also want to speak frankly to you about a most serious business. Among ourselves we must speak openly about it, although in public we will remain silent. I mean . . . the extermination of the Jewish race . . . Most of you know what it means to see 100 bodies lying by the side of a road, or 500 or 1000. To be able to withstand the sight and still remain decent men has made us tough. Every party member says that the Jewish people must be exterminated. That is clear, it is a part of our program. Good, we shall do it. This is a glorious page in our history.'

The most striking feature about the man who presented this speech, at least according to Kersten, was his blind obedience to his Führer. Himmler was always seized by a sort of panic when he was called to see Hitler. Hitler seldom treated him other than as a diligent, trusted, but not especially intelligent, young clerk. Himmler could never overcome his anxiety whenever he was in contact with the 'best brain of all time.' Even a telephone conversation with Hitler threw him into a state. Once, after Kersten had taken a call from Hitler, Himmler was beside himself: 'Mister Kersten, do you

know with whom you have spoken? You have heard the voice of the Führer. What a lucky devil you are. You must immediately write and tell your wife. She will be ever so happy for you that such a thing has happened.'

Hitler, Himmler often maintained, was the greatest man the world had ever known, even greater than Genghis Khan, the Mongol ruler who had conquered a large part of Europe in the thirteenth century and for whom Himmler had a high regard. Himmler held himself to be a reincarnation of Henry I, Duke of Saxony, who in 919 became king and laid the foundations for the creation of the First German Reich.

Himmler's idolization of Hitler, 'Der Führer irrt nie' ('The Führer is never wrong'), stemmed from his serious and genuine belief in the spiritual mission of National Socialism and he was never more happy than when his Führer approved his plans. For example, such was the case when Hitler signed a document drawn up by Himmler in 1943 laying down the rules for the use of language in the future German continental empire. German would be the first language; English and Russian would have to disappear. The other languages could be used for another decade as a means of communication, after which time they would also be banned. Members of the SS who had served meritoriously would have the right to take a second wife, so that as many blond, blue-eyed babies would be born as possible. All measures would be taken to limit the number of births among the indigenous populations in the occupied areas so that after 1000 years the German 'folk' would total 500 million souls, populating the lands between the Urals and the North Sea.

The deportation of the entire Dutch population to the East was planned within the framework of the above-mentioned program. Kersten recounted that he received a 43-page secret state document from Himmler's secretary, Dr Brandt, in March 1941 which showed that Hitler intended to announce the planned transportation of the Dutch population to Poland on 20 April 1941 (Hitler's birthday). This resettlement would take place in two stages: first, the inhabitants of the Catholic south of the Netherlands and Flemish Belgium would be transported, followed by the northern and eastern provinces, and, finally, the inhabitants of the four major cities. A period of 13 weeks and four days was considered necessary for the total resettlement.

According to Kersten, the plans for the movement of these 8.2 million people were ready. The transportable goods of those involved would be shipped by train and sea to East Prussia. The sick and elderly would be sent by train and bus while the younger men and women would have to walk, stage by stage, from their homeland through Germany to Poland. The care of these people would be as laid down in the regulations of the military sanitation services, although handled by the SS. Also, those transported to the east would receive provisions from the Wehrmacht reserves until the new harvest was gathered. Their new home, which would be twice the size of the Netherlands and of which the capital would be Lublin, had good farming land. It was further noted that immediately after the fall of Russia, Lemberg and those lands farther to the East would also be settled. As Germany was not at war with Russia at that time, it was, of course, mentioned in the report that this had to be kept strictly secret.

According to Kersten the move was planned with typical German *gründlichkeit* (thoroughness), with everything thought out down to the last detail. The key staff would be taken from experienced SS leaders, while a special role was reserved for the Dutch National Socialists. It had been decided that they would, at least for the time being, remain in the Netherlands, where they would lend a hand during the resettlement and help to assure a smooth execution of the plan by helping to find and arrest those

Above left: *Himmler enjoys a break from the affairs of state.*

Above: *Hitler receives a group of children in Berlin, 14 June 1938. Goebbels and a smiling Himmler look on.*

Left: *Himmler and the Führer await the arrival of the Leibstandarte Adolf Hitler, 20 April 1939.*

Far left: *Himmler attends the funeral of Reinhard Heydrich who was assassinated by members of the Czech resistance in June 1942.*

Left: *Vidkun Quisling, leader of the Norwegian Nazi Party and head of the country's wartime puppet government, in conversation with Himmler.*

Below: *Senior officers, Hitler and Himmler view the progress of their forces during the invasion of Poland, September 1939.*

trying to illegally avoid deportation. After fulfillment of their service the Dutch Nazis would in turn be purged, leaving only those who had shown themselves to be 'Germans.' The report assumed that at least 50 percent of the Dutch Nazis would be found to be hangers-on. These would also be transported. Resettlement would include the police, the Jews and those Germans who had already been living in the Netherlands for a long time before 1940. The document also referred to a special order regarding the Jews, for which the Reichsführer-SS was directly responsible, wherein it was stated that the Jews from the Netherlands would never reach the point of destination.

Finally, several guidelines were given regarding the disposition of goods remaining in the Netherlands after the departure of their rightful owners. The land, all buildings erected on it and all supplies would automatically become the property of the state administered by the Reich-Commissar for the Settlement of Germans Abroad. The Netherlands would become an SS province, with its farmland divided into lots of 60 to 100 hectares and handed over to young SS *Wehrbauern*, who would be carefully selected on the grounds of race and politics. Utrecht was to be the capital of this province and gigantic fortresses would be built along the entire coast.

A four-year plan had been drawn up for the development of the province. The entire population of the Baltic states was to be transported to the area of Archangel in northern Russia immediately after the defeat of that country. Kersten heard from Himmler why the deportation plan had been drawn up. The Führer, according to Himmler, did not want a hostile populace living on the mouth of

Far left: *Himmler discusses the progress of the war with Hitler, 10 October 1944.*

Left: *Hitler and Bormann greet Himmler on the occasion of his forty-third birthday at the Wolfsschanze, 10 October 1943.*

Below: *A visibly shaken Hitler pictured shortly after the July Bomb Plot. His entourage includes Himmler, Mussolini and Göring.*

the Rhine. During one of his treatment sessions for Himmler's stomach cramps, Kersten was able to convince him that the administration of such an extensive project would be far too taxing for his weak health. Himmler finally agreed with him and was able to convince Hitler to shelve the plan for the time being, according to Kersten.

Dutch historian Dr L de Jong is very critical of Kersten's story: 'Perhaps Kersten invented the entire deportation plan to be in the good graces of the Netherlands.' Shortly after the war Kersten was having great difficulties in Sweden. There was a good chance that being a Finnish citizen he would be deported to Finland, from where he would almost certainly end up in a Russian prison for having been the personal physician of one of the most sinister Nazi leaders.

De Jong added: 'As far as Kersten is concerned: he is, as I came to know him from several meetings and by studying the material re-

Right: *The legacy of the Third Reich – some of the millions of victims of Himmler's death camps await burial by the Allies.*

lating to his person and deeds, a bundle of contradictions: particularly vain and particularly good-hearted; thirsting after a mark of honor and ready to help his fellow human beings; ingenious in trifles, but lacking the power to assess important relationships; crafty and at the same time naive.

'I will repeat what I have already given as an account of my conclusion: in a number of cases Kersten took the trouble for the release of Dutch and others arrested or condemned; he acted as mediator for the release of a thousand Dutch women who had been imprisoned in the concentration camp at Ravensbrück, and he put his own life at risk by these involvements. They were important humanitarian services. But for historical knowledge Felix Kersten is a totally unreliable witness.'

The defeat of the German Sixth Army at Stalingrad in late 1942-early 1943 was the beginning of the end of the Third Reich. From 1943 onward the German armed forces were being pushed back to the German borders. In the meantime Himmler had become Minister of the Interior and commander of the Replacement Army, in addition to being Reichsführer-SS and head of the German police.

On 19 February 1945 a representative of the Swedish Red Cross, Count Folke Bernadotte, had a meeting with Himmler concerning the release of Danish and Norwegian prisoners from the concentration camps: 'The American reporter Shirer had once characterized Himmler as an innocent country teacher and I can attest that this was a very striking characteristic of the Gestapo boss, judging by appearance. When he suddenly stood up for me, with his horn-rimmed glasses and green Waffen SS uniform –

without decorations - he looked most like an insignificant civil servant. If you passed him in the street, you wouldn't notice him. His behavior was remarkably polite, he showed a sense of humor, tending toward gallows humor. He didn't in the least give an appearance of anything diabolical. Of the cold look in his eyes, that is so often mentioned about him, I noticed nothing.'

In these last days of the Third Reich Himmler made all sorts of frenetic efforts to make contact with the Allies through intermediaries. In the strictest secrecy he corresponded with the Swedish representative of the World Jewish Congress and personally secured safe conduct for a Jewish negotiator to fly from Sweden to Berlin to discuss the release of Jewish prisoners from the concentration camps. In the face of total defeat Himmler was obsessed with one idea: after first having let millions be murdered, he now saw himself in the role of the great protector and angel of peace. His main fear was that Hitler would become aware of his plan and take measures against him.

The last meeting with Kersten took place on 19 April: 'The best part of the German people is lost with us. That is sad, but the rest of those still remaining in Germany don't interest us. The Allies can do with them what they want.' While still talking he walked to his car, got in and, once seated, offered his hand to Kersten and said: 'I thank you very much, Kersten, for unselfishly helping me all these years with such skill. No matter what may now happen, you must never think badly of me. If you can, help my family. Keep well.' Kersten said that Himmler had tears in his eyes with these last words.

Bernadotte met Himmler for the last time on 23 April, one week

before Hitler's suicide. Himmler was no longer able to suppress his nervousness during this candlelight meeting. He was convinced that Hitler would name him as his successor and entreated Bernadotte to arrange a meeting with General Eisenhower. 'It was already 2.30 in the morning when we left the building where the meeting had taken place,' said Bernadotte. 'The stars were bright. Himmler got in behind the wheel of his own car. "I am going to drive to the Eastern Front now," he said at our parting, adding with a weak little laugh, "it is, after all, not far from here." Then he drove off. A dull thud was heard a few minutes later: Himmler had driven right into the barbed wire surrounding the villa. With much difficulty and help from bystanders he was hauled out of the car.' 'The manner in which Himmler drove off,' remarked Bernadotte, 'had something symbolic about it.'

On 1 May Himmler heard that Admiral Dönitz had been appointed Hitler's successor. On the 6th Dönitz officially relieved Himmler of all his offices. He and several SS adjutants managed to go into hiding. On 21 May, under the assumed name of Heinrich Hitzinger, without mustache, with a black patch over one eye and in the remnants of the uniform of a sergeant-major in the *Geheime Feldpolizei*, he was picked up by a British control post.

Himmler and his two adjutants stood in a row with several thousand others slowly shuffling over a bridge on the River Oste, near Bremervörde. Their mistake was to present brand new papers to the English guard at a time when hardly anyone had papers. Himmler had wrongly thought that only a person without papers would be suspect. Sometime later he made his identity known.

While being medically examined for the second time at a prison camp at Lüneburg Himmler ended his life with a poison capsule hidden in his mouth. In the early hours of 26 May, Himmler's body was taken away by a British lorry to an unknown destination. Two NCOs picked up the dead man by the head and feet and threw him into the back of the lorry. Himmler was buried somewhere in a forest in the vicinity of Lüneburg. The exact spot is a carefully kept secret. While filling up the grave one of the NCOs said: 'Let the worm go to the worms.' The grass sods were replaced and no mound, no unevenness was left to betray this burial place.

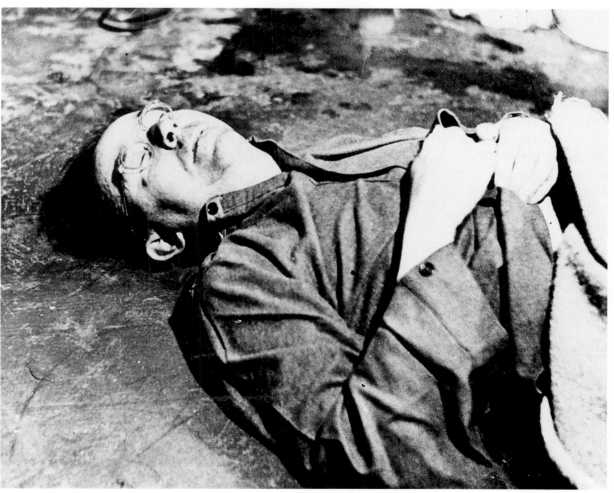

Right: *Himmler pictured after his successful suicide attempt following his capture by the Allies.*

ALBERT SPEER

1905-1981

Left: *Albert Speer, the Führer's leading architect and the driving force behind Nazi Germany's war economy.*

Above: *Speer pictured in later life after his release from Spandau prison in West Berlin.*

ermania, a city with 10 million inhabitants whose center would be punctuated by a 120m-wide boulevard, surrounded by colossal structures attesting to the greatness and might of the German Imperium with its 140 million souls; a 300m-high domed hall topped by a 15m-high Reich eagle holding a world globe in its talons; a Führer palace with an area of two million square meters, more than twice as large as Nero's famous 'Golden House' – these were the building plans Hitler gave to his favorite architect and confidant Albert Speer for the new 'Great Berlin.'

Just how great Hitler's trust in Albert Speer was was shown in February 1942 when he appointed him Minister for Armaments and War Production. Military experts are in agreement that Speer, with his central planning system, prolonged the war by two years. In spite of Allied bombardment and the disruption of the German economy Speer was successful in doubling, and in some cases even tripling, war production in 1944, as compared with 1942.

During his trial in Nuremberg, Speer stated: 'If Hitler had had real friends, I would have been one of them.' Speer was sentenced to 20 years imprisonment for his role in the forced labor system and served out his sentence at Spandau prison in Berlin. He spent his prison years writing the historiography of the Third Reich, and his works have since been published. Upon his release in October 1966 at the age of 61, he retired to his family home in Heidelberg, where he lived until his death in 1981. One way or another Speer had been successful in evading the hangman at Nuremberg. Among Hitler's strange entourage he seemed the most rational and intelligent – a Brahms-like type who had become involved with Wagnerians.

Albert Speer was born in Mannheim on 19 March 1905 and grew up in the protected environment of an upper middle class family. He wanted to become an architect like his father and grandfather. During the turbulent 1920s he studied at the Institutes of Technology at Karlsrühe, Munich and Berlin, and was assistant to Professor Tessenow at Berlin from 1927 to 1930. Speer had as yet shown no interest in politics. On an evening in January 1931 he took several students from his department along with him to one of the many political meetings being held in Berlin at that time. A man known for his passion and clear language would be speaking that evening: Adolf Hitler. Speer gave the following account of that meeting: 'Filthy walls, narrow staircases and an appearance of neglect gave an impression of poverty. The hall was packed. It seemed as though all the students in Berlin wanted to hear and see this man. I was impressed by the enthusiasm of the audience. The man seemed a moderate and easily kept control of the questioners without raising his voice. I had expected a brown-shirted fanatic wearing a swastika armband. However I was facing a man wearing a well-fitted blue suit, revealing noticeably middle-class manners.'

Speer became a member of the NSDAP shortly after this meeting. He received the membership number of 474,481 and, being in possession of a car, ran a courier service for the party. Wrote Speer: 'At that time I chose not for the party but for the man whose personality had made such a deep impression on me at that first meeting, a feeling which I have never lost. His persuasiveness, the strange magic of his by no means pleasant voice, the singularity of his somewhat banal behavior and the seductive, simplifying way in which he handled our complicated problems – this all threw me into confusion and excited me. I knew almost nothing of his political program. He had deeply affected me before I had come to understand him.'

Speer became unemployed in 1932 and moved with his wife to Mannheim to look for work. He was eventually successful, receiving a commission for a small building project for the NSDAP through a friend – the chance he had been waiting for. Speer's first meeting with Hitler took place after the Führer had become Reich Chancellor. Speer received an invitation to visit Hitler and show his designs for the Nuremberg stadium. He met Hitler many times after this while on building site inspection tours in Berlin. On one of these occasions Hitler casually said to Speer: 'Why don't you come and eat with me this afternoon?'

Speer was delighted with the invitation. However, shortly before it was time to leave for lunch Speer was unfortunately hit by a lump of cement. Being covered with dirt he wanted to excuse himself from the luncheon engagement but Hitler lent him one of his own jackets. Speer, as the most honored guest, sat next to Hitler. One of the other guests (Goebbels, Minister of Propaganda) noticed that Speer was wearing the Führer's personal party insignia on his jacket (it had been overlooked in the excitement) and said provokingly to Speer: 'You are wearing the Führer's insignia, that cannot

Left: *The pomp and ceremony of Reichsparteitag in 1936. The lighting effects were created by Speer using dozens of searchlights pointing into the night sky.*

Right: *A model of a massive arena capable of seating 250,000 people. Designed by Speer, it was one element in the redevelopment of Nuremberg.*

possibly be your jacket.' To which Hitler replied: 'That's true. It is my jacket.'

One thing led to another. Speer was to become Hitler's most important architect. In the foreword to a book about the Reich Chancellery built by Speer in 1939 Hitler called Speer 'ein genialer Gestalter und Baumeister' (a brilliant designer and architect). Speer wrote about this period: 'After so many years of searching in vain, at 28 I was bursting with energy to work. Like Faust, I would have sold my soul to the devil for a substantial building contract. I had found my Mephisto . . .' There can be no doubt that the Führer entertained much sympathy for the young builder and saw in him a 'fellow artist.' Hitler, rejected twice from entrance to an art academy, saw in Speer the fulfillment of his own unsatisfied dream of becoming an architect.

Although Hitler knew how to fascinate, he was, according to Speer, unable to give true, human warmth. 'In the center, where his heart should be, Hitler was empty. Not one of us was more than a projection of his gargantuan "I," like the buildings I designed for him . . .'

The extent to which Speer had become one of Hitler's intimates is apparent from the fact that Hitler invited him to come and live on the Obersalzberg. Speer became, after Hitler, Göring and Bormann, the fourth 'Obersalzberger.' His workshop, situated next to his house there, was a simple stone building with a strikingly large window. It was built in typical Alpine style, a style which Hitler insisted upon for most buildings on the Obersalzberg. Behind the large atelier window Speer had his work table. The Führer often paid unannounced visits to Speer, generally accompanied by an adjutant carrying a file full of floor plans that Hitler would study with Speer. The two men often stood for hours bent over the most amazing building plans; they did, after all, want to transform the Reich into a country in which colossal structures would reflect the glory of the Führer, the party and the state. Architecture was more than just a hobby to the Führer, he was obsessed with it. Hitler was still involved in numerous building projects when the end was approaching and Russian soldiers were crossing the borders into the Third Reich.

Speer saw Hitler's sketch book of drawings from the early 1920s several times. What Speer found interesting about Hitler's work was that almost all of the architectural sketches were surrounded

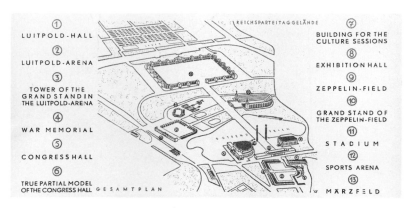

Top: *The layout of the 'new' Nuremberg – boulevards and imposing edifices to awe the masses.*

Above: *A model of the colossal entrance to one of the Reich's autobahns. It was to be built on the border, somewhere near Salzburg.*

Left: *Two SS guards stand in front of the west portal of the Reichs Chancellery.*

Above: *One of the many marble anterooms in the new Reichs Chancellery.*

Right: *The hub of Speer's Reichs Chancellery – Hitler's imposing study. The room was 90 feet long, nearly 50 feet wide and over 30 feet high. The walls were of dark-red marble.*

Left: *The main podium at Nuremberg's Luitpold arena draped with the flags and banners of the Third Reich.*

Above: *The party faithful gather in the Luitpold arena to listen to speeches by leading figures in the party.*

Below: *The Brandenburg Gate in Berlin captured at night.*

by drawings of weapons and warships. Hitler's architectural preference was for the pompous neo-baroque, a style identical to that which accompanied the decline of the Roman as well as the Napoleonic Empires. A true 'Führer style' did not exist, although the party press stated otherwise. What was declared as the official architectural style of the Third Reich was simply the neo-classical style which had been altered and exaggerated, sometimes to a ludicrous extent. As Hitler's power grew, so did the extravagances in his architectural plans.

Hitler always had a mania for breaking records. His mountain retreat near Berchtesgaden was claimed by him to have the 'largest sunken window' in the world. The museum at Linz, the town of his youth, must have the 'largest sculptured frieze on the Continent.' Hitler commissioned designs for the highest domes, the most gigantic triumphal arches and stadiums to hold the largest crowds. He translated the massive, the abnormal, into normal. Because of this childish passion for breaking records, the architecture of the Third Reich was in essence no different from that of earlier dictators. It is as though these dictators wanted to deny the mortality of their rule by creating majestic monuments. On the Reich Party Day in 1937, Hitler announced: 'Because we believe in the eternity of this Reich, our buildings must also be eternal, that is to say . . . they are not intended for 1940, nor for the year 2000, but they, just like the cathedral towers of the past, will still be standing thousands of years from now.'

Speer received his first large building commission from Hitler in early 1934. He was to construct a gigantic complex of structures in Nuremberg for the yearly party days. The complex in its entirety would cover an area of 16.5 square kilometers and would be peppered with stadiums, streets, galleries and halls. The main building was to be 390m long and 24m high, while the elevated stage with its long colonnade would be closed off on the top and flanked by two massive towers. Speer developed his *Theorie der Rüinenwerte* during the construction of this *Reichsparteitaggelände*. His 'Theory of the

Value of Ruins' held that structures such as pyramids should have clearly recognizable forms even after thousands of years. To this purpose Speer developed complicated statistical computations and used durable materials which would survive the ravages of time. Hitler determined that in future all important structures built for the Third Reich were to be constructed on the basis of this 'Ruins theory.'

Hitler once said to Speer's wife: 'Your husband will erect structures for me such as have not been created for 4000 years.' In Nuremberg Hitler organized the largest and most alarming spectacles of mass hysteria known to German and perhaps even European history. At dusk hundreds of thousands of uniformed supporters in tightly closed ranks with their flags and banners, and tens of thousands of swastikas, all illuminated by flaming torches and subtly positioned spotlights, marched in step with rousing music.

Speer also introduced the so-called 'dome of light' at Nuremberg. This impressive spectacle was created by 130 searchlights which had been set up around the mammoth arena throwing their beams upward to a height of six to eight kilometers into the night sky. In addition to this surrealistic spectacle, the searchlights also had a political purpose: namely, the intimidation of foreign diplomats and military observers who had been invited to visit the Nazi festivities at Nuremberg. In their reports to their governments, these observers wrote with awe of the obvious military strength of Germany, a country that could use 130 searchlights from the air force solely for decorative purposes around the Nuremberg arena. Neither the diplomats nor the foreign journalists realized that the Nazis were using all the available searchlights from the area, including reserves, for their spectacle.

On 30 January 1937, exactly four years after Hitler came to power, Speer was given his largest job yet. Hitler commissioned him, giving him a free hand, to transform Berlin within a period of 15 years into a monument of 'imperial greatness' appropriate for the 1000 Year Reich. Berlin would be renamed Germania. Speer was given the title of *Generalbauinspektor für die Neugestaltung der Reichshauptstadt* (Inspector General for the Rebuilding of Berlin). He and his staff moved into the venerable *Akademie der Künste* building, supplanting, under pressure from Hitler, the Minister of Education. Hitler's eye fell on this building because he would be able to visit it via the gardens of the bordering ministries without attracting the attention of the public.

Hitler had for years planned to transform Berlin into a gigantic metropolis with broad avenues, mammoth structures, triumphal archs, domes, stations, meeting halls, and areas for parades. He had often said that Berlin would surpass cities such as London, Paris and Vienna, and that it would be comparable only to ancient cities such as Thebes, Babylon or Rome. The new Germania with its 'imperial greatness' was to be dominated by a huge, copper-domed meeting hall. The building, almost 300m high extending far into the sky, would be the largest building in the world. It would be somewhat similar to the Pantheon in Rome.

The meeting hall, with its dome having an almost unbelievable inner circumference of 250m, would be able to hold a standing crowd of 180,000 people. The dome itself, starting at a height of more than 98m above ground level would soar to a height of 220m. With a capacity of 21 million cubic meters the building could contain St Peter's in Rome 17 times! Standing on the 'Führer' gallery, marked by a towering gold-plated Reich eagle, Hitler would address the crowds of the '1000-Year Great German Reich.' A 50m-wide, 28m-high recess with a gold mosaic floor was to be built across from the entrance to the complex. The only decoration in front of this would be a gold-plated Reich Eagle holding in its talons a swastika set in a wreath of oak leaves. The structure would be surmounted by a 40m-high lantern itself topped by an eagle clasping a swastika in its claws. Hitler already had a model of the project by early summer of 1939. He pointed to the eagle crowning

Below left: *Loyal party members assembled at Nuremberg wait for the arrival of their Führer.*

Right: *Nuremberg at night, Reichsparteitag, 1936.*

the building and said: 'This will have to be changed. The eagle must no longer rise above the swastika, but shall rule the world.' He asked Speer to replace the eagle with a world globe. Hitler's political and military ambitions were reflected in his architectural plans.

The domed building was to be connected to a 110m-high triumphal arch by a five kilometer-long ceremonial thoroughfare crossing from north to south through the heart of Berlin. 'And every year,' fantasized Hitler, 'a troop of Kirgiezens will be led through the streets of our capital city to impress upon them the immensity and the greatness of her stone monuments.' He saw Germania's population growing from four million inhabitants to 10 million by 1950 to become the capital city of a German Empire of 140 million inhabitants with all of Europe under its rule.

An Adolf Hitlerplatz was to be situated in the center of Germania where, on the first day of every May, a million workers could file past. Two-thirds of the ceremonial street were reserved for private building. A luxurious large cinema with seating for 2000, a new opera house, three theaters, a new concert hall, a 21-floor hotel with 500 beds, music halls, both large and first-class restaurants and even a Roman-style indoor swimming pool were all planned to bring life to the surroundings. Quiet courtyards with colonnades, and small tasteful boutiques would entice people away from the noise for a quiet stroll. The rest of the showplace would be taken up by 11 separate ministries.

The southern *Zentralbahnhof*, which would be three times larger than Grand Central Station in New York, would have a station square in front of it measuring 1000m long by 300m wide. The square was to be encircled by seized weaponry. Northern Germania would also have its central station where, looking over the majestic 1100m-long and 350m-wide water garden, people would be able to see the central dome almost two kilometers away. The water garden would also be used as a swimming pool with changing rooms, boat houses and terraces.

A gigantic *Soldatenhalle* would be built in Germania's center to commemorate the German armies. After the ceasefire with France Hitler declared that the first exhibit for the *Soldatenhalle* was to be the dining car used during the signing of the armistice. He also wanted the remains of famous German field marshals to be exhibited. A new building for the Wehrmacht high command would be erected behind the *Soldatenhalle*.

The new 'Führer palace' was an indication of his never-ending ambitions and megalomania. This new building was to be 150 times larger than Bismarck's original Chancellor's residence. Hitler's dream palace would even measure up to Nero's 'Golden House' with its surface measurement of a million square meters. His fortress-like palace in the center of Berlin would have a floor surface of two million square meters including gardens. There would be reception areas leading through a system of hallways to a dining room with seating for thousands. Eight gigantic halls for gala receptions and a theater with the most modern technical equipment and decorated in rococo style with seating for 400 were also planned.

The entire complex would be encircled by innumerable fountains and roof gardens. The total length of the garden frontage would be 670m – surpassing that of the Palace of Versailles. The large reception room at the end of the gallery was to be 21,000 cubic meters (as comparison, the reception room at the White House East Room is approximately 2500 cubic meters). The official driveway for diplomats was to be more than 500m long and laid with smooth, polished marble to impress visitors of the power of the Führer. A new Reichstag was also going to be built which would be four times the size of the existing, partially burnt-out building. Mammoth barracks for the SS and other elite party organizations were also to be erected near the 'Führerpalast.'

Speer, carrying out a strictly top secret commission, had a model of Germania ready in 1936. The model itself was two meters high and more than 36m long. Speer kept it at his workroom on the Pariser Plaz where Hitler would often come, either alone or accompanied by good friends, for a look at his precious dream city. Its scale was 1:1000 and could be dismantled and put on rolling tables allowing Hitler to rearrange the planning, studying the various possibilities. Once when Speer's 75-year-old father (also an architect) visited, he looked at the model and commented: 'You have both become totally mad.'

The urban development project which Hitler had in mind had one major drawback: it was not thought through. He had become so enamored with the idea of a Berlin Champs Elysées, two-and-a-half times longer and 20m wider than the Paris original, that he had not taken the basic structure of the city into account. Upon closer study of Hitler's plans Speer saw some of the important problems, such as the rail system, which were bound to arise. Working with

the Reichsbahn's top planner Speer did, however, see a possibility for a large-scale renewal of the entire railroad network in the capital. Broadening the Berlin circle line by two tracks would increase the capacity to such an extent that it would be possible to concentrate long distance traffic at one point. As a result travelers could arrive at two central stations, one in the south as well as one in the north, making the numerous terminals for through trains superfluous.

The cost of the new line was estimated at one to two billion marks. The line in the center of the city would create a new residential area with a capacity for 400,000 inhabitants. In addition to this, various exit roads connecting to the motorway ringroad network would be built; new residential neighborhoods would be created which, even with inner city redevelopment, would allow for the doubling of the city's population. A system of star-shaped green areas radiating out from the center would prevent the traditional oppressive effect caused by circular building zones.

The road system could be expanded in the future to include five ringroads and 16 exit roads, each with a width of 60m. A planned underground motorway system was to relieve traffic congestion. Land beyond the '*Autobahnring*' was reserved for recreational facilities. Following the example of the Bois de Boulogne in Paris, the Grunewald with its tens-of-thousands of broad-leaved trees would provide walking paths, play areas, restaurants and sports fields for this city of millions.

At the end of January 1938 Hitler commissioned Speer to build the new Reich Chancellery within a year. Hitler found the existing Reich Chancellery 'suitable for a soap firm.' The elongated construction site on the Voszstrasse in the heart of Berlin called for a series of rooms which together formed a long axis: from Wilhelm-Platz the visitor went through grand doors to a presentation hall; a landing brought the visitor to a smallish reception room with its five meter high panel doors opening on to a hall and proceeding through the dome-shaped space to a 145m-high gallery.

Far left: *Speer's home at the Eagle's Nest.*

Below, far left: *One of the massive concrete gun emplacements built by Speer's forced-labor organization to defend the coast of northwest Europe.*

Left: *Speer and Hitler inspect the work in progress on the redevelopment of Nuremberg.*

Below left: *The cover of* Wehrmacht *magazine showing Speer in conversation with a Luftwaffe officer.*

Below: *A poster advertising the 1938 Reichsparteitag.*

Right: *One of the impressive corridors in the Reichs Chancellery.*

Below right: *The Reichs Chancellery's central courtyard.*

Above: *An aerial view of the Luitpold arena in Nuremberg, 1937.*

Right: *Speer and Hitler inspect a model of the reliefs to be used in the Munich Reichs gallery.*

Hitler was very impressed with the gallery because it was more than twice the length of the Versailles mirrored gallery. The structure, with its variety of materials and color combinations had a total length of 220m. From the gallery one reached Hitler's reception hall. Impressed, Hitler said: 'The long route from the entrance to the reception hall will give them an idea of the power and greatness of the Third Reich.'

Hitler started using the new Reich Chancellery on 7 January 1939. He was full of praise for his 'brilliant architect,' although he did not share Speer's opinion that the polished marble gallery floor was a poor choice. Hitler said: 'It is perfect, for diplomats have to walk on slippery ice.' Using two shifts, 4500 workers toiled day and night on the building. In addition to this there were many thousands throughout the country working on various components.

Looking back on the 'supercity' after more than 30 years Speer said that he was surprised by the coldness and bleakness which the ostentatious buildings would have radiated. He said: 'Designs of such immensity indicate an outburst of permanent megalomania. Michelangelo was right when he said that mankind was the measure of everything, especially in building. I didn't see that then.'

When the German Blitzkrieg was brought to a halt at the end of 1941 and the character of the war changed, the National Socialist regime realized that it must change its armaments industry policy. The death of the Minister of Armaments and War Products, Fritz Todt, in February 1942 had been a heavy blow for Hitler. He decided to appoint his 'brilliant' architect Albert Speer as successor to Todt and with Speer a new era began when the entire arma-

Left: *A grateful Führer presents Speer with a gift for his work in improving the Reich's war economy, 4 June 1943.*

ments industry was centralized under his leadership. Todt had already introduced the first measures for the organization of a central planning system in December 1941. Using these initial plans Speer received permission from Hitler, on 4 April 1942, for the establishment of an '*Amt für zentrale Planung.*' This group included Speer, Chairman and Minister of Armaments and War Production; State Secretary and Field Marshal Erhard Milch; Körner, State Secretary and Göring's deputy; and Walther Funk, Minister of Economic Affairs and Schacht's successor.

The Wehrmacht would in future receive top priority in the fulfillment of orders. Speer's ministry took over the control of Wehrmacht orders and determined which companies were to carry them out and the production method to be used. Speer's organizational plan was an enormous success. Arms and munitions production increased by about 60 percent in the first months (March-July, 1942) of his leadership. After mid-1942 arms production concentrated on tanks and airplanes. Within six months the total number of tanks produced increased by 25 percent and the total number of airplanes by 60 percent, with the labour force only increasing by 30 percent. Speer said that these results came from his policy of giving technicians responsibility for entire sections of the armaments industry on the grounds of their professional skill rather than on the grounds of party membership.

However, in spite of Speer's successes alarming reports began to stream in regarding fighting in the east (the battle for Stalingrad was in full swing). Speer: 'It must have been in the second half of November 1942. Stalingrad was going badly when Hitler sought refuge on the Obersalzberg. Dr Morell had advised him, as he often did, to fit in a few days rest to which Hitler, to everybody's surprise, agreed. He entreated me to join him on the Obersalzberg. At the Berghof he brought the familiar circle together, whose trusted faces and jokes put him in a good humor. When I arrived in the evening we greeted each other briefly. Hitler sat, as he so often did in those days, silently before the open hearth staring for hours into the flames.

'The following morning he was still tired and apathetic. Toward the afternoon he asked us to join him for the daily walk. It was one of those bleak days on the Obersalzberg with westerly winds driving the low hanging clouds from the Bavarian valley over the Obersalzberg, bringing a prolonged snowfall. Hitler came down from

upstairs wearing his shabby, grey windbreaker. His manservant gave him his tattered velour hat and a walking stick. Pleasantly, with a somewhat absent-minded cordiality and as though he sought my silent sympathy, he said to me: "Come, I would very much like to speak with you about something." Then, to Bormann: "Stay here with the others."

'We walked down the recently snow-cleared path, the Un-

Right: *Hitler and Speer arrive for a meeting at the Führerhauptquartier, 23 March 1942.*

Left: *A production line of Panzer III tanks.*

tersberg rising in the background. The sky had cleared and the sun hung low. Hitler's Alsatian ran barking through the snow. After walking silently side-by-side for several minutes Hitler said suddenly: "I hate the east. Even the snow depresses me. Sometimes I think that I won't come to these mountains in the winter. I don't want to see or smell the snow." I said nothing. What could I have said? Dejectedly, I continued walking with him. He talked on in a monotone about his aversion to the east, to the winter, to the war. He complained that his destiny of carrying out war was a heavy one. He stopped, poked his walking stick in the snow and turned toward me: "Speer, you are my architect. You know that my wish was always to be an architect. The World War and the criminal revolution of 1918 prevented that. And the Jews! November ninth was the result of their systematic, undermining activities."

'His voice became more forceful, louder, until it turned into a hoarse staccato. I saw him work himself up into his old anger. An old, actually already defeated man standing powerless in the snow spitting out his bitterness, his poisonous resentments: "It was the Jews then too. They even organized the strikes in the munitions factories. We lost hundreds of soldiers because of that just in my regiment alone. The Jews forced me into politics."

'I had never realized so clearly as at that moment just how absolute Hitler's need was for the figure of the Jew: he needed the Jew as an object of hatred and as an escape. With the Jew he found that which his beloved mountain and the winter's walk could not give him. The Battle of Stalingrad, Montgomery's breakthrough at El Alamein, they were completely forgotten. The vague recognition that the war was already lost was also forgotten. He continued, but without excitement, tired and drained as though the outburst had exhausted him. "You know Speer, I have really never lived like other people. I have given my health to it the past 30 years. Before World War I, I often didn't know where my next meal was coming

from. In the war I was just an ordinary soldier at the front. After-ward, the revolution came and my commitment and then the diffi-culties, for 10 long years. Someone else would have given up. But destiny wanted it so; Providence has helped me."

'We started walking a little faster again. "Then, when I was called upon to take up the leadership of my country I wanted to transform it, together with you, Speer, erecting one edifice after the other. It was going to be the most beautiful country in the world. Just think what we would have made of Berlin. Paris would have been nothing compared to it. But they spoiled everything for me. They interpreted my overtures as weakness. They thought that I was afraid. Me, of all people! What does that scum know about the Führer of National Socialist Germany? We'll get them! And then we will settle scores! They will come to know me yet! This time nobody escapes! I have always been too soft! But no more! This time we settle up!" He called his Alsatian, Blondi, who had run on ahead.'

Stalingrad proved to be the definitive turning point of the war. On 18 February 1943, shortly after the German defeat there, Goebbels announced 'total war.' The 'butter and guns' concept was given up. The production of consumption goods (relatively high in Germany compared to England) was to be drastically re-duced in favor of the armaments industry. Speer's central planning again proved to be extremely effective. In spite of heavy Allied air bombardments, production in many areas of the armaments in-dustry reached a high point during the summer of 1944.

Allied air attacks greatly increased from 1943 onward. However, the estimated loss of 9 percent of the total industrial production in that year was, to a large extent, compensated for by greater efforts on the part of the population. Nevertheless, large amounts of war materials were diverted to the extensive air defense measures. Thousands of antiaircraft guns were positioned in Germany and the occupied countries and these could certainly have been used in the Soviet Union as antitank guns or for other purposes. In addi-tion, the 'air front' tied down hundreds of thousands of young soldiers. One-third of the optical industry was working on direc-tional apparatus for the flak batteries, and the electronics industry devoted 50 percent of its production to radar and linkage equip-ment for air defense.

After World War II, experts stated that the war could almost cer-tainly have ended in 1943 if the Allies had used a different air stra-tegy. Instead of the extensive but useless bombing of cities and other heavily populated areas, they should have applied the princi-ple of 'paralysis,' that is to say, concentrated on destroying several carefully chosen targets which were of utmost importance to the German war effort, such as the ballbearing factories in Schwein-furth, Berlin-Erkner, Cannsatt or Steyr, and those factories making synthetic petrol, rubber and nitrogen.

In the second half of 1943 Speer began a plan which almost brought the forced recruitment of workers for Germany from the western occupied countries to an end. In France, Belgium and the Netherlands the policy of 'Arbeitseinsatz' had more disadvantages than advantages. Hundreds of thousands of potential forced laborers went into hiding, and internal and external sabotage caused extensive damage, reducing production. In Speer's plan the above-mentioned countries would be involved with goods on a large scale for the German civilian population which, along with the arms industries in those countries would count as 'Sperrbetriebe' for which those workers were exempt. This plan resulted in a dras-tic reduction of the number of foreign workers transported to work in Germany.

In 1944 the Allies began to concentrate their air attacks on the systematic bombardment of key parts of the German armaments industry. In addition to systematic bombing of German petrol re-fineries, the Rumanian oilfields near Ploesti were also a major tar-get. With the German petrol production already more than halved

Above left: *Speer exhorts the German people to make more sacrifices for the greater good of the Third Reich, February 1942.*

Above: *Speer, Ley and Goebbels in Berlin's Sportpalast, 5 June 1943.*

Left: *Speer in conversation with one of the Todt Organization's senior members.*

by the end of May 1944, Allied attacks on 22 June and 17 July dealt a death blow. Production decreased by 98 percent and reserves had to be tapped. On 6 June 1944 the Allies successfully invaded Nor-mandy. This was soon followed by a large-scale Soviet offensive which quickly led to the loss of 25 entire German divisions.

With his appointment as Minister of Armaments and War Pro-duction, Speer became more involved in the endless power strug-gles between the different Nazi bosses. When Goebbels, after the defeat of the Sixth Army at Stalingrad, gave his address on 'total war,' it was directed not only toward the German population but also to the party leaders. Several days after his address he asked Speer for a meeting to discuss the war situation. Goebbels was ex-tremely concerned with the increasing power and influence of Bor-mann and Hans Lammers, head of the Reich Chancellery.

Speer reported their conversation as follows: 'It can not carry on like this any longer. We are here in Berlin, Hitler doesn't hear what we have to say about the situation; I have no influence with him; I cannot even explain the most urgent measures relating to my own area to him. Everything goes through Bormann. Hitler must be talked into coming to Berlin more often. Domestic policy has totally slipped through his fingers; it is now being conducted by Bormann and he is able to give Hitler the impression that he is

always on top of everything. Bormann is driven only by ambition; he is dogmatic and a danger to any sensible development. His influence must be limited immediately! We have not only a Staff crisis but, strictly speaking, a leadership crisis.'

Speer, sharing Goebbels' concern, suggested calling in Göring, who as head of the council of ministers, was in charge of Reich defense, a position which gave him the power to enact laws without Hitler's prior approval. Speer and Goebbels believed that they were in a position to reduce the power that the superbureaucrats Bormann and Lammers wielded. There were, however, several problems. The initial successes of Göring's Luftwaffe and the prestige that went with them had paled in the course of the war. The heavy Allied air attacks on German cities had undermined Hitler's faith in Göring. In addition the personal relationship between Göring and Goebbels had been soured when Goebbels allowed Göring's favorite Berlin restaurant (Horcher's) to be shut down for reasons of economy. Speer was the obvious man to act as intermediary between them.

Speer left the next day, 28 February 1943, for the Obersalzberg where Göring was staying. He spoke in detail with the Reich Marshal. Speer: 'The atmosphere during our long meeting was friendly and, in line with the relatively small house, unforced. What did surprise me enough to still remember was his red polished nails and clearly made-up face. I was already used to the unusually large ruby brooch on his green silk dressing gown. Göring listened calmly to our proposal and to my report of our meeting in Berlin. While listening, he several times took some unset, precious stones out of his pocket and rolled them between his fingers. He seemed pleased by our having thought of him. He also saw the situation which had developed around Bormann as a danger and agreed to our plans.'

On 2 March Speer and Goebbels returned to Göring's house on the Obersalzberg. Göring was standing outside waiting for them. The two men, who had been on bad terms for some time, withdrew. After the Reich Marshal had given his views on the war situation, commenting that France had aged 15 years in the three-and-a-half years of war, the time came to get down to business. Goebbels proposed to Göring that the future political leadership of the Reich should be in their hands, that the growing power of the sycophants around the Führer be brought to an end. Göring's help for this was indispensable. Goebbels: 'Göring showed enthusiasm for my proposal. I suggested that he find a number of supporters and that I would also try to win some over to our idea. We would, however, tell them nothing about our actual intention of gradually working the 'pact of three' [Field Marshal Keitel, head of the *Oberkommando der Wehrmacht*; Lammers, head of the Reich Chancellery; and Bormann, head of the Party Chancellery] out of the way and shifting the power to the new council of ministers [to be expanded] for defense. Telling them would only create unnecessary difficulties. We had no other intention than of supporting each other and shaping a solid battle array around the Führer.'

Goebbels and Speer were very satisfied upon leaving the Obersalzberg. A mutual basis of trust had been achieved with Göring. Goebbels wrote: 'I believe that even the Führer will be very happy about this.'

Shortly afterward, however, Allied air attacks increased dramatically and, especially after the bombing of Hamburg, Hitler lost all faith in Göring. He held Göring personally responsible for the Luftwaffe's failure. The plan devised by Speer and Goebbels would never be implemented. Göring remained at his house on the mountain for increasingly longer periods.

Speer later stated that he was forced into active resistance when, to his horror, he saw that his idolized Führer was heading for disaster, and seemed to be dragging Europe down with him. The

Above left: *Speer takes a close look at a captured Soviet T-34/76, in 1943.*

Above: *An artillery primemover is put through its paces; Hitler, Speer and Keitel (far left) in attendance.*

Right: *Bormann, Göring, Hitler and Speer head for a meeting at the Führerhauptquartier, 10 August 1943.*

turning point for him was the Allied invasion, at which time Hitler decided to introduce a scorched earth policy in all of western Europe. This monstrous plan for mass destruction would need the full cooperation of technical specialists who received their instructions either from Speer's department or directly from Speer himself. Speer made use of his personal influence to protect those not following Hitler's orders. Moreover, he was able to get Hitler to sign the following *Führerbefehl*: 'The Führer is convinced that the areas in the West already in the hands of the enemy shall shortly be retaken. All measures taken during evacuation should be seen in this light. Factories, mines and electricity plants should be put out of use but not destroyed.'

Speer also says that he tried to kill Hitler in February 1945. He asked a colleague for some deadly nerve gas (Tabun) which he planned to put down the ventilation system in the bunker under the Reich Chancellery. He knew that the inlet opening was at ground level. He chose a time when Hitler's closest colleagues, including Bormann, Goebbels and Himmler, would be present. According to Speer, it took two weeks before the gas became available. He then discovered that Hitler's uncanny intuition, which had saved his life several times before, had again been at work. The Führer had had a high chimney built on top of the inlet with its top covered by a searchlight and guarded by the SS.

On 19 March Speer handed over his last memorandum to the man he had faithfully served for the past 12 years. He reiterated his conviction that the war was lost and that Hitler must accept the consequences of this. Hitler replied: 'If the war is lost, the nation shall also perish.'

Nevertheless, Speer walked down the 50 steps of the Berlin bunker on 20 April 1945, to celebrate Hitler's 56th birthday. Three days later he took his final formal leave. Speer wrote about his last meeting with Hitler: 'It was already three o'clock in the morning of the 24th when I went to Hitler for the last time. The old man stood trembling in front of me. I was both moved and confused. He, on the other hand, showed no emotion. His words sounded as cold as his hands felt: "You are leaving then? Good. Until we meet again." No greetings for my family, no word of thanks, no goodbye. I lost my self-control for a moment and talked of returning again. But he could easily see that it was a thought of the moment and turned toward the others. I could go.

'I wanted to look at the Reich Chancellery, which I had designed, for one last time. The lighting being defective, I restricted my visit to several moments in the *Ehrenhof* from where the outlines could barely be seen against the night sky, requiring me to imagine the architectural lines. There was an almost eerie silence, a silence one only experiences on an evening in the mountains. The sounds of the large city, which in former years even at this late hour would have carried this far, were silenced. I heard the explosion of Russian shells in the far distance; my last visit to the Reich Chancellery. Years before I had designed the building – full of plans, prospects and dreams for the future. Now I left behind me not only the ruins of my building, but also the most valuable years of my life.'

Albert Speer died in London on 1 September 1981 of a heart attack. He had become unwell during preparations for an interview with the BBC and was taken immediately to hospital, where, in spite of all efforts, he died. Thus came to an end the life of a man who, next to Hitler, was most responsible for Germany's war economy. Speer had been Minister of Armaments and War Production from 1942 and his organizational talents undoubtedly helped to prolong the war for two more years.

In the years before 1942, when Speer was still Hitler's favorite

architect, he dreamt of creating colossal buildings which were to demonstrate the power of the Reich. Contrary to what he had always maintained, it was he as much as Hitler who wanted to make German cities ever more monumental. It was Speer who managed to spread the story that he had tried to murder Hitler with poison gas in the last days of the war. From diverse declarations from witnesses it has become evident that the whole story was purely an attempt to get on the good side of the judges at Nuremberg. It is also clear that were the trial to be held today, Speer would almost certainly not escape the gallows. A great deal of incriminating material has surfaced over the years disproving his contention that his role was purely that of a technocrat with no knowledge of the concentration and extermination camps. In short, after Hitler, Speer, together with Goebbels and Himmler, was one of those most responsible for the German effort in World War II.

Above left: *Speer in captivity shortly after the end of the war with Dönitz (center).*

Above: *The trial at Nuremberg. Speer was sentenced to 20 years jail for his slave-labor system.*

Right: *Speer after his release from prison.*

BALDUR VON
SCHIRACH

1907-1974

Above: *Baldur von Schirach, head of the Third Reich's youth movement.*

Right: *Von Schirach gives an address in the Berlin Sportpalast, 1937.*

Left: *Von Schirach pictured at his desk.*

Right: *Massed ranks of the Hitler Youth march through the streets of a German town, 1933.*

Nuremberg, September 1936. Hundreds of thousands have traveled from all corners of Germany to celebrate the yearly NSDAP party day at this former Frankish city. For eight days Nuremberg will be the center of Germany, that is, the center of National Socialist Germany. From early morning until late into the evening the streets of Nuremberg will echo to the steps of marching NSDAP and army formations. The roll of drums and rousing martial music will be heard throughout the city. The Führer of the 1000-Year Reich is also at Nuremberg to speak, to take the salute and to confer with his gauleiters, ministers and political advisors. The main attraction for many, however, is the almost hypnotic display of National Socialist power.

During the rally of 1936, one day was set aside for German youth. Tens of thousands of Hitler Youth members stiffly assembled in military ranks to welcome their Führer. Finally, Hitler approached with his entourage in a column of open cars. Hundreds of trumpets and hunting horns of the Hitler Youth Music Corps announced their Führer's arrival. Deafening cheering and salutes of 'Heil!' broke out from thousands of throats when Hitler stepped out of his car. The young people finally saw in living form the man who had been introduced to them by the most refined propaganda as a true savior of the German people. Raising them out of their deepest misery to create a vast new Reich. After Hitler had mounted the immense podium their voices burst into the Hitler Youth theme song: 'Unsere Fahne flattert uns voran': 'Forward, Forward; resound the clear fanfares; Forward, forward, youth knows no danger. Be the target still so far away, the young will still attain it. We march for Hitler through want and darkness, with the banner of youth for freedom and bread. Our banner waves in front, our banner is the new era. And our banner leads us to eternity. Yes, the banner is greater than death.'

In commentaries young people were compared to the sun and to light. These youths would one day be the leaders of the Great German Reich and everything for which National Socialism had struggled for. 'The Führer never looks friendlier, never laughs so much as when he looks over his young people and sees their glowing faces,' said one newspaper commentary. On that September morning in 1936 the Führer did indeed look amicably towards 'his' young people, 'his' youth and saw 200,000 tense faces looking up at him in wonder.

In his address to the assembled German youth, Hitler spoke

about concepts such as heroism, sacrifice, building the new 'Reich', struggle and hardship and, after praising them, he ended with: 'When the endless columns of our movement march triumphantly through Germany, I know that you will join with them.' After Hitler's speech one of the men from his retinue came forward and, together with the assembled mass of youngsters, gave a thundering '*Sieg Heil!*' It is a young man, not yet 30, but already having the rank of *Reichsleiter*. It is *Reichsjugendführer* (Reich Youth Leader) Baldur von Schirach, a man with an awe-inspiring capacity for work and a worshiper of Adolf Hitler. Hitler totally trusted von Schirach and the other leaders of the Hitler Youth to raise the youth of Germany in a true National Socialist manner. The Hitler Youth was not especially important during the years of the NSDAP's struggle for power, but once power had been gained this changed.

The Hitler Youth was to grow into an organization which had no equal. At its peak its membership included almost all of the German young of certain ages; membership was obligatory and parents who tried to keep their children out of the movement risked imprisonment. In 1932, the last year of the Weimar Republic, the Hitler Youth had about 110,000 members. Compared to nearly 10 million members in the *Reichsausschuss Deutscher Jugendverbände* (the government organization for German youth associations) it was small. In no other country in the world was there such a vital and extensive youth organization as in the Weimar Republic. Hitler placed great value on the Nazification of this movement and Baldur von Schirach would be his closest staff member in this task.

Baldur Benedekt von Schirach was born in 1907 at Weimar. His great-grandfather, Frederick von Schirach, had been a Union officer in the American Civil War. Frederick's wife, Elisabeth Norris, came from Baltimore and was of French origin. Her father was owner of a locomotive factory in Philadelphia. After the civil war the von Schirachs moved to Kiel where Baldur's father was born. He was brought up as an American although living in Germany and even married an American woman from Philadelphia, Emma Tillen. He renounced his American citizenship and became a subject of the kaiser and an officer in the kaiser's guard.

Although both of Baldur's parents were American from birth he was born as a German. He grew up in Weimar and soon showed a talent for both sports and art. He studied German and English literature at the University of Munich and wrote numerous poems, some of which were published in 1927. During his years of study

Left: *Von Schirach and his wife Henriette visit Hitler at Obersalzberg.*

Below: *Hitler and von Schirach receive the salutes of young Nazi supporters.*

Right: *Hitler speaks to 60,000 members of the Hitler Youth on Reichsparteitag, 1934. Von Schirach and Hess watch the proceedings.*

Below right: *The Führer inspects members of the Hitler Youth, Nuremberg, 1934.*

Schirach was active as leader of the National Socialistic Student Union (NSDSB) and made himself useful by mobilizing students in support of National Socialism. In 1931 von Schirach was appointed *Reichsjugendführer der NSDAP* (Party Reich Youth Leader); two years later he was appointed *Jugendführer des Deutschen Reiches* (Youth Leader of the German Reich).

Baldur von Schirach went into action immediately after his appointment as youth leader of the Third Reich. Imitating the tried and tested tactics of older party leaders, he had the offices of the *Reichsausschuss Deutscher Jugendverbänd* occupied. General Vogt, the head of this organization and a former officer in the Prussian Army, was simply chased away. After this takeover von Schirach joined forces with Admiral von Trotha, who had been chief-of-staff of the *Hochseeflotte* during World War I and was now president of the German youth associations. The admiral could also offer no

resistance to the Nazis and was forced to step down. The organization was disbanded and its assets valued at many millions of marks, mainly from the hundreds of youth hostels spread throughout Germany, were confiscated by the NSDAP.

Catholic youth organizations remained untouched for the time being. The Nazi government had signed a concordat with the Roman Catholic Church on 20 July 1933 in which, among other things, it was stated that the Roman Catholic youth organizations would be able to continue their activities unhindered. This, however, came to an end on 1 December 1936, when Hitler enacted a law relating to the Hitler Youth ('*das Gesetz über die Hitlerjugend*'). From that day the Hitler Youth was the only legal organization open to all male and female Germans between the ages of 10 and 18. The *Jugendführer des Deutschen Reiches* received the rank of *Obersten Reichsbehörde* (highest government official), subordinate only to the Führer himself.

The law relating to the Hitler Youth stated, among other things that 'All German young people are to be organized in the Hitler Youth. The youth of Germany shall not only be raised by the family and the school, but also physically, spiritually and morally by . . . the Hitler Youth.' Von Schirach, who had been subordinate to the Minister of Education, was now solely answerable to Hitler. Von

Left: *Hitler, Goebbels, von Schirach, Hess and von Ribbentrop at the National Workers Day celebrations, 1 May 1935.*

Right: *Accompanied by von Schirach and Hess, Hitler returns the salute of the crowd at Nuremberg, 1935.*

Schirach was a sentimental and romantic young man who wrote poems in which he glorified Hitler ('this genius that reaches to the stars'). He was also strongly influenced by the racial ideologies of Rosenberg and Streicher, particularly their vicious anti-Semitism.

The National Socialists attached great importance to creating an obedient and Nazified youth. Von Schirach himself proclaimed: 'The NSDAP is the party of the young.' The words 'youth' and 'young' were often used symbolically by the Nazis. As von Schirach once said: 'Faust, the Ninth Symphony and the Will of Adolf Hitler constitute eternal youth and know neither time nor mortality.' The Nazis knew how to play on the feelings of the young in Germany. Because of the dramatic consequences of World War I and the economic crisis in the 1920s, many of the young felt a great resentment toward the Weimar Republic and had a naive attachment to the concepts of honor, heroism and struggle. Many also held strong feelings against middle-class idealism.

One commentator wrote: 'There is an almost classic alliance among the German youth between social despair, nationalistic romanticism and the generation gap.' It not only affected the younger generation of former World War I soldiers, but also, and mainly, the following generation. They joined the ranks of the NSDAP in ever increasing numbers and marched through Germany. The NSDAP offered them many attractions: the sense of belonging to a group; association with the Führer; the prospect of comradeship; mystical customs; glorification of the people; being of the elect; and, especially, the promise that the future leaders of the new Germany would be chosen from among the ranks of the Hitler Youth. The soldier became an ideal; the Hitler Youth was organized like an army with the motto of the 'German Trinity' – '*Gott, Ich und die Waffe.*'

Baldur von Schirach had to give up his studies at the University of Munich because of the pressures of his NSDAP work. This was not without consequences: he often felt discriminated against by those who had finished their studies and remained a student in his way of working, lacking the mental maturity for leadership and decisiveness. His behavior always remained equivocal. He vigorously tried to keep up the appearance of an academic while trying to cling to the coarse traditions of the Hitler Youth. He adopted the gestures and manners of the Hitler Youth with great difficulty, and was never a true representative of what Hitler in one of his slogans described as the 'ideal' type. Von Schirach was neither harsh, nor tough, nor stalwart, but rather a soft, spoilt

young man from a well-to-do family who only felt safe in his *Reichs-jugendführer* uniform.

Throughout his career, von Schirach was the subject of persistent stories that he had latent homosexual inclinations. His strikingly feminine features, his idolizing poems and lyrical speeches, stories about his all-white bedroom, and his forced manly behavior all combined to feed these rumors. He tried to hide his uncertainty behind an excess of pathos, but this, like his arrogance, was only a transparent disguise. He enjoyed some respect in the Hitler Youth, but he was certainly not popular with the lower ranks of the organization or with party leaders. His speeches and writings were full of flamboyant language but lacked inner warmth. Von Schirach could never disguise the fact that he was not completely genuine and that his status within the Hitler Youth and Nazi Germany was due to his being Hitler's protégé. Once the Führer's respect for him lessened his career, which had begun so successfully, was soon over.

G M Gilbert, the prison psychologist who observed and tested the former leaders of the Third Reich during their trial, wrote in his *Nuremberg Diary*, of von Schirach's explanation to him as to why he became an anti-Semite: 'In my youth I moved in titled circles and never came into contact with Jews. I had no reason to be anti-Semitic. I did notice in the better circles a vague sort of prejudice against the Jews. This did not, however, make an impression on me until someone gave me the American book *The Eternal Jew* which I read at the spiritually weak age of 17. You can not imagine how great an influence this book had on German young people.

'At about the same time I came under the influence of Julius Streicher who gave anti-Semitism a pseudo-scientific tint. Since many older people were socially following the same course, it seemed obvious to us younger people that such opinions would be accepted without question. I became acquainted with Adolf Hitler when I was 18. I must admit that I was enthusiastic about him. I went to study in Munich because he worked there and I became one of his most trusted followers. From that time on I was a convinced anti-Semite until the recent tragedy [the disclosure of genocide in the concentration camps] proved to me the incorrectness of that belief.

'I committed the mistake of agreeing to the evacuation of the Viennese Jews and am ready to die for it. But German youth can and must be re-educated. I do not believe that after this horrible example anti-Semitism will make its appearance in the world

again. But the people must fight this silent, social stigma, which is the breeding ground for the sickness.'

He told Gilbert about his relationship with Hitler and stated that he had noticed a definite change in Hitler over the years: 'Before 1934 he was human; from 1934 to 1938 he was superhuman; after 1938 he was inhuman and tyrannical. I am of the opinion that power went to his head when Hindenburg died and he became Führer of the Reich. And in the end, he was a megalomaniac when the laws and legal institutions were abolished; shortly before the war broke out he became a dictator with plans for conquering the entire world. He disappointed me for the first time when he did not keep to the Munich Agreement, because I could see that Germany's prestige in the world would suffer much damage from this. However, he was successful in convincing me that all would finally end well.

'I believe that I noticed for the first time in 1942 that madness had become his master. His glassy look sometimes became expressionless in the middle of a conversation; he deviated then from the subject; or one would turn around thinking that he was looking at someone else; or he closed his ears to something he did not want to hear.'

With twilight seeping through the cell window, von Schirach continued, his voice becoming softer and softer: 'When all those atrocities became known at the end of the war, my worst fears were confirmed and I understood that I would have to die for them. But I did not want to commit suicide like a coward. I did not duck out of my arrest. I even suggested to the American authorities that all youth leaders should be brought together for a re-schooling course at Buchenwald; I wanted to offer myself as hostage to bear the consequences for my earlier blindly made faults. I hoped with this to make something good from my wrongs.' His voice choked and

silence fell over the cell, writes Gilbert.

The rapid growth of the Hitler Youth brought with it a demand for a rigid structure. A system was introduced within a short period which held that the NSDAP had absolute say over the development of children from their sixth year. Both boys and girls were placed into one of the many sections of the Hitler Youth until their eighteenth year, after which obligatory work service or recruitment into the army followed. Parents who forbade their children from joining the organization received heavy prison sentences.

From their sixth to their tenth year boys were in training for the Hitler Youth as *pimpfs*. Each boy received an achievement book in which his progress in the movement was recorded, as well as his 'ideological growth.' By his tenth year each *pimpf* had to show good results in athletics, camping, night time orientation trips and Nazified history. After this he advanced to the *Jungvolk* for which he had to give the following oath: 'In the presence of this blood banner which represents our Führer, I swear to devote all my energies and my strength to the savior of our fatherland, Adolf Hitler. I am willing and ready to give up my life for him, so help me God.'

At 14 boys entered the Hitler Youth proper and remained there until 18 at which time they entered either the Labor Service or the Wehrmacht. The Hitler Youth was a vast organization with a paramilitary ethos. Its members were systematically indoctrinated with Nazi ideology. Above all they trained for war. On many weekends groups went camping, crawling through forests and over heaths, rifles at the ready and carrying heavy army backpacks.

Girls were not spared the strict regime of the Hitler Youth. From their tenth to their fourteenth years they were in the *Jungmädel* and had to wear a uniform comprising a white blouse, a long blue skirt, socks and heavy walking shoes. Their training was similar to that of boys of the same age, including long marches with heavy backpacks and the usual initiation into Nazi philosophy. At this stage emphasis was placed on their roles as future wives and mothers of as many healthy Aryan children as possible. Even more attention was paid to this point once the girls reached the age of 14 and went on to become members of the BDM (*Bund Deutscher Mädel*), of which they remained members until they reached 21.

At 18 the girls were sent to work on a farm for one year – the *Landjahr* – comparable to work service for the young men. The young women had to do housekeeping as well as work in the fields. They either lived on a farm or in small camps from where they would be taken every morning to the farm by truck. The situation did, however, create problems: it was not uncommon for an entire farming family to break up because of the presence of a pretty young city girl and there were also complaints from the parents of young girls who had become pregnant while carrying out their farm service. Also, their camps were not such a great distance from the labour service camps for young men. A few lines of verse referred to the *Landjahr* for young women, and became known throughout Germany: 'On the field and in the heather, I lose my strength through delight.' Similar moral problems also arose with the housekeeping year in which about 500,000 young women from the Hitler Youth spent a year in a city household.

Toward the end of 1938 the Hitler Youth had almost eight million members. In spite of the strict regulations and the threat of imprisonment, the parents of four million young people were able to keep their children out of the organization. However, in March 1939 Hitler issued a law whereby all boys and girls automatically became members of the Hitler Youth under the same system as that used for recruiting for the army. Parents who were still recalcitrant were threatened with having their children taken from them and put in orphanages.

At the head of this mammoth organization and responsible for all its youthful members was von Schirach. He called on the German youth to devote themselves heart and soul to the movement. All members had to memorize his short poem, '*Beckenntnis zum*

Left: *Von Schirach and Hitler in the Luitpold arena, 1935.*

Führer' ('A Confession of Faith to the Führer'), which read as follows:

We heard so often your voice ring out
while listening silently with folded hands.
We all know; the end comes once,
that shall free us from want and will.
What is one year to eternity.
Of what use a law that forbids us
the pure belief, given us by you,
piercing with certainty our young lives.
My Führer, you alone are the Way and the Purpose!

There were three kinds of school in the Third Reich where future party and political leaders received their training: the Adolf Hitler schools, which fell under the control of the Hitler Youth; the so-called 'Napolas,' the 'national political *Lehranstalten*'; and the 'castles of the order,' the *Ordensburgen*. The last two came under the control of the NSDAP.

The Adolf Hitler schools took the most promising children from the *Jungvolk* at the age of 12 and gave them six years of training for a high position. The students lived-in and endured a spartan lifestyle. Upon completion of the course they had the right to go to university. Ten Adolf Hitler schools were opened after 1937, of which the Academy of Brunswick was the most important.

The Napolas, the political training institutions of the NSDAP, had a special purpose. The Nazis wanted to restore the kind of instruction in honor which had been part of the former Prussian military academies where 'the soldier's spirit, with his attributes of courage, duty and simplicity are cultivated.' In addition there was special instruction in Nazi philosophy. The schools came under the direct control of the SS, which also supplied the heads of the schools and the majority of their teachers. Three of these schools were founded initially and their number grew to 31, including three for women, before the outbreak of the war.

At the top of the schooling pyramid were the *Ordensburgen*. The

148

children of the party elite received their schooling at these institutes where the organization and discipline were similar to that of the Order of the Teutonic Knights. Only the most dedicated young National Socialists were selected for this schooling and came mainly from the best pupils at the Adolf Hitler schools and the Napolas. There were four *Ordensburgen* in Germany, of which those in Sonthofen and Vogelensang were the most famous. The total period of schooling lasted six years, with the first year being spent at a castle following specialized training in the 'science of race' and other aspects of Nazi philosophy.

Emphasis was placed on wide-ranging indoctrination and on discipline, with physical training being secondary. This was reversed during the second year which was spent at a castle where athletics and sports, including mountain climbing and parachuting, took priority. The third castle, where the students spent 18 months, specialized in political and military training. Finally, for the fourth and last stage of their schooling, they were sent for 18 months to the *Ordensburg* in Mariënburg, near the Polish border. Here, inside the same walls which had once been besieged by the Teutonic Knights, political and military schooling concentrated on the 'eastern question' and the 'necessity' of *Lebensraum* at the cost of the Slavic countries.

The minds of Germany's young were being systematically poisoned through education, and they were being brought up to die for their Führer and the Reich. Normal schooling was interrupted and the family was, to a large extent, replaced by the Hitler Youth and the NSDAP schools. There is no doubt that it was seen as a social responsibility to bring together children from all classes and ranks in society. The poor and the rich, the children from working-class families, from farming families, and from the nobility, all must do equal work. In most cases young people from the city were forced into spending a year in the country with the Work Service, where they lived and worked in the open air and learned the value of physical labor, came to value nature and learned how to get along with people from a totally different background.

The youth of the Third Reich grew up with strong and healthy bodies and with a belief in the future of their people and country, but with totally indoctrinated minds. They achieved a feeling of comradeship that crossed all economic and social barriers, but they were also encouraged to compete among each other and to adapt to the strict military discipline of the Hitler Youth. Furthermore, their minds were poisoned with National Socialist racist theories for the ultimate purpose of being prepared to fight and to die for their cherished Führer. Hitler demanded, and got, young people who were 'quick as a fox, tough as leather and strong as [Krupp] steel.'

In 1933, the year in which he became the undisputed leader of the Hitler Youth, von Schirach began to expound the aims of the organization in a flood of writings. From 1934 onward he put forward a motto every year which proclaimed the central points of the organizational as well as the ideological program in the Hitler Youth for that year. His first motto was: *Jahr der inneren Schulung und Ausrichtung* (the Year of Resident Schooling and Organization).

In a speech given in 1938 Hitler commented on the importance of a systematically educated and indoctrinated youth, saying: 'Our young people learn nothing other than to think German, to act German and when these fine children enter our organization at the age of 10, where they often for the first time can breathe fresh air and stay in the open, then, after four years they graduate from the *Jungvolk* to the *Hitlerjugend* and we keep them there another four years and then we do not hand them over to the old class-society educationalists, but take them directly into the party, in the *Arbeitsfront*, in the SA or in the SS.

'And, if after one-and-a-half or two years there they have still not become true National Socialists, they go into the *Arbeitsdienst* working there for another six to eight months under one flag, under one symbol, namely, the German spade. And what is left over of class consciousness or class differences is taken care of by the Wehrmacht, and when they return after two, three or four years we immediately take them back into the SA, SS, etc, so that they will not fall back into their old errors and they shall remain there for the rest of their lives. And if someone says to me: yes, but there will always be a few who are against National Socialism, then I say: National Socialism is not on the point of collapsing, but is only beginning.'

On 1 September 1936 a law came into effect whereby service in the Hitler Youth was put on a par with service in the Wehrmacht or the Labor Service. Speaking to a large audience of parents that same evening, Baldur von Schirach said: 'Each *pimpf* already carries the marshal's baton in his knapsack. It is not only positions of leadership within the Hitler Youth that are within reach, for the doors of the government and of the party also stand wide open for him. He, who from his earliest days has fulfilled his obligations, is diligent, loyal and brave, need have no worries for the future.' It is patently obvious that this sort of exhortation, based on the cultivation of fear, sent many young people running to join the ranks of the Hitler Youth. It was not uncommon for the parents to insist on membership because of fear of reprisals from the Nazis.

The Hitler Youth gave the young a feeling of security, of having been chosen as the future rulers of Germany, of Europe and of the world. It encouraged resistance to authorities outside its own organization such as parents, church functionaries and teachers. The movement also had its own all-encompassing code of honor, its own flag, its own theme song, its own leader and even its own martyrs. Hitler's view was that 'Youth leads youth.' This can not, however, veil the fact that seldom has a generation grown up more dependent than this one. The principle of independence only applied to the world outside National Socialism. The incorporation of the Hitler Youth into the NSDAP completely subjected the young to the orders of the party leaders. It was not for nothing that von Schirach called his Hitler Youth 'the Youth Section of the NSDAP.' With an only slightly veiled, directed campaign German youth were trained to carry out the regime's grandiose plans for the future.

Marksmanship was an important part of Hitler Youth training. In 1943 Arthur Axmann, from 1940 von Schirach's successor, wrote that 30,700 first class marksmen had been trained and that one million Hitler Youth regularly took part in target practice. An agreement had also been reached between the *Oberkommando der Wehrmacht* and the leadership of the Hitler Youth which stated that the Wehrmacht would take an active role in their schooling from the beginning of 1939.

The navy's Hitler Youth included 50,000 young men in 1938; the motorized Hitler Youth enjoyed a strength of 90,000; the air force units counted 74,000; model flying had 73,000; and the *Nachrichten* (messenger service) 29,000 members.

In their ideological instruction the young were taught that to die for the fatherland was most admirable and that the highest honor that a man could attain was death on the battlefield. Hitler stated during an interview: 'My pedagogy is tough. The weak must be swept away. The world shall remember the youth who grew up in my *Ordensburgen*. I want young people who are violent, cruel, fearless. The young must be all of that. They must be able to bear pain and hardship. There may be no weaknesses, no frailties. The eyes of the magnificent, free beast of prey shall gleam again. I shall see my young people strong and beautiful. With this I can create.'

In the spring of 1940 von Schirach volunteered and fought with a unit at the front. At the end of hostilities in the West he was summoned to the *Führerhauptquartier* by Hitler and appointed Governor and Gauleiter of Vienna. Hitler did not want von Schirach back as Hitler Youth leader, as he was afraid that he would become too powerful. Hitler had even heard rumors that the

Reichsjugendführer coveted the position of his official deputy. After his appointment the coolness between von Schirach and the Führer increased. Von Schirach had often spoken out against the invasion in the West. His relations with Hitler were worsened by his American ancestry. Early in 1943 Hitler told Göring that he harbored vague suspicions of von Schirach. When the former *Reichsjugendführer* organized an exhibition in Vienna in which works of so-called 'degenerate art' were also shown, Hitler felt this as a personal slight and admonished von Schirach for advancing the 'cultural opposition' in Germany.

In the end it was Schirach's wife, Henriette, who brought about the definitive break between Hitler and von Schirach. Henriette, the daughter of Hitler's photographer Hoffmann, had known Hitler since childhood. Because of this relationship she and her husband were frequent guests at the Berghof. In 1943 Henriette was invited to the Netherlands by friends in the German occupation forces. She decided to visit Amsterdam first, where she was witness to a round-up of some Jewish women. She was shocked by what she saw and asked her friends for an explanation. Henriette: 'I was told that Jewish women were being deported and didn't I know about it? Even Seyss-Inquart, Reich Commissar for the Netherlands, would tell me nothing about the deportations. My friends, however, advised me to take the matter up with Hitler himself. They were of the opinion that he knew nothing of these horrors. Since it was strictly forbidden to communicate in writing with the Führer regarding the deportation of the Jews, I was the person appointed to relate this information to him by word of mouth and to ask him for his opinion.'

Touching upon political subjects was forbidden at the Berghof, particularly the persecution of the Jews and the concentration camps. Both Speer and Christa Schröder (Hitler's secretary) were convinced that Hitler was well informed, even down to the details, about what was taking place in the concentration and extermination camps. Christa Schröder: 'There will always be those who think that these acts of barbarism took place without the knowledge or permission of Hitler. I know for myself that Hitler was kept well informed by Himmler as to what was happening in the camps. He regarded all these atrocities as necessary for his regime. But in this area, as with many others, he was protecting his good reputation.'

All meetings between Hitler and Himmler took place in private, either behind closed doors or while walking alone together on the Obersalzberg. Only Bormann was occasionally allowed to be present. No one from Hitler's permanent circle dared to mention the words 'concentration camp,' let alone openly ask whether they existed.

Henriette von Schirach broke off her visit to the Netherlands, and after informing her husband who was in Vienna at the time, of her recent experiences, she telephoned the Berghof to make an appointment with Hitler. Henriette: 'It was a splendid, somewhat sultry fall evening when we joined the regular company by the large open fire at the Berghof. I was still confused and had thought out no plan for the manner in which I would approach Hitler. Hitler was reading some telexes about the situation at the front. I understood that the reports were not good. Long after midnight Hitler turned to me and asked in a friendly tone: "You have just come back from Holland, have you not?"

'Although I had already had a double cognac, the moment still came totally unexpectedly. I took a deep breath and answered: "Yes, that is why I am here. I wanted to speak to you about some terrible things I saw; I cannot believe that you know about them. Helpless women were being rounded up and driven together to be sent off to a concentration camp and I think that they will never return." A painful stillness fell; all color had left Hitler's face. His face looked like a death mask in the light of the flames. He looked at me aghast and at the same time surprised and said: "We are at war." He very cautiously stood up; there was still a macabre silence in the room, with only the crackling of the burning wood to be heard. I also stood up. At that moment he screamed at me: "You are sentimental, Frau von Schirach! You have to learn to hate! What have Jewish women in Holland got to do with you?" Then he grasped my wrists as he used to do and clung to them with both hands so that I would be able to concentrate on him better. Suddenly he released me. "Do you not understand? Every day tens of thousands of my best, my most precious soldiers are killed. These others are not killed; they live in the concentration camps. The inferior live on and what will be the face of Europe in a hundred years? Or a thousand years? I am only accountable to my people and to none other."

'The rest of the company were quiet as mice. Nobody looked at me. I walked out of the room and once in the vestibule I began to run. One of Hitler's adjutants came running after me. The Führer was furious. I was asked to leave the Obersalzberg immediately. I

Left: *Von Schirach launches the model ship* Bremen *in Potsdam.*

Right: *Von Schirach at the opening of a festival in Vienna.*

got Baldur who had been talking to several chauffeurs in the canteen and told him what had happened. We quickly packed our things, got the car out of the garage and drove, as carefully as possible, down the mountain.'

During the last years of the war von Schirach intentionally kept in the background, both out of fear of Hitler and because his romantic ideals of sacrifice and heroism were clearly out of step with the reality of the war.

After the war Baldur von Schirach was brought before the International Military Tribunal at Nuremberg. His first written reaction to the indictment read: 'The entire disaster was due to racial politics.' According to the prison psychologist Gilbert he was reconciled with death, and was serious and nervous during his trial. Even in prison he could not do without his poetry and wrote, among others, a poem titled: 'To Death.' In spite of the circumstances he seemed to be thoroughly conscious of his origins. He said to his lawyer on their first meeting: 'So long as I still have my head, I shall hold it high.'

Before the trial began he displayed an attitude of deepest remorse, and it seemed at first that he, as had Speer, would confess to his guilt. However, during the trial, he fell under the influence of Göring and all efforts to get him to repent came to nothing. His answers remained vague and unclear and, in the end, von Schirach let himself be used by Göring as a sort of messenger boy to make the 'party view' clear to those 'turned' defendants such as Speer. Von Schirach did not have the courage to follow Speer's example. Nothing came of their original plan to draw up an indictment against Hitler for treason. Out of concern for the fate of his family, who had been arrested, he concentrated all his attention on the 'maltreatment' and the 'guilt' of the Allies.

Göring took full advantage of this. After Göring labeled him a 'young weakling,' Gilbert renewed his efforts to make von Schirach aware of the reality of his situation: 'As usual, he offered me the comfortable chair he had made by putting blankets on his wooden plank. He immediately began talking about the arrest of his family. He showed me the letter that General Truscott had written to the tribunal, evidently as a result of a request encouraged by me. The general explained why the von Schirach family was being held prisoner. Von Schirach disparagingly tried to brush aside the reasons for his family's arrest and criticized the poor treatment of the Germans by the Allied occupation forces. After I

had read the letter, I said that everything appeared to me to be in order. That safety measures such as these were understandable and necessary such a short time after the war, and certainly during the trial – he knew very well that his family were not being badly treated, let alone murdered, as they would have been by the Gestapo. My sharp tone frightened him. It had not been his intention to criticize the Americans as much as the Russians. I advised him to pay close attention during the trial and he would come to understand why the Russians were so "merciless."'

However, von Schirach remained in awe of Göring and said that condemning Göring was political folly because he was so popular – even in America. Von Schirach was of the opinion that his enemy von Ribbentrop bore much more guilt for the war and that it was he who had actually influenced Hitler, not Göring.

Von Schirach began his defense with the announcement that he accepted full responsibility for the education of German youth. He said that he had propagated not only National Socialism but also the works of Goethe and German literature in general. He had to be repeatedly interrupted and advised to restrict himself to the point in question. He painted a picture of the Hitler Youth as a sports-loving Boy Scout organization in which military training played no role. He further declared that he and Germany's youth had hoped for a peaceful solution to the Jewish question. He had had nothing to do with the Nuremberg racial laws and had been of the opinion that the problem had already been solved and that the laws were superfluous. The solution of that problem had been, in his opinion, purely a government affair over which German youth could exercise no influence whatsoever. The infamous Crystal Night pogrom against the Jews had been named a cultural outrage and a crime by himself as well as by the German youth. This was why he had thought it would be better for the Jews if they left Germany.

Furthermore, he admitted to having given permission for the deportation of the Viennese Jews and that he had supported this action in his capacity of Gauleiter of Vienna during a speech given on 15 December 1942. He further said about this: 'I put my morals to the side when, out of misplaced faith in the Führer, I took part in this action. I did it. I cannot undo it.'

With regard to Auschwitz he stated: 'It was the most all-encompassing and diabolical genocide ever committed by man. But Höss was not the murderer. Höss was only the executioner. Adolf Hitler gave the order. That is recorded in his testament. The testament is real. I have seen a photocopy of it. Hitler and Himmler together started this crime against humanity which will remain a blot on our history for centuries. It is a crime which fills every German with shame. I am guilty in front of God, my people and my country, for bringing up the young of this country to follow a man whom I had for many years regarded as Führer and inviolable head of state – for bringing them up in such a way that they saw Hitler as I saw him. I am guilty of encouraging the German young to follow a man who turned out to be a mass murderer.'

Prosecutor Dodd showed in his cross-examination that von Schirach had had very good reason for showing remorse. He told the court several things von Schirach had neglected to mention. In the early days of the war von Schirach had praised himself for having brought up the German youth to be patriotic fighters. He had even composed songs which had warlike and anti-Semitic sen-

timents. Countless youths were trained in the use of small arms and in gliding. The young were encouraged to have an anti-Semitic outlook and reject their parents, their teachers and the church. Finally, Dodd proved that von Schirach had even reached an agreement with Himmler to put boys from the Hitler Youth to work in the concentration camps and that he received weekly reports regarding the extermination camps from the SS.

During the course of the trial Dodd forced von Schirach into admitting that he had suggested to Bormann that an English cultural center be bombed and that Vienna be cleared of all Czechoslovakians in reprisal for the assassination of Heydrich. Furthermore, he had to admit that he, together with Himmler and Frank (Governor General of occupied Poland), had discussed the forced deportation of the last 50,000 Jews in Vienna to Poland. Frank had protested against the proposal on the grounds that he had no room in Poland for them. Von Schirach also tried to deny responsibility

Left: *Hitler Youth drummers beat a tattoo at Nuremberg.*

Left: *Baldur von Schirach as the Gauleiter of Vienna, 8 August 1940.*

for the exploitation of 10-to-14-year-old foreign children for the purpose of carrying out war-related activities. Schirach denied having read reports sent to him about the extermination of the Jews and of partisans in the occupied eastern countries. While under cross-examination by the Russian prosecutor, General Alexandrov, von Schirach stated that the militarization of his Hitler Youth had not gone as far as that of the Russian youth. Governor General Frank, the butcher of Poland, laughed until he became red in the face.

Baldur von Schirach poisoned the minds of an entire generation. He taught German youth the principles of National Socialism, formed them into legions for the Wehrmacht and the SS, and delivered them to their Führer. The deportation of the Jews had already begun when he became Gauleiter of Vienna. In a speech given on 15 September 1942, he said: 'Hundreds of thousands of

Jews have been driven to the ghettos in the East as a contribution to European culture.' The International Tribunal at Nuremberg had no hesitation in condemning Baldur von Schirach to 20 years imprisonment.

When he was brought back to his cell after hearing his sentence, Gilbert visited him: 'von Schirach's face looked serious when he entered his cell with uplifted head. "Twenty," he said, when the handcuffs were removed. I told him that his wife would be relieved that he had not been sentenced to death. "Rather a quick death than a slow . . ." he said.'

On 1 October 1966 after precisely 20 years of imprisonment, he was, together with Albert Speer, released from Spandau Prison. Baldur von Schirach was destined to live for less than 10 years. The former leader of the Hitler Youth died on 8 August 1974, almost totally blind as a result of an eye disease.

JOACHIM VON RIBBENTROP

1893-1946

Left: *Joachim von Ribbentrop, Hitler's Foreign Minister from 1938.*

Above: *Von Ribbentrop strikes an heroic pose for the camera at the Führerhauptquartier.*

The once-arrogant Nazi ambassador to Britain and later the Third Reich's Minister of Foreign Affairs was barely recognizable in cell number seven. Joachim von Ribbentrop, the man who had forged the Berlin-Rome-Tokyo Axis had become a defeated, confused and morally bankrupt figure after the collapse of Nazi Germany. He asked everyone for advice on his defense – from the prison doctors to the barbers – and was writing endless memoranda which were supposed to prove his innocence. Of all the 21 defendants on trial at the Nuremberg International Military Tribunal, von Ribbentrop was to make the worst impression.

June 1945. In ravaged Hamburg the sun shines on the remains of what had once been a beautiful city. For Germany the war is over, and the country is in a state of flux. It is only a short time since the

Gestapo, SS and SD ruled here and the city was being hit with a daily rain of bombs. Then, at the beginning of May, a deathly silence suddenly reigned. Germany had surrendered unconditionally, bringing an end to the hostilities. People came stiffly out of cellars and bomb shelters, their eyes blinking in the harsh light. Their last months had been spent almost entirely underground. Dazed, the people, mainly women, stood about talking to each other. It was only very slowly that something approaching normality returned. Several visible reminders of the Nazi period, such as street signs and swastikas, were removed from the townscape as quickly as possible. Civilians and demobilized soldiers (those not in POW camps) were pressed into removing the rubble.

With the fall of the Third Reich, the hunt for senior party, military and government officials moved into top gear. In March 1945 Britain's Foreign Minister, Anthony Eden, made it known that Adolf Hitler topped the list of the foremost war criminals that had been compiled by the London Commission for War Criminals. In answer to the question by Labour representative Ivor Thomas: 'Would a British soldier who found Hitler be obliged to kill him or capture him?' Eden answered: 'I am of the firm conviction that the decision regarding this matter should be completely left to the judgment of the relevant British soldier.' Laughter and applause in the British House of Commons. The Commission for War Criminals had more than one million Germans on its list. Every underground cellar, every prison camp and every group of refugees needed to be combed. 'From northern Germany to the Bavarian Alps the largest manhunt in history has been set in motion,' Eden stated during the session.

By mid-June 1945 almost all the leading figures of the Third Reich had been either arrested or were dead. However, von Ribbentrop, the most arrogant of Hitler's closest advisers, who with his 'whiplash' diplomacy spat out his orders to the German ambassadorial and diplomatic corps, could not be found. Apparently, von Ribbentrop had ended up in northern Germany where, restlessly travelling to and fro like a hunted animal, he offered his services to Hitler's successor, Grand Admiral Dönitz, shortly before the end of the war. Dönitz wanted nothing to do with the strained Ribbentrop and showed him the door. Ribbentrop then dropped out of sight.

Ribbentrop, who for seven years had controlled Nazi Germany's foreign policy and had 'appropriated' numerous magnificent country houses, villas and castles began, according to the British Military Commission, a new life. He rented a room on the fifth floor of a modest apartment block in Hamburg. Although his photograph was hanging in many Allied barracks and investigation centers, von Ribbentrop walked around Hamburg dressed in an elegant suit with a black diplomatic hat and sunglasses. He had secret talks with former business associates from his days as a representative for a champagne firm in an attempt to go under-

ground. A wine dealer from Hamburg hesitated. His son, on the other hand, went to the police. Shortly thereafter Allied military police were on the trail of the man with the dark glasses.

The dramatic denouement took place on the morning of 14 June 1945 when one Belgian and three British soldiers stormed up the stairs to the fifth floor of the apartment building. They knock on a door, and when they get no answer, start beating on it with their

Far left: *Von Ribbentrop makes a point to Julius Streicher during the Reichsparteitag of 1936.*

Center left: *Von Ribbentrop's wife and daughter.*

Below left: *Von Ribbentrop pictured on his forty-fifth birthday, 30 April 1938.*

Left: *Hitler, Chamberlain and von Ribbentrop in conversation during the Munich crisis, September 1938.*

fists and kicking the door panel with their heels. Just as they are on the verge of smashing in the door, it opens slightly. One of the soldiers, Sergeant RC Holloway, whistles through his teeth with surprise. The men see a young brunette; her eyes, as well as her sloppily painted lips, are wide open with terror. 'House search,' says Lieutenant JB Adams, and the soldiers push the woman aside.

In the fourth room they find an unmade bed with a pile of blankets on it. Under the pile, and in spite of all the racket, a man seems to be sleeping. 'Hey, get up!' On hearing this shout from one of the soldiers, Lieutenant Adams enters the room; he shakes the sleeping man, but it is only after protracted shaking that he shows some life. He slowly turns over, still half asleep, involuntarily blinking his eyes in the strong daylight and stares incredulously at the strange soldiers by his bed. 'What's the matter? What's the matter?' he asks with a sleepy voice. 'Stand up,' says Adams, 'and get dressed – hurry!'

Joachim von Ribbentrop throws back the down quilt. Without saying a word, he crawls out of bed and puts on his slippers. He is wearing pink and white striped pajamas and his face is covered with a heavy stubble. 'What is your name?' asks Adams. 'You know perfectly well who I am,' replies von Ribbentrop with an unpleasant smile. Bowing stiffly, he says ironically: 'I congratulate you.' 'Good, Mister von Ribbentrop,' says Adams, 'get dressed. You are under arrest.'

'I should like to shave first.' 'You can shave later. You are to come along immediately.' Von Ribbentrop quickly dresses, combs his hair in front of the mirror and packs his things in a Wehrmacht toilet bag. The group then proceeds outside to a waiting jeep, where von Ribbentrop is shown to the front seat.

At British headquarters he was given a thorough body search for cyanide capsules, as several prominent Nazis had slipped through Allied fingers by taking poison capsules. Several hundred thousand Reichsmarks – carefully bundled up – were found in Ribbentrop's toilet bag. According to later statements he was going to quietly wait 'until everything was over.' Three letters were found in his jacket pocket: one to Field Marshal Montgomery, one to the British Minister of Foreign Affairs, Eden, and one to – those present could hardly believe their eyes – 'Vincent' Churchill! More than anything else, this minor detail, Vincent instead of Winston, revealed the dilettantism of the former Foreign Minister, the man who so readily saw himself as 'a second Metternich.' During his transfer to an internment camp in Luxembourg, von Ribbentrop still wore his elegant gray suit and a black fedora.

Who was von Ribbentrop? Born on 30 April 1893 in Wesel, a garrison town on the Rhine, he grew up in Kassel. His father, an officer in an artillery regiment, had been transferred there shortly after Joachim's birth. His family descended from the Ribbentrups, whose country estate was near Salzuflen in Detmold. In 1908 the mother of the 15-year-old Joachim, 17-year-old Lothar and the 12-year-old Ingeborg died. When he was 17, Joachim left for Canada where he stayed for four years. He had various jobs there including serving as a bank clerk and working for the Canadian Bridge Company helping to build the Quebec Bridge.

In 1914, just before the outbreak of World War I, he returned to Germany and became an officer in the Torgauer Husarenregiment Nr 12. He spent some time at the Russian and Polish fronts and was awarded the Iron Cross, Second Class, but quickly exchanged the front for a quiet office job at the Ministry of War, where he stayed until the end of the conflict. After the war he was a member of the 'lower ranks of cafe society' until his marriage to the daughter of the wealthy champagne manufacturer, Henkell, in 1920 allowed him to enter high society. In his father-in-law's wine business he spent most of his time traveling abroad as a sales representative. He was able to add the noble 'von' to his name thanks to a 'von Ribbentrop' aunt who was willing to adopt him. From 1925 onward, instead of Joachim Ribbentrop, he was known as Joachim von Ribbentrop.

Ribbentrop's doubtful nobility, his blatant displays of arrogance and his snobbishness (which earned him the nickname '*Ribbensnob*') made him particularly disliked by the other party leaders. Goebbels once remarked with derision: 'He bought his name, married his money and got his job through fraudulent means.' Goebbels's hostile attitude most likely came from the fact that Ribbentrop became a party member only in 1932.

In August 1932 von Ribbentrop met Hitler for the first time. Negotiations between Hitler, von Papen and von Schleicher relating to the formation of a new cabinet had broken down due to Hitler's refusal to accept the office of vice-chancellor. Ribbentrop, who knew von Papen quite well, was asked by several party leaders to act as an intermediary in negotiations between him and Hitler. Even the arrogant Ribbentrop seemed willing to bow to the 'genius of the Führer.'

On 10 January 1933 von Papen's cabinet fell and von Schleicher became chancellor. However, Hitler now wanted not von Papen but von Schleicher as vice-chancellor in his cabinet. But at the insistence of Ribbentrop, Hitler discarded this plan and decided to take his chances with von Papen, at least according to von Ribbentrop, who offered the use of his Berlin-Dahlem villa for the secret talks. On 22 January the decisive meeting, which led to the formation of the Hitler-von Papen coalition government, took place there.

Ribbentrop had by now succeeded in convincing Reich Chancellor Hitler that he (von Ribbentrop) could provide more reliable information about what was happening outside Germany than could the officials of the Foreign Office. Using money from the NSDAP (the National Socialist German Workers' Party), von Ribbentrop set up a *Dienststelle* (literally, office-service) *Ribbentrop* in the Wilhelmstrasse across the street from the Foreign Office. His personnel were businessmen, journalists and party members eager for a diplomatic career. Having served as Special Commissioner for Disarmament in 1934, his big chance came in 1935 when he successfully negotiated the Anglo-German Naval Treaty. His reputation, especially with Hitler, had now been definitely established. From Reichsführer-SS Himmler he received the honorary rank of Gruppenführer-SS.

The arrogant, vain, humorless and vindictive Ribbentrop was undoubtedly one of the worst choices that Hitler ever made for a high post. However, he enabled Hitler to take a firmer control of foreign relations; he shared many of Hitler's own social rancors; and he saw in Hitler a father – just as he saw a mother in his domineering wife.

In 1936 Hitler appointed Ribbentrop ambassador to London. It now became Ribbentrop's ambition to replace von Neurath as Minister of Foreign Affairs. He accepted his appointment as ambassador to London with reluctance, being convinced (not without justification) that von Neurath was trying to get him out of the way. He showed his reluctance by taking up his post in London three months after his appointment. Once there, he traveled back and forth between London and Berlin so often that the British satirical magazine *Punch* called him 'the roving Aryan,' while a highly placed official in the Foreign Office suggested the possibility that von Ribbentrop regarded his appointment to the Court of St James's as a part-time job. Ribbentrop made the unforgivable mistake of greeting the King of England with 'Heil Hitler' at a court reception in 1937. He was rejected by British society as a result, which deeply offended him. After this episode he had a deeply ingrained hatred for everything British, a hatred that certainly played a role in the turbulent developments leading up to the outbreak of World War II in 1939.

He also received due criticism in Germany for his astounding *faux pas* at the English court. Göring described him as an extremely egocentric person, a successful wine merchant who had neither the background nor the tact for diplomatic service. 'I tried to convince Hitler to relieve him of his position, and for two reasons,' said Göring from his Nuremberg cell in 1945. 'In the first place he was *persona non grata* to the British, and even Hitler wanted to remain on good terms with England. The British did not like von Ribbentrop because of his coarse tactlessness. On his mission to London he had hardly stepped out of the train before giving expert advice on controlling the balance of power with Russia, and he did not notice at all that the British regarded themselves as experts in the area of power politics and were more interested in hearing from us how we could protect ourselves from the east.

'When he was introduced to the King and responded with "Heil

Above right: Hitler and von Ribbentrop meet with David Lloyd George.

Right: Mussolini adds his signature to the Munich agreement as von Ribbentrop looks on.

Above, far right: Hitler and von Ribbentrop at ease at the Eagle's Nest.

Far right: Ribbentrop and some of his staff.

Hitler," which the British, of course, saw as an insult to the Crown, I was able to convince even Hitler of the impropriety of his action. I said to Hitler: "Imagine that Russia sent you a diplomat who greeted you with 'Long live the communist revolution!'"' Göring gave the communist raised-fist salute and burst into laughter. 'The second reason was that von Ribbentrop did not have an international diplomatic background. Hitler could not judge this as he himself had never been abroad. But because there had been several Counts among the wine merchants that von Ribbentrop had worked with, Hitler believed that he was a man with connections.'

In order to gain a higher position than that of ambassador, Ribbentrop developed a plan for the restructuring of the Foreign Office in 1937. He suggested reorganizing the ministry and modeling it on the lines of a general staff, which would be used as an aggressive instrument of Nazi foreign policy. His reward came in the form of his appointment as Minister of Foreign Affairs in 1938. In spite of his slavish manner toward Hitler, Ribbentrop did actually influence his foreign policy. According to many witnesses, he gave Hitler false information about British politics during the crisis years of 1938-39, drawing a picture of a country that had withdrawn into itself to such an extent that any aggressive action on the part of Germany would be accepted without reprisal. Hitler acted on the basis of this catastrophic and shortsighted thesis. He was more willing since his own views regarding the 'weak and corrupt western democracies' were in accordance with those of Ribbentrop.

Ribbentrop's prestige and influence were further increased after his prediction of a passive reaction from Britain to the Austrian and Czechoslovakian crises proved to be true. Two other high points in his career were the Munich Pact in 1938 and the Nonaggression Pact with Russia in 1939. It was Ribbentrop who repeatedly suggested to Hitler that he could risk war because the western powers would, in the end, not react. He never forgot the indignities inflicted on him by the British. An example of this comes from a Dutch journalist who met von Ribbentrop shortly before the crisis which was to lead to the outbreak of World War II. 'The foreign journalists were having supper with several members of the *Auswärtige Amt* [Foreign Office] when von Ribbentrop came in. The guests were seated at small tables and von Ribbentrop moved from table to table during the course of the evening to talk with them. When he came to our table he said that he did not want to talk about

foreign affairs, and suggested a conversation about art. Von Ribbentrop regarded himself as an expert in this area. He by chance sat next to me and started elaborating on Dutch painting. He saw a similarity between our flourishing Golden Age and the Golden Age brought about by Hitler in German art. After all, the Dutch government had, according to von Ribbentrop, done much for its painters in the sixteenth and seventeenth centuries, even giving them financial support.

'When it was pointed out to the minister that this was not totally true as many of our greatest painters had died in the most abject poverty, and that it was only those artists like van Dijk and Rubens, who had either inherited or made their own fortunes, who were well-to-do throughout their life, von Ribbentrop changed the subject and started talking about renovations to the German embassy in London. When I asked him whether the British were able to appreciate the new style (which was certainly not the case, as in its transition to the Führer-style practically nothing was left of the original beautiful, imposing building), his face became contorted. "The English," he said, "do not have the least notion of art, as with so many other things. They cling to their Queen Anne woodwork and Chippendale furniture and understand nothing about modern times. That will be their downfall!"'

A short time before this conversation took place Ribbentrop had scored another diplomatic success: the signing (with the aid of

Hitler's personal intervention) of a Nonaggression Pact with the Soviet Union in August 1939. After Austria and Czechoslovakia had fallen into Hitler's hands, he turned his eyes to Poland. However, since Hitler was not yet ready to risk war on two fronts (in view of Britain and France's guarantees of Polish independence) the Soviet Union would have to be neutralized. Hitler told Ribbentrop to open negotiations with the Soviets. The Führer decided, in the meantime, to solve the Polish question in his own way; the attack began on 1 September 1939.

Ribbentrop's first diplomatic maneuvers in Moscow were not successful. The Soviets, already negotiating with Britain and France, were stalling for time. This could have meant that the attack on Poland planned for 1 September would have to be postponed. It was at this decisive moment that Hitler himself intervened. He swallowed his pride and asked, by telegram, 'Mr J Stalin' to receive his Foreign Minister immediately.

The telegram, sent on 20 August went on: 'The conclusion of a nonaggression pact for me means the fulfillment of a long-standing German policy. Germany now resumes a political course that was beneficial to both states in past centuries. In view of the intention of both states to enter into a new relationship to each other it seems to me best not to lose any time. I therefore propose that you receive my Foreign Minister on Tuesday, 22 August, or at the latest on Wednesday, 23 August. The Reich Minister has the fullest power to draw up and sign the nonaggression pact as well as the protocol. In view of the international situation a longer stay by the Minister in Moscow is impossible. The tension between Germany and Poland is becoming impossible. A crisis may arise any day. Germany is determined to use all means at her disposal to protect the interests of the Reich. I should be glad to receive your early answer.'

On the evening of 21 August, dinner was served late at the Berghof. Hitler was handed a telegram during the meal. According to Speer: 'His eyes flew over the paper, he turned bright red, stared a moment into space, hit the table so hard that the glasses clinked, and cried with a catch in his voice: "I have got them. I have got them!" Within several seconds he controlled himself again; nobody ventured a comment and the meal continued. After the meal he had the male members of the company come to him: "We are going to close a nonaggression pact with Russia. Here, read it! A telegram from Stalin!"'

The telegram from Stalin read as follows: 'To the Chancellor of the German Reich, A Hitler: I thank you for your letter. I hope that the German-Soviet nonaggression pact will bring about an import-

Left: *Von Ribbentrop with his children.*

Top: *The Governor of Rome meets with von Ribbentrop, 27 May 1939.*

Above: *Molotov and von Ribbentrop converse in Berlin.*

Left: *Von Ribbentrop speaks after the signing of the Tripartite Pact between Germany, Italy and Japan, 27 September 1939.*

Below: *Von Ribbentrop and Hitler arrive in Munich to meet Mussolini, 18 June 1940.*

ant improvement in the political relations between our countries. The peoples of our countries need to live in peace with each other. The Soviet government have instructed me to inform you that they agree to receiving your Herr von Ribbentrop on 23 August in Moscow.'

Ribbentrop left for Moscow on the 23rd to sign the pact. Even with the telegram from Stalin, Hitler was very anxious that day. Shortly before 0200 hours in the morning, 24 August, Ribbentrop telephoned to report the signing of the Nonaggression Pact; he had already had telephone contact with Hitler earlier that evening. During the negotiations Stalin had made claims on the Baltic states of Estonia, Latvia and Lithuania. Ribbentrop had said that he would first have to contact the Führer. A map of the relevant area, hastily spread out, lay next to the telephone at the Berghof. After studying the map for several moments, Hitler authorized Ribbentrop to accept the Russian proposal. The accompanying protocol was made known only after the war. All of Eastern Europe had been divided up into spheres of influence between the two countries.

Göring's comment in 1943 that 'this war is von Ribbentrop's war' goes too far, but is not entirely lacking in truth as is demonstrated by von Ribbentrop's efforts to torpedo any peace talks in 1939. The Italian Foreign Minister Count Ciano wrote in his diary: 'When we were walking in the garden at von Ribbentrop's castle, Schloss Fuschl, I asked him: "Well now, Ribbentrop, what more do you want to have? Danzig or the Corridor?" "No more, now," and he stared at me with his cold, fish-eyes, "we want war. . .!"' Ciano closed with the comment that 'Germany, even if all its wishes were acceded to, would still start a war, since she was "possessed" by the devil of destruction.'

A close colleague of Goebbels inadvertently overheard the following conversation between von Ribbentrop and Hitler, a conversation that highlights their cynicism in a revealing way. Von Ribbentrop was heard to say in a boasting tone: 'Once the war is finally over, I am going to have a richly carved chest and put in it all the pacts and other agreements that I will have broken during my term of office, and for all those to be broken in the future.' Hitler replied, 'And I shall send you a second chest when the first is full.' In spite of all his boasting, Ribbentrop must also have been anxious when, on 3 September, the British ultimatum over Poland reached the Reich Chancellery. Hitler's only comment was an angry: 'What now?'

Before von Ribbentrop became minister, the Foreign Office had

been a bulwark of conservatism and anti-Nazi feeling. Diplomats from the old school, such as von Neurath, von Bülow, von Hassel, von Dirksen and others, wanted nothing to do with their parvenu boss. However, von Ribbentrop was soon on good terms with several officials, some of whom held key positions at the ministry. Shortly after his appointment, von Ribbentrop had special uniforms made for his officials and forced them to become members of the NSDAP. Ribbentrop also placed many of his friends, devoted National Socialists, in high positions (Luther, Likus, Hewel, von Thadden, Sonneiter, Gottfriedsen, Abetz, and Ritter).

In addition, he appointed a number of amateurs from the party as *Sonderaktionen*, who as agents and *Stosstruppführer* carried out National Socialist diplomacy, and were also active in bringing about the downfall of governments, making the preparations for a German invasion or creating protectorates. The new Office of the Reich Ministry of Foreign Affairs and the *Deutschlandabteilung* led by a friend of von Ribbentrop (also State Secretary) were attached to the Foreign Office. Contacts with other *Dienststellen* within the NSDAP, especially those with the SS, were carried out by the *Deutschlandabteilung*. It was in the appointment of *Polizeiattaches* to a succession of German embassies in southeastern Europe, whose task was seeing to the deportation of Jews or recruiting 'folk German' or 'German' SS troops in the occupied areas, that cooperation between Ribbentrop and Himmler was most marked.

The contrast with the former ministry was even more sharply emphasized when, after the outbreak of war, Ribbentrop and a group of close colleagues were hardly ever in Berlin, spending

most of their time near the *Führerhauptkwartier*. After war broke out with Russia Ribbentrop set up a mobile headquarters (first in Himmler's *Sonderzug* (special train, the 'Heinrich', and later in his own *Sonderzug*, the 'Westfalen'). Von Ribbentrop's directives to German ambassadors and representatives abroad were often sent directly from his mobile headquarters and he also received the most important communications from abroad there. Those in his immediate circle (such as Hewel, his liaison officer; and his personal consultants von Rintelen and Sonneiter) were often better informed than the State Secretary at the Foreign Office. The gulf between the older career diplomats and von Ribbentrop's new men became increasingly greater.

Also characteristic of the new diplomacy was the fact that during the war diplomats of the old school were not involved with small and dependent states, as Ribbentrop gave party members the function of *Reichsstathalter des Grossdeutschen Reiches* instead. In 1941 Ribbentrop set up his own intelligence service, the *Sicherheitsdienst* (SD), as a counterpart to the intelligence service of the SS. After the outbreak of war the Foreign Office had more and more newly authorized agents, special departments and official bodies for the purpose of carrying out the often chaotic diplomacy of the National

Socialist regime. The quality of these various bodies can be gauged from Hitler's comment made when Germany invaded the Soviet Union on 22 June 1941: 'It is just as though I have opened the door to a room in total darkness – a room that has never been entered before – without knowing what to expect.'

On the first day of the trial at Nuremberg those indicted for war crimes received a written copy of the charges against them. Each defendant was requested to provide a written comment on the indictment. Ribbentrop wrote: 'The indictment is directed against the wrong person.' He wanted to add 'we only stood in Hitler's shadow' but was afraid to put it in writing. During the preliminary examination by the committee of prosecutors he stated that he was suffering from partial amnesia and asked the others what they thought about everything. He spent his time writing endless memoranda. He asked everyone – and literally everyone – for advice about his defense, from the guard who brought his food to the prison barber. He repeatedly complained that he was not being given enough time to prepare his defense and that 'This trial is truly a great mistake. It will not be an edifying spectacle to watch Germans humiliating other Germans!'

Meanwhile he fought his fears with sleeping pills and with his innumerable notes. After several months Ribbentrop was even more pessimistic. He spoke in a monotone; he had become an old man waiting to die. 'Ah, we are only living shadows. The remains of a dead era, an era that died with Hitler. Whether a few of us live another 10 or 20 years is of no importance. The old days died with Hitler. I should have drawn the consequences on 30 April. Yes, it is a great tragedy!'

Ribbentrop took the stand on 29 March 1946. In a weary tone he gave an account of the prewar situation, of the party's accession to power, of the difficulties resulting from the Treaty of Versailles, and other aspects of the Third Reich. He added nothing that was not already known. He was repeatedly urged to keep to the point. The other prisoners would have less and less to do with him. Ex-minister Schacht mimicked him during a meal by letting his shoulders hang and saying in a sleepy voice: 'I went, therefore, to London. Mr so and so came to meet me at the train. Then I dressed.' Schacht straightened himself up again and said contemptuously: 'And so speaks the German Foreign Affairs mini-

Above: *Goebbels forcibly makes a point to Party Treasurer Schwartz.*

Right: *After the signing of the Tripartite Pact, von Ribbentrop socialises with Japanese General Oshima and Italian Dino Alfieri.*

ster!' Ribbentrop's predecessor, von Neurath, also held only contempt for him: 'Just from the way in which he speaks you can see that he did not have the faintest idea of foreign politics when he was minister. And yet he played the great expert!' 'True,' said von Papen, 'not the faintest idea! You can see from the way he talks about the Munich Pact and the Anti-Comintern Pact that the man simply did not know what he was doing.' Göring, not hiding his maliciousness, said: 'He bored the tribunal to death! I told him that if he wanted to be successful with his long enumeration he would have to make it a bit exciting like I did. After all, the judges and journalists want at least to hear something interesting – otherwise they do not even listen!'

During the course of his testimony, Ribbentrop twisted and denied almost everything that was part of his policy. He undoubtedly made by far the worst impression of all the defendants during the trial. He just could not understand why the prosecutors were being so unfair in their assessment of his character. 'Why are they trying to make an anti-Semite of me?'

The prison psychologist, GM Gilbert, reminded him that Paul Schmidt (head interpreter for the Foreign Office) had confirmed that he (Ribbentrop) had told the Hungarian Horthy that the two solutions to the Jewish problem were extermination and concentration camps. 'He could not have said that? Or I did not completely understand. It is so difficult to concentrate. But I could never have said something like that. It is totally against my character,' von Ribbentrop said to Gilbert. 'In any case,' he continued, 'the prosecutor should not paint my character so black. History will judge otherwise. And the German people will not believe him. I know what my people think of me. I have only tried to help them.'

On 1 April, the longest day but one of his examination, the British prosecutor, Sir David Maxwell-Fyfe, crossexamined Ribbentrop. By the use of evasion, contradiction, unimportant and irrelevant arguments, clinging to certain points, diplomatic bragging and stuttering Ribbentrop tried to refute the incriminating evidence against him. He denied all aggressive intentions, and by the afternoon the crossexamination had reached a high point in absurdity when Ribbentrop denied having put Hácha under unbearable pressure so that he, in violation of the Munich Agreement, would hand over Czechoslovakia. 'What further pressure could you put on a Head of State than to threaten him that your army of overwhelming strength would march against his country and that your air force would bomb his capital?' Sir David wanted to know. 'War, for example,' answered Ribbentrop naively. The entire courtroom shook with laughter.

Judgment was pronounced on 1 October 1946: 'The accused Joachim von Ribbentrop! In accordance with all counts of the indictment, of which you have been found guilty, the International Military Tribunal sentences you to death by hanging.' Von Ribbentrop's face looked ash-gray; his eyes were half-closed. He was holding a file of dossiers under his arm. Back in his cell he walked restlessly back and forth, continually whispering to himself: 'Death, death! Now I will never be able to write my memoirs. Ah, ah! So, I am hated so much, so hated. . .'

The grounds given for his sentence were that he had participated in the plans for the invasion of Czechoslovakia. That from March 1938 onward he was in close association with the Sudeten Germans. He continued to apply pressure after the Munich Agreement, the purpose being the occupation of the rest of Czechoslovakia. Ribbentrop played a special diplomatic role during the events which led up to the invasion of Poland. He played, as well, an important role in the 'solution' of the 'Jewish question.' In 1942 he gave the German diplomatic representatives from the puppet states orders to speed up deportation of the Jews to the East. Furthermore, he was involved with all of Germany's invasion plans, from the occupation of Austria to the invasion of Russia.

On 16 October 1946 shortly before 0100 hours the bolts were thrown back on von Ribbentrop's cell door. 'I trust in the blood of the lambs, that carry the sins of the world,' said Ribbentrop with closed eyes. Two MPs with white belts and silver helmets took him between them and proceeded to the gymnasium where the gallows were waiting. His hands were tied. He was asked to give his name. He said: 'God protect Germany! It is my last wish that Germany retains its unity and that East and West can come to an agreement on this.' A heavy thump; the trap door. So ended the life of Joachim von Ribbentrop. Once wholly dedicated to his alter-ego and substitute father Adolf Hitler, he had followed his orders with utmost servility. Now he was no more than a caricature of himself.

Left: *Von Ribbentrop pictured after his execution.*

163

ALFRED
ROSENBERG
1893-1946

Left: *Rosenberg makes a speech in the company of Field Marshal Erwin von Witzleben who was later to be executed for his part in the July Bomb Plot.*

Above: *Alfred Rosenberg, the Nazi Party's chief philosopher.*

Alfred Rosenberg was the author of *The Myth of the Twentieth Century* which, after Hitler's *Mein Kampf,* was the second bestselling book published in Nazi Germany. Alongside the ideas of Fichte, Hegel, Treitschke, Nietzsche, de Gobineau and Chamberlain those of Alfred Rosenberg were, at least in the early years of National Socialism, an important source of inspiration to Hitler in developing his threatening and morbid ideas regarding race and *Lebensraum* (living space). Rosenberg, as well as the poet Eckart, served mainly as 'intermediaries' who would present various ideas and opinions to Hitler. Rosenberg's influence should not be underestimated; he was a muddled theoretician with dangerous ideas who got mixed up with Hitler's unwholesome company.

Nuremberg, 30 September 1946. The day of judgment for the most prominent war criminals had finally arrived. In his closing speech Robert M Jackson the American prosecutor said: 'The past 40 years of the twentieth century will be recorded in the annals of history as the bloodiest time of all. Two world wars have assured a death toll greater than for any army participating in any war whether in ancient times or in the Middle Ages. No single period of less than half a century has ever undergone wholescale massacre to such an extent, such atrocities and barbarities, such wholesale subjection of peoples to slavery, such massive extermination of peoples regarded as inferior. The horrors of Torquemada pale in comparison with those of the Nazi inquisition.

'These deeds are somber historical facts which will be remembered by the future generations of this century. If we can find no way of removing the causes of these barbaric events, thereby preventing a repetition, one may predict that the twentieth century will possibly succeed in delivering the death blow to our civilization... We have not judged them [the war criminals] for their loathsome ideas. The intellectual bankruptcy and moral decay of the Nazi regime would not have become a matter for international law if they had not been used to goose-step the *Herrenvolk* across international borders. It is not their thoughts but their overt deeds that we charge as criminal...'

The British prosecutor, Sir Hartley Shawcross, stated: 'There can be no doubt that the accused took part in and are morally responsible for crimes of such atrocity that even fantasy reels against it... Large cities such as Coventry, Rotterdam and Stalingrad in ashes... the land ravaged... and the unmeasurable results of a war carried out in this way – hunger and sickness spread through the world; millions are without a homeland, are maimed, are in mourning... In their graves lie 10 million victims, who could have lived now in peace and happiness, soldiers, sailors, aviators, civilians... war crimes which never should have taken place... and then the slavery to such an extent that seven million men, women and children were dragged out of their homes... were starved, tortured and murdered...'

Sir Hartley then quoted Goethe: '"The German people shall lend an ear to the first scoundrel who calls up the lowest in the Germans and teaches them that nationalism means isolation and coarseness." With what a prophetic voice he spoke! Since the mad scoundrels who have all these things on their consciences are sitting in the dock.' One of the accused cursed softly under his breath on hearing these words, namely the official 'philosopher' of National Socialism, Alfred Rosenberg.

On this 30 September the cordon of guards surrounding the Nuremberg courthouse is thicker than usual. Control has been tightened, with the guards searching the contents of briefcases more thoroughly and examining identity cards more carefully. People have streamed here from all corners of the world. The glass-enclosed radio cubicles are filled with technicians and radio reporters. Photographers and film crews are in position, and there is not a single space left in the press gallery. The stenographers and interpreters have taken their places, as have defense counsel, who had been escorted in by the military police. Only the dock, two rows of simple hardwood benches, is still empty. The minutes creep slowly by...

The accused enter at last; they leave the small lift which has brought them down to the courtroom on the lower floor in groups of two or three, escorted by white-helmeted MPs. The majority of the accused give an impression of good-humor. They greet their fellow-accused with a wink or a handshake.

An officer of the tribunal enters the courtroom. Everyone stands; silence prevails. The eight judges solemnly enter the room; it is 1003 hours. Hour after hour slips by while the judges in turn read the documents aloud. At 1345 hours, the first part of the judgment is completed. A preoccupied Rosenberg has in the meantime heard 'guilty' pronounced on all four counts of his indictment, namely conspiracy, crimes against peace, war crimes and crimes against humanity. The court now adjourns for lunch. The sentences will be delivered after the adjournment.

Well over an hour later the tribunal returns to the courtroom for the 407th, and last, sitting. The atmosphere is completely different from that of the morning session. The courtroom is no longer

Left: *A gathering of early followers of the Nazi Party in Munich. Rosenberg is fourth from left in the third row.*

Above right: *Hitler and Rosenberg pictured in 1923 at the time of the putsch.*

Right: *Rosenberg arrives at the Reichstag, 1930.*

floodlit. Only the dull, bluish glow from the florescent lights casts a shadow over the paneling, the empty dock, the faces of the judges, the prosecutors, defense counsel, stenographers, assistants and members of the press. A court order has barred all photographers and film crews from the room. The faces of the accused are not allowed to be photographed or filmed during those moments in which they will learn their fate. The minutes pass agonizingly slowly and the accused, who will be brought in one by one to hear their sentence, have not yet arrived.

Suddenly, the elevator doors slide eerily open – no hand has touched them. Hermann Göring emerges from the dark opening and enters the gray light of the courtroom. Behind him, side-by-side, follow two military policemen. Göring grips the headphones and hears his sentence. The sixth accused, Alfred Rosenberg, enters. He is pale and nervous. When the two MPs have taken up position next to him he takes the headphones. 'Accused Alfred Rosenberg! In accordance with the counts of the indictment, of which you have been found guilty, the International Military Tribunal sentences you to death by hanging.' Rosenberg clearly had difficulty in controlling himself. Once back in his cell, this priest of the *Herrenvolk*, who had created a doctrine of hatred and provided the rationale for the extermination of the Jews, said to the prison psychologist Gilbert: 'The noose, the noose! That is what you wanted, isn't it?'

The sentences were to be carried out on the night of 15/16 October. The hour was a tightly guarded secret. The condemned are under strict security; the guards must keep the prisoners in sight all the time. The noise from the builders can be heard in all the cells. The Bible suddenly becomes a very popular book among the prisoners. But not for Rosenberg. He is reading *Die Geige*, a novel by Binding. He receives a number of letters, but writes none.

On the morning of 16 October at 0130, Alfred Rosenberg was taken from his cell. Two American MPs led him to the inner court where the gymnastics room was. Three black-painted stands had been set up in the strongly lit room. Thirteen wooden steps wend their way upward to a platform on which the gallows rested. The clergyman who asked Rosenberg whether he would like a prayer to be said for him received a surly 'no, thank you' as reply. Reporters, hiding on the Hall of Justice roof, heard the clap of the trapdoor.

At 0400 that same morning, two American army trucks drove up and stopped in the courtyard. Eleven coffins were loaded into them. Via a roundabout route the bodies were taken to Munich to be cremated the same day. Their ashes were strewn in the River Isar to prevent a memorial from ever being erected. 'Ash is innocent' wrote *The New York Times* at the time. 'The ash of the innocent and the ash of the unspeakably criminal is made up of the same elements, carried away by the same winds, joined in the same waters. And we in our valley of darkness must now hope and pray for the advent of a new world.'

Alfred Rosenberg was born on 12 January 1893 at Reval (now Talinin) in Estonia. His father, a shoemaker, was of German extraction; his mother of Baltic. Rosenberg studied architecture in Riga and Moscow, receiving his diploma in Moscow in 1918. During his stay in Moscow he was witness to the revolution which filled him with loathing for Bolshevik ideas. To escape the upheaval, Rosenberg fled to Reval where he carried out various 'anti-Red' propaganda activities. When the Red Army later marched toward Estonia Rosenberg fled to Germany. He reached Munich in 1919 filled with a deep hatred for Bolshevism, a hatred that he soon linked to a fanatical anti-Semitism. He was convinced that the Jews were behind all the events in Russia and Estonia. In Munich the young Rosenberg made contact with the *Thule-Gesellschaft*, an organization from which, to a degree, the NSDAP was later to emerge.

The *Thule-Gesellschaft* was a focal point for extreme right-wing forces in Bavaria shortly after World War I and maintained relations with many groups in Bavarian society. Approximately 1500 members (some influential) used the swastika as their symbol and with the *Munchener Beobachter* they had a newspaper at their disposal. Members had to be of Aryan descent. The *Thule-Gesellschaft* was notable for its rabid anti-Semitic propaganda: the Jews were the 'arch-enemy' of the German people. There were various lines of communication running from the *Thule-Gesellschaft* to Russian emigré circles with their headquarters in Munich. That Rosenberg soon came into contact with this group is no surprise.

In October 1918 the sports journalist Karl Harrer and the fitter Anton Drexler set up a *Politische Arbeiterzirkel* on the order of the *Thule-Gesellschaft*; its purpose was 'the discussion and study of political matters.' The aim was to use this group to spread the message of those wanting greater national rights. On 5 January 1919 Anton Drexler, together with 25 workers, established his own party – the *Deutsche Arbeiterpartei* (DAP). On 12 September one of the local DAP agitators, Gottfried Feder, spoke at a gathering which had more the character of a drinking party than a political meeting. Among the approximately 40 persons present were Rosenberg and Hitler. When one of the company argued that Bavaria should withdraw from the German Empire and enter into union with Austria, Hitler angrily stood up and made an unusually strong counterargument. Chairman Drexler whispered to the man sitting next to him: 'My, he has a mouth. We could use him.'

When Hitler was leaving the meeting immediately after his speech Drexler quickly ran after him to ask him to return. At the door he pressed a pamphlet he had written, *Mein Politisches Erwachen* (My Political Awakening), in Hitler's hand. Hitler would later write of how the following morning at the barracks, with the mice still breakfasting on a few breadcrumbs he had thrown them, he started to read the pamphlet and found it contained numerous things in common with his own life. He joined the DAP and, after some hesitation, became committee member number seven. His tasks included recruitment and propaganda.

Dietrich Eckart played an important role in the first meeting of Hitler and Rosenberg. Eckart, a not very successful journalist, poet and playwright, had numerous contacts in Munich and was a member of the *Thule-Gesellschaft*. Eckart was editor-in-chief of *Völkischer Beobachter*, the DAP paper. The name of the DAP would be changed in March 1920 to NSDAP, *National Sozialistische Deutsche Arbeiterpartei*.

Eckart was somebody who had read a lot: he had translated *Peer Gynt* into German and was knowledgeable about Schopenhauer. Moreover, he held strong nationalist, anti-democratic, anti-clerical ideas, was a theorist on race and was interested in Nordic folk-

Left: *Rosenberg studies a model of a Viking longship, 12 February 1937.*

Above right: *Rosenberg photographed on his forty-fifth birthday, 12 January 1938.*

Above, far right: *Hitler congratulates Rosenberg on his birthday.*

lore. He was an excellent speaker and had a sparkling wit. He undoubtedly had a great deal of influence on the younger and still very inexperienced Hitler. He lent him books, corrected the manner in which he expressed himself, and took him, when possible, to visit his numerous acquaintances. It was Eckart who first introduced Hitler to Berchtesgaden, where they occasionally stayed at the Platterhof on the Obersalzberg. Among Eckart's acquaintances was the wealthy Bechstein family (piano manufacturers). Mrs Bechstein organized numerous parties where people could meet the new 'prophet' and gave substantial donations to the money-troubled NSDAP.

It is obvious that a qualified architect like Rosenberg would make a deep impression on someone like Hitler who had failed to get into architecture school. Hitler was, moreover, impressed by Rosenberg's learned manner. Hence, shortly before Eckart's death in 1923, Hitler appointed him editor-in-chief of the *Völkischer Beobachter*. Hitler came into contact with violently anti-Semitic and anti-Bolshevik emigrés through Rosenberg. This group included Scheubner-Richter, a German from East Prussia, who soon became one of Hitler's close friends but was shot to death during the unsuccessful putsch of 1923.

Hitler saw Rosenberg as the heir of the extreme right-wing 'folk' ideologists and the great prophet of the new racist *Weltanschauung* (philosophy of life). The horrors that Hitler would unfold in *Mein Kampf* were partially taken from Rosenberg, but Hitler also incorporated numerous ideas from philosophers such as Nietzsche, Hegel and Fichte. Hitler's anti-Semitism was partly inspired by Karl Lüger, mayor of Vienna during the years that he stayed there. Also, Professor von Treitschke, propagandist of 'Prussiandom' and glorifier of war as the highest form of expression in man, had an influence on the young Hitler, as did the mystically charged operas of Richard Wagner. It should also be mentioned that Hitler's racial theories were taken mainly from the Frenchman De Gobineau and the Englishman Houston Chamberlain.

From the time that he joined the small NSDAP, especially in the early years when he was in charge of propaganda and membership recruitment, Hitler was inspired by a sacred belief. The National Socialist Party program was launched on 24 February 1920. Although Hitler had helped draft the policy, the actual compiler was Gottfried Feder, an economist from Munich. Strictly speaking, the program combined arbitrary, hastily assembled elements from 'folk' ideology which had been chosen for their emotional appeal. It was anti-Marxist, anti-parliamentarian, and anti-Semitic; it railed against the consequences of World War I, especially against those measures in the Treaty of Versailles which imposed an enormous war debt on Germany.

With unlimited energy Hitler, by now absolute leader of the NSDAP, went to the beer halls, often long into the night, canvassing for new members. He was now calling himself 'Führer,' in imitation of Mussolini, who was known as 'Il Duce'. Hitler's activities resulted in a slow but steady increase in membership. By January 1923 the NSDAP had 55,000 members. After inflation set in the flow of new members became even greater; 35,000 joined in the period February-November 1923.

One result of the inflation that swept through Germany in the early 1920s was that millions of people lost their savings and, as a result of the drop in purchasing power, could barely afford life's basic necessities. From a political viewpoint, the depression led to the strengthening of right-wing extremism. When, in 1923, Germany could no longer fulfill its reparation obligations, France occupied the Ruhr, a move which led to the total collapse of the German monetary system. Hitler thought that with the crisis that was now ravaging the country at its worst, the time was ripe to seize power by means of a violent putsch.

On 8 November 1923, Hitler, with a number of cronies including Göring and Himmler, forced his way into a right-wing political meeting where he proclaimed that the 'national revolution' had begun. With pistol drawn he tried to convince the poli-

Left: *Dr Ferdinand Porsche shows off a Volkswagen Beetle to the Führer.*

Below left: *Rosenberg and Hitler in conversation with Reichsminister Dr Lammers.*

Right: *Rosenberg on the Eastern Front.*

tical leaders present to participate in a 'March on Berlin,' in imitation of Mussolini's 'March on Rome.' The 'march' was nipped in the bud when, at the cost of several lives, the demonstrators were dispersed in front of the Feldherrnhalle in the heart of Munich. Numerous arrests were made; the NSDAP was dissolved and banned by the government. Hitler was sentenced to five years imprisonment for treason. Rosenberg managed to escape as he was not considered by the authorities to have taken part in the putsch.

Before his arrest Hitler sent Rosenberg a letter which contained a brief message: 'Dear Rosenberg, as of now you have the leadership of the movement.' As Rosenberg himself admits in his memoirs, this was a surprising decision. He was certainly not a man of action and had not taken an active role in the small group which had prepared the putsch. As a leader he was unsuitable; he found it difficult to reach decisions or to assert his authority. However, it was precisely the lack of these qualities that attracted Hitler to him. With Rosenberg as his deputy there would be no threat to his own position in the party. Rosenberg was an intellectual, a rather stiff, fairly respectable man who was always falling out with the cruder elements of the party. Using the revealing pseudonym Rolf Eidhalt, an anagram of the name Adolf Hitler, he tried to keep the rest of the former followers of the NSDAP together as the *Grossdeutsche Volksgemeinschaft.*

Rosenberg visited Hitler several times each week during his imprisonment. There is no doubt that Hitler, busy writing *Mein Kampf*, took over or adapted a number of Rosenberg's ideas about racism and nationalism for his work. The most important elements in *Mein Kampf* are *Lebensraum* (living space), anti-Marxism and anti-Semitism, with all three linked together by a Darwinian ideology of struggle. Hitler vehemently struck out at 'the Jewish doctrine of Marxism,' a connection that was certainly influenced by Alfred Rosenberg.

'The world,' Hitler used to say, 'is just like a challenge cup; it always wants to be in the hands of the strongest. For tens-of-thousands of years. . . man became great by eternal struggle, and eternal struggle will destroy man.' This iron law of nature, the right of the strongest, was the point of departure for everything: that history was nothing other than the struggle of peoples for living space, a struggle in which all conceivable means are permissible. 'Struggle, subjection, extermination are irrevocable', said Hitler. 'One being drinks the blood of another. Its death feeds the other. One must not talk idly about humanity. . .'

This diatribe shows Hitler's total lack of understanding of justice and the right to happiness of others, and his unbridled amorality. Being influenced by Hess and Rosenberg, Hitler firmly believed in the appropriation of *Lebensraum*. He indicated the direction his quest for expansion would take while still in prison: 'The appropriation of new land is only possible in the East. . . If one seeks expansion in Europe, one has practically no choice but to take land from Russia, which means that the new [German] Reich will have to tread in the footsteps of the Teutonic Knights who, in the past, conquered land and gained bread for their people by the sword. . .' He wanted to destroy Marxism to its very roots, as he was in the habit of saying, and thought that Marxism could be brought down by another doctrine with a greater truth, but one willing to use brutality in equal measure.

It has been claimed that National Socialism was a 'nihilist revolution.' However, neither Hitler nor the movement he led followed a definite philosophy. Rather, the party made use of votes and events, but only in so far as they brought either followers or results. National Socialism knew no boundaries; ideology was no more than a camouflage that hid a desire for power in which each success was regarded purely as a starting point for savage and ambitious adventures. The movement's ruling elite was utterly deliberate, cold and refined. No objective existed that National Socialism would not abandon if need be, or would not embrace for the sake of the movement.

With their unquenchable thirst for power, Hitler and his associates showed that they were prisoners of their own prejudices. Just as National Socialism absorbed no ideological themes without

Above: *Hitler greets von Schirach while Rosenberg and Himmler are deep in conversation. Martin Bormann (far right) watches the proceedings.*

Left: *Speer, Rosenberg and Dr Seyss-Inquart, Reichs Commissioner for the Netherlands, listen to a speech by Hitler, 26 April 1942.*

considering the possibilities they held for the enhancement of power, the overriding importance of their declarations of power can only be understood by taking into account ideological motives such as *Lebensraum*, a concept linked to strident anti-Marxism and anti-Semitism and held together by the theory of Darwinian struggle.

The leading National Socialists, insofar as they tried to combine practice and ideology, were able to say that National Socialism did not lend itself to definition, because it was subject to continuous and irreversible change.

With the exception of the concept of a struggle for supremacy National Socialism gave up all its principles, at one time or another, for the sake of power. Its *Weltanschauung* consisted of numerous heterogeneous components arbitrarily lumped together. The result was that there was not one specific type of NSDAP leader. 'National Socialism was solely what "so and so" said or did, whereby each representative thought that he was carrying out National Socialism in its true meaning,' wrote Hans Frank, later to become the infamous Governor-General of Poland, who in his Nuremberg cell converted to Catholicism. He added: 'There were just as many kinds of National Socialism as there were leading functionaries.'

The result of this was that the drive for more power came to take a dominant position, one based on continually changing personal obsessions, ambitions and resentments which were linked only by a blind obedience to the Führer. This, to a large extent, explains why there were so few firmly committed to the leadership of the party. Those who put their ideological principles above their struggle for actual power soon saw themselves pushed into a position of isolation.

This factor goes some way to explain the career of Alfred Rosenberg: a leading National Socialist who allowed himself to be totally led by his ideological views and stubbornly defended them against opponents. One of his well-known sayings was: 'National Socialism stands or falls by its ideology.' Rosenberg's decision to become the new apostle of a 'new' message made of him a curious, strange and absurd figure within the NSDAP leadership (for the most part pragmatists) – the philosopher of a movement whose sole philosophy was the struggle for more power, with the end justifying the means. As the party's power increased and its ideological trimmings were pushed into the background, Rosenberg became a forgotten and lonely philosopher, no longer taken seriously, passed over when important party posts were handed out, a relic from the early years of the NSDAP. Goebbels sneeringly called him *'Beinahe' Rosenberg* ('almost' Rosenberg), because he had 'almost' become a scholar, a journalist, a politician in his career – but always 'almost.'

With his loss of prestige and power, Rosenberg was unable to reach Hitler and had very few friends in the NSDAP. His weighty manner and the wall of ideological terminology with which he surrounded himself only strengthened his isolated position in the party.

Yet the picture of Rosenberg as a somewhat pathetic, powerless and inept figure with little importance is only partly true. Rosenberg did have considerable influence on the thinking and behavior of many National Socialists who were poisoned by the anti-Semitic, anti-Marxist and warmongering articles in his newspaper, the *Völkischer Beobachter*. Rosenberg sowed, to a large extent, the seeds of widespread racial hatred, hatred of communists and an all-embracing amorality.

Rosenberg's ideas came mainly from the secret *Thule-Gesellschaft* which, with its sinister horror stories about Jews, Freemasons and Bolsheviks promoted the idea of a sectarian Aryan and 'Germanic' cult. He borrowed heavily from the ideas of the *Thule-Gesellschaft* in his efforts to give National Socialism a philosophy of its own. The titles of his first publications demonstrate this influence: *Die Spur der Juden im Wandel der Zeiten (The Tracks of the Jews Through the Ages), Unmoral im Talmud (Immorality in the Talmud)*, both published in 1920; *Das Verbrechen der Freimaurerei (The Crime of Freemasonry)* from 1921; and *Der Sumpf (The Morass: A Plague in Russia)* from 1922. He was also involved in the distribution of the forgery *Dir Protokolle der Weisen von Zion und die Jüdische Weltpolitik (The Protocols of the Elders of Zion)* from 1923, which he had reprinted in 1940.

In 1930 his *Der Mythus des 20 Jahrhunderts (The Myth of the Twentieth Century)*, was published and became, next to *Mein Kampf*, the most important book on Nazi theory. This strange, difficult to read book was also known as the 'catechism of NSDAP racial religion.' Rosenberg believed that all races had specific and different physical and mental characteristics. He divided Europeans into five general racial types which, he admitted, had become so interbred that it was impossible to distinguish them from each other. However, the 'Nordic' race, to be found in Germany, Scandinavia and England was the purest of the five. Actually the answer was very simple, according to him. All the Germans had to do to 'purify their race of impure elements' and regain their 'own Nordic character' was to prevent further interbreeding, especially by the 'Oriental Jewish race.' After a certain period of time the blood would revert to its pure 'Nordic' state. 'Nordic' blood would, according to Rosenberg, cleanse itself of impurities.

These ideas were inspired by Darré, the NSDAP agricultural expert who, in his book *Blut und Boden (Blood and Soil)*, related the blood of the German farmer to the ground he worked. Darré developed a 'theory' of the 'eternal blood cycle' which held that the farmer who worked the soil would be buried in the same soil. Therefore, the farmer's daily bread was, in fact, the blood of his forefathers. German blood would be passed on from generation to generation by means of the soil and contained, therefore, 'special' German characteristics.

Rosenberg also developed the 'theory' that only the 'Nordic race' would ever be able to climb to great cultural and political heights. He proclaimed in inflated, barely comprehensible language the struggle against the unwholesome 'Christian-Syrian-Liberal' tradition, a contest to create a new world in which, through toil, *Lebensraum* would be won.

In spite of the wearying prose of *The Myth of the Twentieth Century* the book sold hundreds-of-thousands of copies. The public saw it as the standard work on party ideology, although Hitler called it 'trash that nobody can understand, written by a petty Balt who thinks in a terribly complicated way,' and 'a step back to the Middle Ages.' During the Nuremberg trial all the accused denied having ever read the book. Rosenberg's proud comment in his diary for 19 January 1940 'that hundreds-of-thousands are slowly being inwardly motivated toward revolution by my book,' sprang out of the necessity to replace an unsuccessful political career with the status of a great philosopher.

It was becoming increasingly clear that Rosenberg had hardly any true political power and that when important decisions were being taken he made hardly any contribution. Rosenberg had once hoped to become the party's most important diplomat, a hope based on the fact that he had been Hitler's closest advisor during the NSDAP's *'Kampfzeit'* (time of struggle). However, after his unfortunate blunder while on a visit to England – he laid a wreath with a large swastika on the grave of the unknown soldier – his diplomatic missions and activities ended. His obstinacy and his unwillingness to compromise made for difficulties. In addition, his neurotic paranoia about seeing a Jew, a Marxist or a Freemason in every opponent worked against him. As he saw himself being brushed aside, his hatred of men such as Goebbels and Ribbentrop greatly increased.

He had expected to receive the post of Minister of Foreign Affairs; although he subsequently received the impressive title of 'Deputy to the Führer of the National Socialist Party for the Entire

Spiritual and Ideological Training of the Party,' it only gave him control over the rather unimportant *Aussenpolitische Amt* of the NSDAP. In spite of all the activities that Rosenberg organized, he was not much more than the head of an office for receiving foreign visitors. Göring stated during his trial that the *Aussenpolitische Amt* had never had a say in foreign policy questions.

One of Rosenberg's most bitter experiences was Hitler's decision to give the Minister of Foreign Affairs post to his rival von Ribbentrop in 1938, passing him over for the second time in doing so. He believed von Ribbentrop to be totally unsuitable for the post and, when the pact with Moscow was settled in 1939, his bitterness knew no bounds. Referring to this he wrote in his diary: 'I have the feeling that the pact with Moscow shall, one way or another, break National Socialism apart. How can we speak of saving Europe when we must apply for help to those destroying her?' Rosenberg's naive loyalty to Hitler gave way to a sort of disdain after the pact with Moscow. From then on it seemed to him that National Socialism had lost its direction.

Rosenberg was a prominent member of numerous organizations and societies dealing with art and culture. By means of the *Kampfbund für Deutsche Kultur*, already established in 1929, he could engage in battle against the 'foreign, non-Aryan impurities in German art.' He 'cleansed' all German museums and collections of Marxist and Bolshevik-Jewish impurities. He saw himself as the great organizer of 'German iconoclasm' and, where possible, furthered 'true Aryan art.'

After the fall of France in June 1940 Rosenberg asked Hitler's permission to scour the country's libraries and archives in occupied areas for objects of value. The request resulted in Rosenberg's appointment as head of the '*Einsatzstab Reichsleiter Rosenberg*,' an organization which would gradually become involved in systematic robbery and plunder. Rosenberg was in fact authorized to transport back to Germany any cultural treasures which he thought valuable. The following division was made for art objects from the Louvre (Paris): 1 Art objects of which the Führer himself will decide how they will be used; 2 . . . which will complement the collection of the Reichsmarshal (Göring); 3 . . . those suited to be sent to German museums.

The French government's protests, referring to the Hague Convention, were disregarded. In January 1941 Rosenberg estimated the value of the art treasures taken from France alone to be about one billion Reichsmarks. According to a secret German report, up to July 1944 approximately 137 freight cars loaded with 4174 cases of works of art, including 10,890 paintings, were transported from France to Germany. In addition to this looting the party philosopher saw an opportunity of using his *Einsatzstab* to implement a number of his ideas. Thus he also confiscated 550,000 books intended for the 'Advanced Schools of the NSDAP' which would be established after the war. These schools, for which Rosenberg had already made detailed preparations, were to teach 'pure National Socialist doctrine.'

On 20 April 1941, two months before the German invasion of the Soviet Union, Hitler appointed Rosenberg Reichsminister for the Eastern Occupied Territories. Obtaining *Lebensraum* in the East had for years been a favorite dream of the Führer. Hitler saw German cities being built with magnificent governor's palaces and splendid buildings, while strategic highways were to open up the gigantic eastern empire, especially a major railroad system to the ore-rich mouth of the Dönetz. Double-decker trains with a speed of 200 kilometers per hour were a favorite 'tea-time' topic of the Führer. The cities would be encircled by a ring of 'beautiful villages,' peopled with 'able-bodied' country folk.

The standard of living of the Slavic population would be kept as low as possible. It would be best if they were taught 'sign language,' with the radio being used for information and entertainment – endless music which, according to Hitler, increased the pleasure in

Below, far left: *Rosenberg after his capture by the Allies.*

Below left: *Rosenberg's wife and daughter after their arrest in May 1945.*

Right: *Rosenberg pictured after his execution.*

work. Further, European migration would be directed eastward and finally, after 10 years he wanted to hear that 'at least 20 million Germans live in the Eastern provinces.' Rosenberg, in one of his many memoranda, wrote with regard to this wish: 'The Baltic Sea will again become a Germanic inland sea.'

Two days before the German attack on the Soviet Union, the Reichsminister for the Eastern Occupied Territories addressed his Reich Commissars (the eastern territories were to be divided up into four Reich Commissariats: Ostland, Ukraine, Moscow and Caucasia): 'The job of feeding the German people stands at the top of the list of Germany's claims on the East. The southern Russian territories will have to provide food for the German people. We know that this is a harsh requirement and feelings must be put aside. . . . The future will hold very hard years in store for the Russians.'

One major proposal of the Reichsminister for the Eastern Occupied Territories was not accepted by the Führer. Rosenberg pleaded in vain for a division of the Soviet Union into politically autonomous nations. Rosenberg knew, for example, that the Ukrainians would welcome the Germans as liberators. He firmly believed that if the Germans liberated the Russian people from the Bolshevik-Stalinists and held out an offer of eventual self-government, Germany would obtain the greatest benefit from the *Ostreich*. However, the Führer's intentions lay elsewhere.

On 23 July 1942, with the Germans approaching the Volga and the Caucasian oilfields, Bormann, Hitler's secretary and right-hand man, wrote to Rosenberg setting out the Führer's views on Russia: 'The Slavs are to work for us. Insofar as we do not need them, they may die. Therefore, compulsory vaccination and German health services are unnecessary. The fertility of the Slavs is undesirable. They may use contraceptives or practice abortion – the more the better. Education is dangerous. It is enough if they can count up to a hundred. . . Every educated person is a potential enemy. We can leave them their religion as a means of diversion. As for food they will not get more than is absolutely necessary. We are the masters. We come first.'

Dr Otto Bräutigam, Rosenberg's deputy, made an official protest, with Rosenberg's approval, on 25 October 1942. In an embittered report, he risked calling attention to the mistakes being made in Russia. The report was like a voice crying out in the wilderness.

Hitler could now finally carry out his *Lebensraum* plans and neither man nor report could stop him. In spite of his title of Reichsminister for the Eastern Occupied Territories, Rosenberg had hardly any political clout. From the outset he saw his power being restricted by Göring, authorized coordinator of the Four-Year Plan and influential in the field of the eastern economies; by Himmler, Chief of Police and Reichsführer SS, who as Reichs Commissar was also responsible for the colonization of the East, the '*Festigung des Deutschen Volkstums im Osten*;' by Saukel, Hitler's authorized representative for the deportation of 'usable' work forces to Germany; and, finally, by the Wehrmacht. These persons and institutions had extensive authority at their disposal and were responsible only to Hitler, thus bypassing Alfred Rosenberg's *Ostministerium* (Eastern Ministry), mockingly called 'Cha-Ostministerium' by Goebbels.

Rosenberg could not keep his brutal Reich Commissars in line, especially Koch and Lohse who stopped at no savagery in carrying out Hitler's wishes in the eastern occupied territories. Goebbels spoke of Rosenberg as a 'Monarch without land and without subjects.' Rosenberg was gradually reduced to writing endless memoranda which nobody read, and making protests which no one took seriously until, finally, toward the end of 1944, finding his situation impossible, he resigned.

Rosenberg, because of his weak character, contributed to the slaughter of hundreds of thousands of people in the eastern territories where he had, after all, been the highest civil authority. He knew of the inhuman horrors being perpetrated by the occupation forces. His subordinates committed (formally, in his name) mass murder and he himself gave the orders for the massive deportation of workers from the eastern territories. He did occasionally protest against excesses and atrocities, but remained in a position of power until the fall of 1944.

Rosenberg was a man who truly believed that a sailor on a submarine who was oily and grimy from crawling out of the machine room would gladly reach out for his *Myth of the Twentieth Century*. He was, and remained, a theoretician totally incapable of dealing with political figures such as Göring, Himmler and Bormann. This did not, however, make him less dangerous, for he was one of those who spread the poison of amorality and racism among the German people.

EVA
BRAUN
1912-1945

Above: *An informal portrait of Eva Braun.*

Right: *Three images of Eva Braun, each capturing her youthful vitality.*

It is 28 April 1945, shortly before midnight. A somber marriage ceremony is taking place in the eerie bunker under the Reich Chancellery. A civil servant from the Record Office has been found after much difficulty from among the soldiers of the *Volkssturm*. In his crumpled uniform the nervous man asks the bride and groom to sign the marriage certificate. The bride, overcome by emotion, at first forgets herself and starts writing her own surname; she then crosses it out and begins again, signing: Eva Hitler. The bridegroom's signature is the same as that which has, over the past 12 years, signed numerous laws, regulations and decrees: Adolf Hitler. Goebbels and Bormann signed as witnesses. The ceremony is repeatedly interrupted by falling shells which send shock waves through the sandy earth, causing the bunker to quake. After the ceremony champagne is opened to toast the newly-wed couple. Although Hitler then leaves, Eva and the others present celebrate until the early hours of the morning. Eva Braun was to be called Mrs Hitler for two days.

One of the most successfully guarded secrets of the Third Reich was the existence of and role played by Eva Braun, mistress and, in the end, wife of Adolf Hitler. She was carefully kept out of the public eye for all those years. Among the many hundreds-of-thousands of official photographs of the Führer, not one exists of him and Eva Braun together. To the outside world Eva remained one of the Fuhrer's secretaries. This bland function was also given in her passport and entrance passes to the Obersalzberg and the Reich Chancellery. She traveled several times with the Führer's official retinue in this capacity during visits to Italy and Austria. She was not recognized on these trips as the Führer's lover.

It was only after World War II, when hundreds of photographs and letters were discovered, that it became clear that this young woman from Munich had been Hitler's lover for years and had en-

Above: *Eva Braun (right) and her sister Ilse.*

Left: *Eva Braun at work as a secretary, 1933.*

joyed his unbridled trust. Shortly before his suicide in the chancellery bunker, Hitler said of her: 'Miss Braun is, besides my dog Blondi, the only one I can absolutely count on.'

Eva Braun was born in 1912. She grew up with her sisters Ilse and Gretl in an overprotected environment. Her father was a teacher in a Munich school. She was a moody child who liked to create trouble, seldom did her homework and excelled in gymnas-

tics. Besides swimming and skiing, Eva was enthusiastic about skating; in her daydreams she was already an Olympic champion. The three sisters took music, painting and dancing lessons. Eva especially liked jazz and American musicals and was also fond of acting, which went well with another favorite pastime: dressing-up parties and wearing bright red lipstick.

In 1928, at the age of 16, she was sent to the convent school at

Right: *A family portrait showing (from left to right) Eva Braun, her sister Margarethe, her mother and her sister Ilse, 1935.*

Below right: *Eva Braun photographed at the age of 23.*

Simbach, a small town on the River Inn. On the other side of the river, on Austrian soil, lay the small, sleepy village of Braunau. There, more than 23 years earlier a baby whose fate would be inextricably bound to that of Eva beheld the light of day. Having followed only one year of the two-year course at the convent – no boys and strict discipline were not for her – Eva returned to Munich to look for work. Her first employer was a doctor but after a short time she had had enough of sitting for hours in the waiting room listening to the patients' woes. She was later to give the impression that the medical world held no secrets for her, an attitude that Hitler believed. Her second job as a typist also did not appeal to her and she quit after several weeks. Near the end of 1929, following up an advertisement in the newspaper, she applied for a job as assistant in a photography shop. The owner of the business was Heinrich Hoffmann, already the *hoffotograaf* (official photographer) to Adolf Hitler. Eva was taken on and put to work. According to Henriette Hoffmann (also born in 1912, daughter of Heinrich Hoffmann and later to become Henriette von Schirach) Eva preferred working in the darkroom.

The first meeting between Hitler and Eva Braun took place after she had been working in Hoffmann's shop for several weeks. Eva, in a letter to her sister Gretl wrote about this meeting: 'I had stayed after closing time to straighten up several things and was standing on the ladder putting something away on the top shelf. Then I heard the door open and saw the boss come in with a somewhat older man carrying a felt hat in his hand. I tried to watch them without their noticing. I had shortened my skirt that morning and felt rather embarrassed because I noticed that the man was looking at my legs. Besides, I was not certain whether the seam was straight. You can understand that I had not asked mother to help me with the skirt. When I came down off the ladder the boss introduced us. He said: "Mr Wolff, this is our little Miss Eva." Then Hoffmann sent me out to get some beer and sausages from the corner pub.'

After Hitler, alias Herr Wolff, had left Hoffmann asked Eva: 'Don't you know who that was? Don't you look at our photos? That was Adolf Hitler.' To which Eva answered: 'Who is Adolf Hitler?' At home, Eva asked her father the same question. Father Braun looked angrily at his daughter and said: 'That is the fellow who is a

Left: *Eva Braun practices her gymnastics against a backdrop of a fiord.*

Right: *The audience room in Hitler's residence at Obersalzberg.*

Far right: *Eva Braun's own room at the Eagle's Nest.*

Left: *An exterior view of Hitler's residence on the Obersalzberg.*

jack-of-all-trades and master of none, an idiot who thinks he knows best and will reform the entire world.' In spite of this, the meetings between Eva and Hitler became more frequent – especially after the suicide of Hitler's niece Geli in 1931.

Angela Maria, called Geli, was the daughter of Hitler's half-sister Angela Raubal, Hitler's housekeeper on the Obersalzberg where he had rented a modest chalet (later the Berghof). A romance started between Hitler and his niece. Hitler, who was almost 20 years her senior, even gave her her own room in his Munich apartment. In September 1931, the young woman committed suicide in her uncle's residence. The reason for her suicide was never discovered. Perhaps she was driven to this desperate deed because her insanely jealous uncle allowed her absolutely no freedom. Moreover, she had found a letter to Hitler from a young Munich woman whose name was often being mentioned in the intimate circle around her uncle: Eva Braun.

Eva's affection for this man with 'the funny Charlie Chaplin mustache' was slowly but surely growing. Illustrative is a short letter written in 1931 by the 19-year-old Eva: 'Dear Mr Hitler, I would like to thank you for the pleasant evening at the theater. It was unforgettable. I shall always be grateful for your friendship. I count the hours until the moment when we shall meet again.' When, in 1932, he started to become more occupied with politics, the time he had available for Eva gradually lessened. She sat evening after evening longingly waiting for a sign from her lover, a lover who seldom showed up any more.

On 1 November, at her wits end, she took her father's pistol, put it to her head and fired. Nobody was at home at the time and Ilse was the first to find her. The bullet had, however, lodged itself next to an artery and could easily be removed by the doctor. Upon hearing the news, Hitler rushed to the Munich clinic to visit her. As he said to Hoffmann: 'This will never happen again.' Hitler did feel

flattered by this clear evidence of Eva's love for him. What he valued most in Eva was her selflessness, for she never asked him for even the slightest favor; and her discretion, a virtue no woman should be without according to Hitler. Eva was able to convince her parents that she had accidentally pulled the trigger while looking at the pistol.

In 1943 Dr WC Langer, commissioned by the American intelligence service, brought out a psychological report on Adolf Hitler. It would subsequently appear to be a masterpiece of psychological-historical reconstruction.

If Hitler's behavior pattern is studied one gets the impression that there were two personalities living in the same body, both struggling for supremacy. One was extremely soft, sentimental and indecisive, with hardly any energy and would have done nothing other than be entertained, loved or pampered. The other was exactly the opposite – a hard, cruel and resolute man with a tremendous amount of energy who seemed to know what he wanted and was willing to go after it regardless of the consequences. It was the first Hitler who wept on the death of his canary and the second who, at a public hearing, shouted: 'Heads will roll!' It was the first Hitler who found it difficult to dismiss an assistant, and the second who ordered the murder of hundreds, including his best friends, and could say with conviction: 'There shall be no peace in this country until a body is hanging from every lamp post.'

According to Dr Langer this characteristic is common among psychopaths. In Hitler's case, however, there is no indication of total dissociation for, if such were the case, the two personalities would switch back and forth at random. That was certainly not the case with Hitler as he seemed to choose which personality he wanted. When the situation demanded he could call forth the 'Führer-personality,' which was almost always the case with his speeches. At first the 'person Hitler' was often evident, hesitating, uncertain, not knowing how to begin. Once he had 'tuned in,' the 'Führer-personality' would start to take over. Once he had whipped himself into the 'Führer-personality,' he could play the leader to perfection. The result was such that the Führer could say things that were the complete opposite of what the other 'Hitler' had said only a few minutes earlier, and with total conviction. Hitler wanted to believe that this was his true self and he did everything he could to convince the German people that it was his only self.

Yet the 'Führer-personality' was greatly exaggerated and was a distorted representation of maleness as Hitler perceived it. In Langer's opinion, the 'Führer-personality' showed all the characteristics of a substitute satisfaction which is unconsciously built up as a form of compensation, acting as a mask for the deep-lying tendencies that he abhors. This mechanism is often found in psychopaths and its aim is always the destruction of the true self by the creation of a 'shadow-self.'

Left: *Eva Braun and her sister Margarethe enjoy the view from the Kehlsteinhaus on the Obersalzberg.*

Right: *Eva Braun captures life with Hitler and his closest advisers on the Obersalzberg.*

Below: *Hitler reads a morning paper at the Berghof.*

Hitler had, by this time, become so impressed by the 'Führer-personality' that he did his utmost to forget that behind it lay a completely different Hitler – compared to the 'Führer,' a contemptuous and miserable little man. Hitler's foremost ability was his capacity for convincing others of his 'true I,' the leader. This psychological maneuver, however, is never totally successful. Hidden fears and desires which threaten this 'reality' continue to arise, undermining self-confidence and self-assurance. He can rationalize these fears, or suppress them, but they continue to pursue him. Hitler, for example, suffered for years from a cancer phobia, fear-

ing he had stomach cancer. Since he did have intestinal problems none of his doctors could convince him that his fear was groundless. He was also afraid of being poisoned, of being murdered, of losing his health, of losing weight, of being betrayed, of failing mystical abilities, of anesthetics, of an early death, and of not being able to fulfill his earthly mission.

Hitler's sexual life has often been the subject of speculation and has led to all sorts of conjectures. Some experts maintain that he was a 'chronic masturbator,' others that he was a voyeur. Many say that he was impotent. Still others, perhaps the majority, that he was homosexual. Dr Langer thought he was possibly impotent, but definitely not homosexual in the ordinary usage of the word, and that his true sexual proclivities, suspected only by a few, were of a totally different nature. According to Langer, Hitler was a masochist who derived sexual gratification from being beaten, kicked and urinated on by a female.

One important fact was not mentioned in Langer's report. When Russian doctors performed an autopsy on Hitler's remains in May 1945 they found that his left testicle was missing. The syndromes of monorchysm (the absence of a testicle) and cryptochysm (an undescended testicle) are rare. Psychological studies of prepubertal boys with a similar pattern of behavioral disorders combined with monorchysm, show the same pattern of disorders as did Hitler. The situation and the lifelong consequences of his defective genitals also help to explain why the Führer-concept, as developed by Hitler, took on the form of an exaggerated maleness, a representation of the self which, as Langer noted, 'showed all the characteristics of substitute fulfillment.'

Eva was a more frequent visitor to the Obersalzberg after Hitler became Reich Chancellor in 1933. Her parents eventually accepted the fact that their unmarried daughter was the Führer's mistress. Eva's presence on the Obersalzberg considerably cooled

Right: *Hitler and Eva Braun entertain guests at the Berghof. Also present are Speer (second row, third from left) and Martin Bormann (first row, second from right).*

the relationship between Hitler and his half-sister Angela, Geli's mother. Toward the fall of 1936 tensions had risen to such a degree at the Berghof that Angela decided to leave her job as Hitler's housekeeper. She married a professor from Dresden a short time later. According to the official press bulletin, Hitler was too busy to be present at his half-sister's wedding.

With the departure of Angela, Eva became mistress of the household. The personnel at the Berghof called her 'boss,' and she was one of the few who, besides calling Hitler *'mein Führer'*, used the informal personal pronoun *'du'* when speaking to him. Hitler used various pet names for her, such as *'gnädiges Fräulein,'* 'Schnaksi,' 'Patscherl' or 'Tschapperl.' This last is a typical Austrian expression meaning 'little one.' Later Hitler often used an Austrian variation of Eva – 'Effie' or 'Feferl.'

When in the company of others, Hitler and Eva were extremely formal toward each other, although Hitler would occasionally caress her hand. Heinz Linge, for years Hitler's manservant, said: 'Hitler and Eva occasionally stayed on alone in his study talking for a short while before retiring. On those occasions Eva, generally wearing only a dressing gown, would have some wine and Hitler a cup of tea. One evening I went in without knocking and saw Eva and Hitler standing embracing ardently in the middle of the room. Blushing, I turned around, withdrew and closed the door again. For those of us who knew of Hitler's relationship with Eva from personal observation the motto was: see nothing, hear nothing, say nothing.'

Albert Speer later said that he had never understood why everything that could have indicated an intimate relationship was strictly avoided. (Such a relationship could of course not be kept hidden from Hitler's small inner circle.) Speer said that Eva kept her distance from everyone in Hitler's immediate circle: 'As we came to know each other better over the years I noticed that her reserved bearing, which gave some an impression of arrogance, was nothing other than shyness.' However, for many visitors to the Berghof, even for those regular guests to the 'top' of the Obersalzberg, the relationship always remained hidden. Dr Blaschke, a racist, quick-witted Berliner, was their dentist for the years 1933-45. He was questioned by the Allies after the war and in reply to the question as to whether Hitler and Eva had had a relationship he answered: 'In all those years I never once noticed that he loved that woman. That is something a man would notice.'

Eva often received her mother, sisters and female friends at the Berghof. Her best friend, Herta Schneider (born Ostermayer), and her sister Gretl even had their own rooms there. Eva fre-

quently gave parties, mainly when Hitler was not present. They would dance until far into the night to the accompaniment of an accordion-playing SS guard. They never missed the Munich carnival and would hold crazy dressing-up parties in preparation. Eva was a fanatical sportswoman. She often went swimming in the Köningssee with her friend Anni Brandt, the former Olympic championship swimmer and wife of Hitler's surgeon. She often made long skiing trips beyond the closed off terrain of the Obersalzberg with Speer and his wife. Speer: 'Once Hitler even gave her eight days vacation. Obviously, during one of the periods when he was not staying at Berghof. She went with us for a few days to Zürs where she would not be recognized and fervently danced with the young officers until the early hours of the morning.'

The sports-loving Eva was also a chain-smoker; something that Hitler did not know about since he hated smoking. There was an absolute ban on smoking around him and woe betide anyone who broke it. The guilty party would have a good chance of being permanently banned from Hitler's close circle of acquaintances. There were no ashtrays at the Berghof. He once let drop to Gretl, Eva's sister: 'Before I retire I shall give the order that a fire-red strip be put on every packet of cigarettes sold in Europe with the words: 'Dangerous, smoking causes cancer and can kill you.' When Hitler would rant on against the evils of tobacco Eva would often hum the popular song 'Smoke gets in your eyes.' This often led to great hilarity among the company and to a slightly surprised Führer who was not familiar with the song.

An important hobby of Eva's was photography. While working as Hoffmann's shop assistant she had picked up quite a reasonable amount of knowledge about it. Whenever she had the chance she would be filming or taking photos. Because her photographs were intended strictly for private use, she could often take the most informal snaps as Hitler never looked up when Eva was walking about with her camera or filming equipment. There were many photo albums and films of hers found after the war, offering a treasure of information about Hitler's private life. Without realizing it Eva had made a valuable, historical record of the Third Reich and its leaders, including a revealing picture of life at the Berghof.

Over the years Eva's position at the Berghof grew into that of unofficial hostess. Since Hitler gave her a substantial allowance she could indulge herself in one of her favorite hobbies – buying clothes and footwear. Eva was soon the best dressed woman in the Berghof intimate circle, seldom wearing the same clothes twice. She liked unpatterned dark colors, especially black. Traudl Junge, one of Hitler's secretaries, described her first meeting with Eva as

follows: 'In addition to being so well-dressed and well cared for, it struck me that she was so natural and open. She was not at all the "ideal" German girl that you saw on the propaganda posters or in the magazines. Her hair had been dyed blond and the style suited her; her pretty face had been tastefully made up. She was not tall, [1.63 meters], but had an excellent figure and she carried herself well. She knew how to dress with style and taste. That evening she wore a Nile-green, thick wool dress with a closely fitting bodice. The flared skirt was set off by a wide, leopard skin border.'

Speer, who became a good friend of Eva over the years, emphasized her openness and naturalness: 'Eva was not a true lady, but a simple woman of the people. I liked her very much. She had managed to preserve her natural manner during all those years. She always remained in the background and never pushed herself forward in political matters. The only one she did not like seeing was Bormann, because the *Reichsleiter* was to everyone, even a loved one, an obstacle not to be endured with his unmistakable quest for power.'

Eva Braun was no longer the shy, almost timid girl from Hoffmann's shop. The luxurious life had also had an effect on her and she sometimes behaved like an insufferable film star. Ilse Braun said: 'Sometimes I did not recognize my sister any more. Eva was arrogant, tyrannical and insensitive toward us. . . Associating with the greats of the world makes a person egotistical, even cruel. . . She acted like the queen of the manor.'

The one who certainly did not see her as a queen was Hitler. Although Eva could play the first lady at the Berghof, the true first lady of the Reich was Emmy Göring, wife of Hitler's official successor. Eva was allowed to be present when veteran party members visited Hitler, but was banished to her rooms when other distinguished guests from Germany or abroad arrived at the Berghof. Eva would have to keep out of sight even when the Görings came to visit. Emmy Göring: 'In spite of the efforts I undertook, I was not allowed to get to know Eva Braun because of Hitler's character. Once when I was visiting the Berghof and asked Hitler if I might invite all the ladies from the Berghof to tea he realized what I was up to. He blushed and stammered: "Of course, naturally, if you want to."'

'The next day General Bodenschats [Göring's adjutant] delivered the invitations to the Berghof and all the ladies, including Eva and her sister, accepted. Very late that same night, we were already sleeping, my husband was telephoned and asked to report to the Führer. Hermann returned at three o'clock in the morning and told me the reason for his visit to Hitler. "Do you know Emmy why he had me called? It was actually a most rare and totally peculiar affair. He does not want Eva to come to tea with you. According to him Eva is afraid of you." I heard later that Eva had very much wanted to come with the others, but that Hitler had forbidden it.'

Eva was on a very friendly footing with Mrs Margerethe Speer and Mrs Gerda Bormann. She always wanted to know everything about their children and spent a lot of time playing with them.

Eva did not tolerate the slightest criticism of her loved one. It was perfectly clear to her that Germany would achieve the *Endsieg* (final victory). Her Führer had told her so. Defeat was simply not conceivable. Christa Schröder, one of Hitler's private secretaries, wrote: 'It can be said without exaggeration that in a political sense Eva was equally ignorant and indifferent. Whenever she noticed from the alarmed faces of Hitler's staff members that something dreadful had happened, she would try to find out from us what it was. She often complained that nobody kept her informed as to what was happening. But if a piece of bad news was announced, she always faithfully cried out: "But I knew absolutely nothing about those terrible things," immediately adding: "Is it not better that I know nothing of what is going on elsewhere? After all, there is nothing I can do."'

The pressures of work eventually began to push their relationship into the background. Eva complained frequently in her diary that Hitler had so little time for her and only truly loved her when it suited him. However, even when Hitler was not on the Obersalzberg, he never forgot his Effie. Linge: 'He telephoned her every second day. If his adjutants or Bormann were flying to Munich he would give them letters for Eva. . . When the Berghof became *Führerhauptquartier* again during one of Hitler's stays, the old idyll would blossom again.'

The period from 1938 to 1942 was the happiest time of Eva's life. With Gretl, Herta Schneider and her mother she made several trips to Mussolini's Italy – usually to Rome, Florence or Venice. And, in addition to this, it was during these years that Hitler sought more often than ever rest and inspiration on the Obersalzberg. Hitler began to value Eva more and more. He often paid her all sorts of small compliments and gave her expensive presents. He treated her parents with total respect. Eva began to invite her parents frequently to the Berghof. The family stayed so often on the mountain that Göring once remarked to his friends: 'There are as many Brauns on the Obersalzberg as there are brown shirts in Munich. Hitler should rename the Berghof the *Braunhaus*.' (The *Braunhaus* was the official NSDAP headquarters in Munich; the brown shirt, a part of the Nazi uniform.)

Between 1935 and 1945 Eva spent about 70 percent of her time at the Berghof. When the Führer was present life would carry on with a definite routine. Mornings were deathly quiet; it was absolutely forbidden to make noise because Hitler, who usually worked into the early hours of the morning, slept late. He would appear downstairs at about 1100 hours, read the newspaper clippings and go over his agenda with the ever-present Bormann.

The Berghof started to come to life around midday: Mercedes

These pages: *Scenes from the daily life enjoyed by Eva Braun in the luxurious and beautiful surroundings of the Obersalzberg.*

coming and going, and arrogant boots stamping up and down the asphalt in front of the chalet. The visitors were, for the most part high-ranking officers, especially during the war. During fine weather they often waited outside on the large terrace, sometimes having a quick smoke while waiting for their appointment with the Führer. For Hitler's private circle, often having waited several hours for him, these conferences seemed endlessly long. But Linge would finally appear and announce that the Führer would be with them in 10 minutes. Speer: 'After the announcement about Hitler's arrival, the tone of the various conversations would become muted and the laughter sounding here and there die down. Only the women carried on talking in soft voices about clothes and traveling. Everybody present made a conscious effort to give a good impression.'

After Hitler's arrival the company would proceed to the table. Hitler was painfully precise as regards service and table arrangement. He often checked beforehand whether everything was correctly placed and woe betide the waiter who had laid a spoon askew. Hitler would choose a partner and, followed by Eva Braun on the arm of her permanent (since 1938) dining partner Martin Bor-

mann, the rest of the party joined them and all proceeded to the dining room.

Meals at the Berghof were well-prepared, abundant, but austere. Hitler preferred simple dishes, with green beans, peas and lentils being his favorite vegetables. Meals with the Führer were vegetarian; meat was, after all, a dead and rotting substance according to the Führer. People who ate meat were cruel and merciless and totally alienated from nature. One of Hitler's favorite mealtime stories was about a visit he paid to a Polish slaughterhouse where he had stood in blood up to his ankles. If he noticed that the unappetizing description was creating its due impression, particularly among the ladies present, he would elaborate further. If there were guests from outside the intimate circle, he would, however, refrain from such stories.

He also often lapsed into lyrical descriptions about the way in which the ingredients for the meal had come into being. He would paint a picture of the farmer, who with wide majestic gestures, sowed the field to later harvest a sea of golden brown, sun-ripened grain. The only exception to his vegetarian menu was the Bavarian *Leberknödel* (liver and dumplings) soup. Viennese cakes were often served for a sweet.

After the meal the company would go to the tea-house, 30 minutes from the Berghof and Hitler's favorite walk. The path to the tea-house was only wide enough for two people to walk beside each other, giving an impression of a procession. After tea, the procession would return and two hours later they would meet again for the evening meal, following almost the same ritual as that at midday. Hitler retired after supper for military and political discussions and upon returning to the company, a film would be shown.

Hitler favorites were musicals and cowboy and adventure films. *Gone with the Wind* made an extraordinary impression on Eva Braun. Another popular pastime of the group was playing records after the movie. The numbered records were kept in a large black box. Bormann had the task of acting as disc jockey. Hitler's greatest favorites were Franz Lehar's operetta *The Merry Widow* and *Die Fledermaus* by Johann Strauss. Christa Schröder: 'I remember a time when he would sit in front of the large fireplace evening after evening listening to Lehar records. Even in his office he would sometimes drop his work, stare out of the window into the clear, blue air and, with his hands in his pockets, whistle tunes by Lehar.' The monotonous repertoire included, besides Lehar, Strauss, Wagner, Beethoven and Hugo Wolf. Hitler was also a worshiper of Wagner's music. Eva occasionally livened the company up by putting on a modern American number. 'What a nice record,' Hitler would often remark. 'Oh yes,' Eva would reply triumphantly, 'our friend Goebbels has just banned this one.'

The events would be repeated again, following the same order, the next day. Speer: 'The atmosphere was very informal, but undeniably boring and without the least variation. In the long run we had not much to say to each other any more. The majority of the company were simple souls and seldom or never entered into discussion with Hitler. They had to listen to his stories time and time again, taking no notice of the fact that he was telling the story for the tenth or twelfth time. I did not blame Hitler, for taking into account his many problems, he needed people around him who would hang on his every word as mindless worshipers.'

'After several days I would catch, as I called it then, "mountain sickness," that is to say I would begin to feel weary and empty from the continual waste of time. It was only when Hitler's idleness was broken by meetings that I had the time to work with several colleagues on my [building] plans. Being a privileged, long-term guest and resident on the Obersalzberg, I could not, no matter how boring it was, withdraw from these evenings without appearing to be discourteous.'

After the outbreak of war Eva was gradually allowed to appear more often in public. She was allowed to be present on Hitler's birthday (20 April); she was invited to a reception at Berchtesgaden in honor of Mussolini; and she dined with generals and high party officials. In the early spring of 1945 Hitler, because of the growing danger from air attacks, decided to permanently withdraw to his bunker and direct the war from there. On 20 April a noticeably aged Hitler celebrated his final (56th) birthday. Almost all of his important staff members were present. They all tried to talk him into fleeing. Ribbentrop, Minister of Foreign Affairs, implored Eva: 'You alone have any influence over him. If you tell him that you want to go he will do it for you.' Eva refused. The thunder of shells could be heard far in the distance when the birthday party was underway. Someone had an old record player upon which they played again and again the only song they had left: 'Blutrote Rosen erzählen dir,' by Gluck. Eva danced tirelessly. The final exodus of high party and government officials began the next day.

On the evening of 22 April Eva wrote a farewell letter to her best friend:

Berlin, 22-4-1945

Dearest little Herta,

These are to be my last words and, thus, my last sign of life. I dare not write to Gretl [she was pregnant]; you shall have to explain everything to her using the necessary caution considering her condition. I am sending you my jewels which are to be divided up in agreement with my will, which can be found in the house on Wasserburgstrasse. I hope that these jewels will help you keep your head above water for a time. Please leave the Berghof. It is too dangerous for you there and you could all be killed. We are fighting here to the bitter end and I am afraid that the end is dangerously near. I cannot tell you how much I suffer for the Führer. Forgive me if this letter seems to be rambling, but the six children of G [Goebbels] are in the room next door and making a lot of noise. What more can I say? I do not understand how all this can happen;

Left: *Celebrating Hitler's birthday at the Berghof, 20 April 1942. In attendance are Speer and Eva Braun.*

Above: *Eva Braun at her sister Margarethe's wedding celebration, also present is SS Gruppenführer Fegelein (center), Obersalzberg 1944.*

Right: *Hitler and Eva Braun in conversation. The child belongs to Hertha Schneider, one of Braun's friends.*

Right: *Hitler and Eva Braun enjoy a meal together.*

DAS LETZTE BILD

Einen sensationellen Fund machten Angestellte des CIC (Counter Intelligence Corps) bei Zell am See bei der Mutter eines ehemaligen SS-Führers. Sie fanden dort ehemaliges Eigentum von Frau Eva Hitler geb. Braun, darunter ein Photoalbum mit Bildern von ihr. (Unsere Aufnahme zeigt sie beim Frühstück an der Seite Hitlers.)
Photo: AP

Below: *The ruins of Hitler's bunker in Berlin, 1945.*

it could cause one to lose faith in God!

The man is waiting for my letter. Say hello to father and mother; they must go to Munich or Traunstein. My warmest feelings and thoughts go out to you, my trusted friend! Give my greetings to all my friends. I shall die as I have lived. It is not difficult. You know that.

With the warmest love and kisses, your Eva.
PS
Keep this letter confidential until you hear what has become of us. I know that I am asking much of you, but you are courageous. Perhaps everything will yet turn out satisfactorily, but HE has lost confidence and as for us, we hope in vain. . .

Yet 28 April 1945 would be a grand day for Eva Braun. Hitler had finally asked her to marry him. In his personal testament Hitler dictated: 'Although during my years of struggle I believed I could not take the responsibility of marriage, I have now decided at the end of my life's journey to marry the young woman who, after many years of true friendship, came of her own free will to this city that was already almost completely under siege, to share. . .'

The Russians had by 30 April advanced to little more than 100 meters from the bunker and were clearing a path from house to house. After Hitler had taken his leave from those secretaries and close staff members still present, he and his wife retired to their suite at about 1530 hours. A single pistol shot was heard shortly after and when the suite was entered Hitler was found sitting on the left side of the sofa, blood flowing from his head. He had first poisoned himself, then shot himself through the left temple. Eva was on the right side of the sofa and looked as though she was sleeping. She had bitten through a cyanide capsule. The room smelled strongly of acid and almonds. The bodies were carried upstairs and taken out to the garden where they were placed in a shallow pit near a concrete mixer and set alight. 'Hitler's whore is dead,' said a neighbor to Ilse Braun, not knowing to whom she was talking. So ended the life of Adolf Hitler's closest female companion, the misguided Eva Braun.

Bibliography

AHREND H.: **The Origins of Totalitarianism**, New York 1966.

ANDERS K.: **Im Nürnberger Irrgarten**, Nürnberg 1948.

ANDRUS B.: **I was the Nuremberg Jailer**, New York, Coward, McCann & Geoghegan, 1969.

AUTERBACHER H.: **Erlebt und Mitgestaltet**, Preussisch Oldendorf 1984.

BAUER H.: **Ich flog die Mächtige der Erde**, Kempten 1960.

VON BELOW N.: **Als Hitlers Adjudant**, Mainz 1980.

BERNADOTT F.: **Het einde**, Den Haag 1946.

BESYMENNSKI L.: **The Death of Adolf Hitler**, New York 1968. De laatste notities van Martin Bormann, Amsterdam 1974.

BEWLEY C.: **Hermann Göring and the Third Reich**, Devin-Adair 1962.

BIRD E.K.: **Rudolf Hess**, London 1972.

BLOOD-RAYAN A.W.: **Göring, the Iron Man of Germany**, London 1938.

BOBERACH H.: **Meldungen aus dem Reich**, Neuwied 1965.

BOELCKE W.A.: **The Secret Conferences of Dr. Goebbels**, New York 1970.

BORMANN M.: **The Bormann Letters. The Private Correspondence between Martin Bormann and his Wife from January 1943 to April 1945**, London 1954.

BRACHER K.: **The German Dictatorship**, New York and Washington, Praeger, 1970.

BRAMSTEDT E.K.: **Goebbels and National Socialist Propaganda**, Michigan 1965.

BROSZAT M.: **German National Socialism 1919-1945**, Santa Barbara, Calif., Clio Press, 1966.

BULLOCK A.: **Hitler, A Study in Tyranny**, New York, Bantam, 1961.

BRÜNING H.: **Memoiren 1918-1934**, Stuttgart 1974.

BUTLER E. & YOUNG G.: **Marshal without Glory**, London 1956.

CALIC E.: **Ohne Maske: Hitler-Breiting Geheimgespräche 1931**, Frankfurt am Main 1969.

VAN CAPELLE H.: **Himmler in: Intermediair, Joachim von Ribbentrop in: Intermediair, Goebbels in: Intermediair, Waardeloos geld in: Intermediair 1977; idem: De Nazi-Economie**, Assin 1978.

VAN CAPELLE H. & VAN DE BOVENKAMP A.P.: **The Eagle's Nest**, in press.

CARR W.: **A History of Germany 1815-1945**, New York, St. Martins, 1969.

CECIL R.: **The Myth of the Master Race**, London 1972.

CHARLIER J.M. & DE LAUNAY J.: **Eva Hitler, nee Braun**, Paris 1978.

CZICHON E.: **Wer verhalf Hitler zur Macht**, Köln 1967.

DELARUE J.: **The Gestapo**, New York, William Morrow, 1964.

DIETRICH O.: **Zwölf Jahre mit Hitler**, München 1955.

DOLLMANN E.: **The Interpreter**, London, Hutchinson, 1967.

DOMARUS M.: **Hitler. Reden 1932-1945**, Wiesbaden 1973 deel 1, 2.

VAN DOMBER Y.: **Ik leefde met Martin Bormann**, Amsterdam 1969.

ENGEL G.: **Heeresadjutant bei Hitler 1938-1943**, Stuttgart, Deutsche Verlags-Anstalt, 1974.

EUCKEN W.: **On the Theory of the Centrally Administered Economy in: Economica 1948.**

FEST J.C.: **The Face of the Third Reich**, London 1973.

FISCHER W.: **Deutsche Wirtschaftspolitik 1918-1945**, Opladen 1968.

FRANK J.: **Eva Braun**, Preussisch Oldendorf 1988.

FRAENKEL H. & MANVELL R.: **Doktor Goebbels**, Amsterdam 1960.

GALLAND A.: **The First and the Last, the Rise and Fall of the Luftwaffe Fighters Forces, 1938-1945**, New York 1954.

GEHLEN R.: **The Service**, New York, World, 1972.

GEISS J.: **Der Obersalzberg**, Berchtesgaden 1975.

GIESLER H.: **Ein anderer Hitler**, Landsberg 1977.

GILBERT G.M.: **Neurenberg Diary**, New York 1950.

GISEVIUS H.B.: **To the Bitter End**, Boston, Houghton Mifflin, 1947.

GOEBBELS J.: **The Early Goebbels Diaries**, London 1962.

GOEBBELS J.: **Tagebücher 1945**, Hamburg 1977.

GOERING E.: **An der seite meines Mannes**, Preussisch Oldendorf 1980.

GRITZBACH E.: **Hermann Göring, Werk und Mensch**, Berlin 1938.

GRUENBERGER A.: **A Social History of the Third Reich**, London 1971.

GUN M.E.: **Eva Braun**, New York, Bantam Books, 1969.

HALM G.N.: **Economic Systems**, London 1970 3e druk.

HANFSTAENGL E.: **Biographical Sketch of Hitler and Himmler**, OSS Report, 3 Dec. 1943.

HANFSTAENGL E.: **15 jahre mit Hitler**, München/Zürich 1970.

HART F.T.: **Alfred Rosenberg. Der Mann und sein Werk**, München 1937.

HEIDEN K.: **Der Führer**, London 1944.

HENNIG E.: **Das industrialisierte Deutschland 1914 bis 1972**, München 1974.

HESS I.: **Engeland-Nürnberg-Spandau**, Leoni 1953.

HESS R.: **Der Stellvertreter des Führers**, Zeitgeschichte, Berlin 1933.

HESS R.: **Reden**, München 1938.

HESS R. & I.: **Prisoner of Peace**, London, Britons, 1954.

HEYDECKER J.J. & LEEB J.: **Opmars naar de galg**, Amsterdam 1960.

HILLGRUBER A.: **Staatsmänner und Diplomaten bei Hitler**, 2 delen, Frankfurt am Main, Bernard & Graefe, 1967-1970.

HITLER A.: **Hitler's Secret Conversations**, New York, Signet, 1961.
— **Hitler's Secret Book**, New York, Grove Press, 1961.
— **Mein Kampf**, Boston, Houghton Mifflin Company, 1943.
— **Mein Kampf**, München, Eher, 1925-1926.
— **The Testament of Adolf Hitler, The Hitler-Bormann Documents**, London, Cassell, 1961.

HOFFMANN H.: **Hitler was my Friend**, London 1955.

HOEHNE H.: **The Order of the Death's Head**, New York, Coward, McCann & Geoghegan, 1970.

INFIELD G.B.: **Eva and Adolf**, New York 1974.

IRVING D.: **Hermann Goering**, London 1987.

JANSSEN G.: **Das Ministerium Speer. Deutschlands Rüstung im Krieg**, Berlin 1968.

JOCHMANN W.: **Im kampf um die Macht**, Frankfurt-am-Main 1963.

JUNG G.: **Memoirs**, not published.

KELLY D.M.: **Cells in Nürnberg**, London 1947.

KERSTEN F.: **Klerk en beul. Himmler van nabij**, Amsterdam 1948; **Totenkopf und Treue: Heinrich Himmler ohne Uniform**, Hamburg 1953.

KORDT E.: **Wahn und Wirklichkeit. Die Aussenpolitik des Dritten Reiches Versuch einer Darstellung**, Stuttgart 1948.

KRAUSE K.: **Zehn Jahre Kammerdiener bei Hitler**, Hamburg, Laatzen, 1949.

KRAUSNICK H. etc.: **Anatomy of the SS State**, New York, Walker, 1968.

KREBS A.: **Tendenzen und Gestalten der NSDAP**, Stuttgart 1948.

KROLL G.: **Von der Weltwirtschaftskrise zur Staatskonjuntur**, Berlin 1958.

VAN LANG J.: **Der Hitler Junge: Baldur von Schirach**, Hamburg 1988.

LANGER W.C.: **The Mind of Adolf Hitler**, New York, Basic Books, 1972.

LINGE H.: **Bis zum Untergang**, München 1980.

LOCHNER L.: **Die Mächtigen und der Tyrann**, Darmstadt 1955.

MANVELL R. & FRAENKEL H.: **Hermann Göring**, London 1962; **Heinrich Himmler**, London 1965; **Rudolf Hess**, Baarn 1972; **Inside Adolf Hitler**, New York 1973.

MASER W.: **Adolf Hitler**, München 1975.

MASON T.: **Der Primat der Politik-Politik und Wirtschaft im National-Sozialismus in: 'Das Argument' nr. 41, 1966.**

MILWARD A.S.: **The German Economy at War**, London, Athlone Press of the University of London, 1965.

MOSLEY L.: **De Rijksmaarschalk**, Den Haag 1974.

NEUMANN F.: **Behemoth, The Structure and Practice of National Socialism 1933-1944**, New York 1963.

NEURENBERG: The Trial of the Major War Criminals before the International Military Tribunal, Proceedings, Volumes I-XXIII, Documents of Evidence, Volumes XXIV-XLII, 1946-1949.

NIEHANS S.H.: **Das Autarkieproblem in der Weltwirtschaft**, Berlin 1955.

NOLTE E.: **Der Nationalsozialismus**, München 1963; **Der Faschismus in seiner Epoche**, München 1963.

O'DONNELL J.P.: **The Bunker**, Boston 1978.

PAYNE R.: **Hitler, een leven voor de dood**, Amsterdam 1974.

PENZLIN K.: **Meister der Rationalisierung**, Düsseldorf 1963.

PETZINA D.: **Autarkiepolitik im Dritten Reich**, Stuttgart 1968.

PICKER H.: **Hitler's tischgespräche im Führerhauptquartier, 1941 bis 1942**, Bonn 1951.

PRICE G.W.: **I Know These Dictators**, London, Harrap, 1937.

RAUSCHNING H.: **Die Revolution des Nihilismus**, Zürich/N.Y. 1938; **The Voice of Destruction**, New York 1940.

REIMANN V.: **Joseph Goebbels**, Wien/München/Zürich 1971.

REITSCH H.: **Flying is My Life**, New York Putnam, 1954.

VON RIBBENTROP J.: **Zwischen London und Moskau**, Leoni 1953.
— **Ribbentrop Memoirs**, London, Weidenfeld & Nicolson, 1962.

RIESS C.: **Joseph Goebbels**, New York 1948.

ROBERTS S.: **The House that Hitler Built**, London, Methuen, 1937.

ROSENBERG A.: **Der Mythus des 20. Jahrhunderts; Das politische Tagebuch Alfred Rosenbergs**, Göttingen 1956.
— **Alfred Rosenberg, Selected Writings**, London, Cape, 1970.

SCHACHT H.: **Account Settled**, London, Weidenfeld & Nicolson, 1948.

SCHAFFING F.: **Der Obersalzberg**, München 1985.

SCHELLENBERG W.: **Hitler's Secret Service**, New York, Pyramid, 1958.

SCHMIDT M.: **Albert Speer: Das Ende eines Mythos**, Bern/München 1982.

SCHMIDT P.: **Hitler's Interpreter**, London, Heinemann, 1951.

SCHOENBAUM D.: **Hitler's Social Revolution**, New York 1967.

SCHULZ G.: **Die nationalsozialistische Machtergreifung**, Köln 1960.

SCHWARTZ P.: **This Man Ribbentrop**, New York 1943.

SCHWEITZER A.: **Big Business in the Third Reich**, Bloomington 1964.

SEABURY P.: **Die Wilhelmstrasse, Die Geschichte der deutschen Diplomatie 1930 bis 1945**, Frankfurt am Main 1956.

SEMMLER R.: **Goebbels, the Man Next to Hitler**, London 1947.

SHIRER W.L.: **The Rise and Fall of the Third Reich**, New York, Simon & Schuster, 1960.

SIEMSEN H.: **Hitler Youth**, London, Lindsay Drummond, 1940.

SIMPSON A.J.: **Hjalmar Schacht in Perspective**, Mouton 1969.

SMITH B.: **Heinrich Himmler**, Stanford, Stanford University Press, 1971.

SMITH B.F.: **Reaching Judgment at Nurnberg**, New York 1977.

SPEER A.: **Inside the Third Reich**, New York, Macmillan, 1970.

SPEER A.: **Technik und Macht**, Esslingen 1979.

SUSSKIND W.E.: **Die Mächtigen vor Gericht**, München 1963.

THOMAS W.H.: **The Murder of Rudolf Hess**, New York 1979.

THYSSON F.: **I Paid Hitler.**

TOLAND J.: **Adolf Hitler**, London 1976.

TREVOR-ROPER H.R.: **The Last Days of Hitler**, New York, Macmillan, 1947.

TURNER H.A.: **Faschismus und Kapitalismus in Deutschland**, Göttingen 1972.

WAGENFUEHRER R.: **Die deutsche Industrie im Kriege 1939-1945**, Berlin 1963.

WULF J.: **Martin Bormann, Hitler's Schatten**, Gütersloh 1962.

WURM F.F.: **Wirtschaft und Gesellschaft in Deutschland 1848-1948**, Opladen 1969.

WYKES A.: **Himmler**, New York 1972; **Goebbels**, New York 1973.

ZENTNER K.: **Illustrierte Geschichte des Dritten Reiches**, München 1965.

ZOLLER A.: **Douze ans auprès d'Hitler. (Memoires Christa Schröder)**, Paris Julliard.